Coexistence and Other Fighting Words

Selected Writings of Judea Pearl, 2002–2025

Praise for *Coexistence and Other Fighting Words*

Judea Pearl is a north star for anyone who cares about truth, integrity, and justice. This book—and his wisdom—are essential.

Bari Weiss, Founder and Editor of *The Free Press*

Judea Pearl once said, speaking of his dear son, Danny: "[He] gave humanity a banner with which to fight hatred, fanaticism, and intolerance." I would add that Judea Pearl, himself, has also embodied this banner for decades and is a relentless warrior for truth and good. A ray of hope and light despite the indescribable darkness he has faced, there is no better person to offer intellectual ammunition to navigate our complex time. One of the West's bright minds and moral voices, Judea Pearl has written an essential book, *Coexistence and Other Fighting Words*, which should be required reading.

Bernard-Henri Lévy, Philosopher and Author of *Israel Alone*

Wise reflections on some of the most pressing issues of the day, from the man who, more than anyone, understands why things happen.

Steven Pinker, Johnstone Professor of Psychology, Harvard University, and Author of *Rationality*

Coexistence and Other Fighting Words is a book we might be afraid to open because it forces us to confront humanity's darkest truths—but we must, because within its pages lie the pearls of wisdom essential for our survival. Through the tragic loss of his son, Daniel Pearl, Dr. Judea Pearl transformed personal grief into a global mission for unflinching truth. Like *The Diary of Anne Frank* and Elie Wiesel's *Night*, this collection serves as a witness to history and a call to action, offering a roadmap to confront hatred, challenge moral relativism, manifest post-traumatic growth, and defend our shared humanity.

Asra Q. Nomani, Author of *Woke Army: The Red-Green Alliance That Is Destroying America's Freedom,* Cofounder of Muslim Reform Movement, Editor of Pearl Project

Ideas matter. Words have consequence. Hate and blame can get out of control and burn down the whole world. Dr. Judea Pearl is among those who know this better than most. He has been warning the world since hate took the life of his own son, *Wall Street Journal* reporter Daniel Pearl. In *Coexistence and Other Fighting Words*, we have the opportunity to hear him anew. He addresses the Jewish story, Muslim-Jewish dialogues, and the anatomy of hate. We must listen to his voice. Bracing, precise, and an urgent part of our twenty-first century conversation.

Van Jones, CNN Host and Founder of DreamMachine.org

Coexistence and Other Fighting Words

Selected Writings of Judea Pearl, 2002–2025

Judea Pearl

TORONTO · CHICAGO

Copyright © 2025 Judea Pearl

All rights reserved. No part of this book may be reproduced, stored in a retrieval system, or transmitted, in any form or by any means, without permission in writing from the publisher or a licence from The Canadian Copyright Licensing Agency (Access Copyright). For a copyright licence, visit accesscopyright.ca.

Political Animal Press
www.politicalanimalpress.com

Distributed by the University of Toronto Press
www.utpdistribution.com

Cataloguing data available from Library and Archives Canada
ISBN 978-1895131-73-4

Typeset in Adobe Garamond Pro, designed by Robert Slimbach.

Edited by Karen Kedmey

Cover design by Nic Taylor
www.thunderwing.com

To Ruth, for being my compass and comfort for the past 5,786 years.

Contents

Introduction, or Why I Wrote This Book

What compels me, today, to share my writings of the past twenty-three years with readers troubled by the madness of 2024–2025? The simple answer is that the madness did not start today, but at least twenty-three years ago. More specifically, as we are grappling with the worldwide surge in anti-Westernism, antisemitism, and anti-Zionism in the wake of October 7, we must understand the latent forces that had been fueling these convulsions for decades before they exploded into our view.

Most people know me as the father of Daniel Pearl, the *Wall Street Journal* reporter who was kidnapped and murdered by al-Qaeda terrorists in Karachi, Pakistan, in 2002. Danny's horrific death, along with the last words he spoke in front of his abductors' camera, captured the headlines and turned him into a symbol: millions of people worldwide came to see him as a true citizen of the world, an embodiment of Western values, and an icon of Jewish pride. As people became hungry to hear from Danny's family about who he was and what we can learn from his tragedy, I, too, was thrust into the public eye as a speaker and writer for audiences outside of my usual scientific activities.

In scientific circles, I am known as a computer scientist specializing in artificial intelligence (AI), human cognition, and the philosophy of science—three fields in which I have solved some longstanding problems, especially in reasoning about cause and effect. The tragedy of Danny's death spurred me to step beyond algorithms and equations and directly examine the social and political forces that are shaping our troubled world. This pursuit has led me to produce hundreds of op-eds, essays, and talks covering a wide range of topics, including Jewish identity, the history of Israel, the war on terrorism, the intricate dynamics of East-West confrontations and dialogues, and the puzzling Israeli-Palestinian conflict. In this book, I present a minimally edited selection of forty-five of these writings, showcasing my principal thoughts on these subjects.

The decision to compile these writings into a single volume was inspired by numerous requests from colleagues and friends, who observed that the language, perspective, and logic in my analyses deserved wider exposure to the many people who are trying to understand the complex and pressing challenges of our era. These challenges include the escalating menace of terrorism and extremism; the fundamental aspects of the Arab-Israeli conflict; and the barbaric attack and aftermath of October 7.

The book opens with "Hope from the Horror of My Son's Murder" (2002), a personal article I wrote just six months after Danny's murder. This piece echoes the camaraderie, humanity, and pursuit of truth that Danny embodied throughout his life, as well as the message his killing conveys to us globally. Ultimately, the selection culminates with "Oslo Failed Because It Never Started" (2023), wherein I identify Zionophobia—my preferred term for the obsessive rejection of a Jewish homeland—as the primary catalyst inflaming and prolonging the century-long Arab-Israeli conflict. I explore Zionophobia, its origins, logic, and consequences, in several chapters throughout my journey, because it is universally and unforgivably ignored—it's the elephant in the room. We see this clearly today. Since October 7, many people have been shocked by the sharp rise of antisemitic incidents in America and Europe, failing to see the root cause: Zionophobia. The rejection of Israel's right to exist has been gradually and clandestinely intensified in academia and other institutions of the West, and Zionism, the ideological expression of that right, has become synonymous with the most hateful legacies of colonialism. Naturally, Jews, as the organic carriers of Zionism, have become the direct target of this rising hate.

Has my scientific background influenced my analysis of social and political issues? In many ways, yes. In the field of AI, we are trained to imbue brainless robots with human knowledge. This requires a precise language for representing knowledge and a rigorous understanding of its various components: how it is substantiated by evidence and how it should be used to guide actions and policies. This rigor extends to issues of evidence, knowledge, actions, and policies in social and political arenas. It enables AI researchers to precisely distinguish facts from theories, data from models, definitions from assumptions, and, crucially, causes from effects. This principled methodology helps avoid pitfalls and fallacies that often undermine social and political analysis. The logic of cause and effect is often the first victim in the absence of this methodology.

My family experience, as well, has shaped these writings. Born to a family that escaped the Holocaust from Europe, and married into a family that fled a major pogrom in Iraq, I have been influenced by a generation of nation-building pioneers, driven by dreams and self-reliance. I witnessed the creation of the modern State of Israel, the Israeli War of Independence and its consequences, as well as Israel's struggle for survival a decade later while serving in the Israel Defense Forces (IDF). My efforts to foster peace and mutual understanding have led me to participate in dozens of dialogues with Muslim scholars and activists. Similarly, I have engaged with hundreds of Jewish communities across the U.S. and Europe, sharing insights and helping them fight rising antisemitism and Zionophobia in higher education. Most importantly, despite leaving Israel in 1960, I have remained intimately connected to the pulse of its people, the dynamism of its culture, and the ups and downs of its politics. Through my family, friends, teachers, and students in Israel, I have sustained a firsthand understanding of both their deep-seated existential anxieties and their profound yearning for peace with their neighbors.

So, to return to my opening question: what compels me to share my writings with readers now? To be honest, it is my confidence that these writings reflect a coherent, evidence-based, and compelling worldview that could guide fellow travelers, so many of whom are perplexed by our era's slogans, doubts, conflicts, misinformation, and moral relativism. In particular, I find great joy in conveying the miracle of the Jewish people, the heroic narrative of Israel's establishment, and my certitude in the rightness of her struggle for peaceful coexistence. I hope to make this joy contagious.

Judea Pearl
Los Angeles, CA
July 2025

Daniel Pearl

Daniel Pearl disappeared on January 23, 2002. As the *Wall Street Journal*'s South Asia bureau chief, he was on a reporting trip in Karachi, Pakistan, investigating leaders of the al-Qaeda network. The night of his disappearance, Judea's wife, Ruth, had a nightmare. She dreamt that she was in a foreign place, as she recalled in an oral history interview in 2014, where she saw Danny: "He was very scared. I said, 'Danny, what happened?' He goes, 'Oh, they were pushing water through my throat.' I figured he's cold, I need to get him something. I said, 'I'll get you tea or something.'" After waking up, Ruth went to the computer and wrote an email to her son: "Danny, this is the dream that I had. Please humor me and answer this email immediately."[1]

Silence from Karachi. The next day, Ruth and Judea got a phone call from Danny's wife, journalist Mariane (van Neyenhoff) Pearl, who informed them that he had not returned from his interview the evening before. Mariane was with Danny, since the couple traveled together whenever possible. She was pregnant with their first child. So began a family's hell. As events unfolded, their hell became international news: American journalist Daniel Pearl kidnapped by al-Qaeda terrorists in Karachi, Pakistan.

It took until February 21 to find out what happened to Danny. That morning, FBI agents showed up at Judea and Ruth's door with a changed demeanor and told them to sit down, that there's bad news. The agents put Judea on the phone with John Bauman, the United States consul general in Karachi, who informed him that Danny was dead. Judea asked how they could be sure, and that was when the Pearls learned that his kidnappers had made a ghastly videotape of his murder. On the videotape, Danny says his last words: "My father is Jewish, my mother is Jewish, I am Jewish." Then, he added a final sentence, referring to Judea's grandfather: "Back in the town of Bnei Brak, there is a street named after my great-grandfather, Chaim Pearl, who was one of the founders of the town."

—Karen Kedmey

1 Ruth Pearl, in USC Shoah Foundation, "Intl Day to End Crimes Against Journalists | Iraqi Jewish Survivor Ruth Pearl | USC Shoah Foundation," https://www.youtube.com/watch?v=NvXlhfo1jE4.

AND OTHER FIGHTING WORDS

Selected Writings of JUDEA PEARL 2002–2025

Op-Eds, Essays, and Talks

2002–2025

1.

"Hope from the Horror of My Son's Murder," *The Sunday Times (London)*, August 18, 2002

This was among the first pieces I published after Danny's murder. It was a few months after we established the Daniel Pearl Foundation, and I felt that it was important to publicize its mission: To fight the hatred that took Danny's life. Today, more than twenty years later, it is obvious that we have not fully achieved this ambitious goal. However, I know it has had a transformative impact on thousands of people; journalists, musicians, Muslims, and Jews.

Daniel Pearl, the *Wall Street Journal* reporter who was kidnapped and murdered in Pakistan more than six months ago, was laid to rest last Sunday in Los Angeles, California. Danny was my son.

I last spoke to him on January 21, two days before his abduction, when he called to tell us the great news: he and Mariane had discovered their child would be a boy.

Danny's remains were flown back from Karachi after months of searching for the body and procedural delays. The funeral was private and simple: family and close friends gathered to pay last respects to their beloved Danny; a violinist friend played selections from Bach; the rabbi reflected on the significance of Danny's life and work; I said the Kaddish (the Jewish prayer of mourning) and Danny's body was finally laid to rest in his hometown, overlooking the concert hall where he loved to perform with his youth orchestra.

But who was this young man, and why has the world been so shocked by his death? After all, Danny was not a political leader, military hero, or famous celebrity, yet millions of people worldwide identify with his life, tragedy, mission, and legacy.

For his family and friends, Danny was "a walking sunshine of truth, humor, friendship, and compassion" with "not one shred of malice in his bones" (the description comes from *At Home in the World*, a recently published anthology of Danny's articles for the *Wall Street Journal*).[1] Among

1 See Daniel Pearl, *At Home in the World: Collected Writings from The Wall Street Journal*, ed. Helene Cooper (New York: Simon & Schuster, Inc., 2002).

his colleagues, Danny was known as a fiddler, storyteller, and a bridge-builder who formed connections wherever he went. To his readers, he was a truth-seeker who made the world seem friendlier.

The shocking aspects of Danny's death exceed any imaginable account. A cold-blooded killing of a reporter is in itself a barbaric act. Coupled with the fact that this reporter was a gentle soul, with a pregnant wife who appealed for his release, and that the brutal murder was enacted in front of a camera, the killing of Danny marks a new dimension of savagery.

The irony of this tragedy is that Danny was the antithesis of the "ugly American" that the terrorists were hoping to capture and destroy. Wherever he went, Danny radiated friendship and respect for all. In death he came to personify tolerance, humanity, and dialogue, and his death turned him into a symbol for these values. Furthermore, his lively prose and sensitivity made him a perfect emissary for the West and the Muslim world to understand each other better. Therefore, Danny's murder represents a betrayal of humanity.

Another shocking element of this tragedy is the role played by Danny's Jewish background in the planning and execution of the murder. His captors did not hide their underlying motives. Whereas their early communications expressed anti-American passions, the videotape depicting Danny's murder exposes raw anti-Jewish hatred. Danny's captors showed no interest whatsoever in his background or work except his "crimes"—Danny's Jewish and Israeli heritage. Clearly, knowing the mentality of their prospective audience, the murderers were confident that Danny's Jewish connections were sufficient to license the gruesome actions they planned.

So, how are we, his family and friends, coping with this tragedy? The answer is not easy. Our personal loss is amplified by the fact that Danny's killers seem to have achieved their objectives. They embarrassed Pakistan's President Pervez Musharraf, gained publicity, recruited more terrorists, inflicted pain and humiliation on the West, and scared foreign journalists. They even managed to find publicity-seeking publishers to help disseminate their gruesome propaganda tapes.

On the surface, then, they seemed to have won on all fronts—a thought that caused us great pain. Fortunately, we became aware of positive developments beneath the surface that have given us the strength to endure and to turn his death into a source of hope.

My son's death has generated an enormous awakening of goodwill worldwide; we have had thousands of letters, emails, donations, and ideas on how to prevent such tragedies in the future. This awakening has called our attention to the good things that can come out of our tragedy and has prompted Danny's family, friends, and colleagues to establish the Daniel Pearl Foundation in his honor. The Foundation aims to continue Danny's mission; to create positive connections among people of different cultures, to reduce cultural and religious hatred, to encourage responsible and creative journalism, and to enrich people's lives through music.

We have been fortunate indeed to enlist prominent public figures and activists as board members and volunteers, with representatives from all parts of the political spectrum. In particular, we were gratified to receive tremendous encouragement from Pakistanis. The prospect of saving some communities from the deadly claws of hatred fills our lives with hope that some good may come from this.

The antisemitic component of Danny's murder has also generated a counteroffensive. In April, President George W. Bush said: "We reject the ancient evil of antisemitism whether it is practiced by the killers of Daniel Pearl or by those who burn synagogues in France." Such statements made us realize that if Danny's death can raise people's awareness of intolerance and inspire them to speak against it, this would be a giant step toward a hate-free world. By killing Danny, the terrorists have in effect destroyed the "ugly West" image that they and their ideological supporters have labored to erect in the past few decades, be it explicitly or implicitly.

Instead, what emerged from this killing was an image of Westerners as exporters of values. It has reminded many that in addition to colonialism, materialism, arrogance, selfishness, and other ills and maladies that we are constantly accused of practicing, the West is also the world's largest exporter of pluralism, tolerance, and basic freedoms, values Danny personified in his life. I became aware of this aspect of Danny's legacy when letters started to arrive suggesting monuments, memorials, and awards in Danny's honor.

I understood then that something good can come out of Danny's death and that if my new grandson Adam asks me ten years from now, "What good came out of it?", my answer will be: "Your father gave humanity a banner with which to fight hatred and fanaticism and intolerance. And a banner is a very powerful weapon! It makes each soldier feel an inch taller, it calls for duty new recruits, and it makes armies march in unison."

My hopes are that I will be able to add: "You see? Your father's banner helped us win that battle."

2. "Formula Could Combat Campus Racism," *Jewish Journal*, June 9, 2005

This is one of my early pieces trying to alert people to my realization that anti-Zionism, not antisemitism, is the issue plaguing Jews today. The formula I present in the last paragraph, "Anti-Zionism = Racism," is the seed from which the term "Zionophobia" eventually sprouted.

In the past three months, I have visited four "troubled" campuses—Duke, York (Canada), Columbia, and UC Irvine—where tensions between Jewish and anti-Zionist students and professors have attracted national attention. In these visits, I have spoken to students, faculty, and administrators, and I have obtained a fairly gloomy picture of the situation on those and other campuses.

Jewish students are currently subjected to an unprecedented assault on their identity as Jews. And we, the Jewish faculty on campus, have let those students down. We have failed to equip them with effective tools to fight back this assault. We can reverse this trend.

Many condemn anti-Zionism for being a flimsy cover for antisemitism. I disagree. The order is wrong. I condemn antisemitism for being an instrument for a worse form of racism: anti-Zionism. In other words, I submit that anti-Zionism is a form of racism more dangerous than classical antisemitism. Framing anti-Zionism as racism is precisely the weapon that our students need for survival on campus.

Anti-Zionism earns its racist character from denying the Jewish people what it grants to other collectives (e.g., Spanish, Palestinians), namely, the right to nationhood and self-determination. Are Jews a nation? A collective is entitled to nationhood when its members identify with a common history and wish to share a common destiny. Palestinians have earned nationhood status by virtue of thinking like a nation, not by residing where their ancestors did (many of them are only three or four generations in Palestine). Jews, likewise, are bonded by nationhood (i.e., common history and destiny) more than they are bonded by religion.

The appeal to Jewish nationhood is necessary when we consider Israel's insistence on remaining a "Jewish state." By "Jewish state," Israelis mean, of course, "national Jewish state," not "religious Jewish state"—theocratic states (like Pakistan and Iran) are incompatible with modern standards of democracy and pluralism. Anti-Zionist racists use this anti-theocracy argument repeatedly to delegitimize Israel, and I have found our students unable to defend their position with conventional ideology that views Jewishness as a religion.

Jewishness is more than just a religion. It is an intricate and intertwined mixture of ancestry, religion, history, country, culture, tradition, attitude, nationhood, and ethnicity, and we need not apologize for not fitting neatly into the standard molds of textbook taxonomies—we did not choose our turbulent history.

As a form of racism, anti-Zionism is worse than antisemitism. It targets the most vulnerable part of the Jewish people, namely, the people of Israel, who rely on the sovereignty of their state for physical safety, national identity, and personal dignity. To put it more bluntly, anti-Zionism condemns five million human beings, mostly refugees or children of refugees, to eternal statelessness, traumatized by historical images of persecution and genocide.

Anti-Zionism also attacks the pivotal component of our identity, the glue that bonds us together—our nationhood, our history. And while people of conscience reject antisemitism, anti-Zionist rhetoric has become a mark of academic sophistication and social acceptance in Europe and on some U.S. campuses.

Moreover, anti-Zionism disguises itself in the cloak of political debate, exempt from sensitivities and rules of civility that govern interreligious discourse. Religion is ferociously protected in our society; political views are not. Just last month, a student organization on a University of California campus hosted a meeting on "A World Without Israel." Imagine the international furor that a meeting called "A World Without Mecca" would provoke.

So, in the name of "open political debate," administrators would not think twice about inviting MIT linguist Noam Chomsky to speak on campus, though his anti-Zionist utterances offend the fabric of my Jewish identity deeper than any of the ugly religious insults currently shocking the media. He should be labeled for what he is: a racist.

Strategically, while accusations of antisemitism are worn out and have lost their punch, charging someone with racism makes people ask why anyone would deny people the right of self-determination in a sliver of land in the birthplace of their history. It shifts the frame of discourse from debating Israel's policies to the root cause of the conflict: denying Israelis their basic rights as a nation.

Charges of "racism" highlight the inherent asymmetry between the Zionist and anti-Zionist positions. The former grants both Israelis and Palestinians the right for statehood, the latter denies that right to one, and only one, side. This asymmetry is the most effective weapon our students should use in campus debates, for it puts them back on the high moral ground of "fair and balanced" and forces their opponents to defend an ideology of one-sidedness.

For example, I have found it effective when confronting an anti-Zionist speaker to ask: "Are you willing to go on record and state that the Israel-Palestine conflict is a conflict between two legitimate national movements?" Western audiences adore evenhandedness and abhor bias. The question above forces the racist to unveil and defend his uneven treatment of the two sides.

America prides itself on academic freedom, and academic freedom entails freedom to teach hatred and racism—we graciously accept this fact of life. However, academic freedom also entails the freedom of students to expose racism, be it white-supremacy, women-inferiority, Islamophobia, or Zionophobia, wherever it is spotted. Not to censor, but to expose. Racists stew in their own words.

In summary, I believe the formula "Anti-Zionism = Racism" should give Jewish students the courage to both defend their identity and expose those who abuse it.

3. "Dialogue of the Deaf," *The Jerusalem Post*, June 16, 2005

In 2005, I was invited to the U.S.-Islamic World Forum in Doha, Qatar through the Brookings Institution's Doha branch. I believe they invited me because for the two years prior I had been traveling with the Islamic scholar and Pakistani diplomat Akbar Ahmed, wrestling with how we can bridge community differences in a series we called the Daniel Pearl Dialogue for Muslim-Jewish Understanding. The Doha forum was my first exposure to the sad fact that Muslims had not even begun to grapple with Israel's rightful place in the region and, therefore, the notion of a "two-state solution" was nowhere in their consciousness. Moreover, these were moderate Muslims, who claim to champion modernity and human rights! So, everyone wanted to believe that this forum could help bridge East-West relations. I arrived hopeful and left totally discouraged; the Muslim spokesmen essentially told us, "If you want us to progress, erase Israel for us."

The age of terror, it seems, has sprouted an era of dialogue. A host of conferences meant to bring together East and West have been cropping up. There was the World Economic Forum's recent Middle East regional summit in Jordan. A few weeks before that star-studded Mideast "Davos" conference, I had the opportunity to attend the similarly high-level U.S.-Islamic World Forum, held in Doha, Qatar.

The Doha conference was packed with hundreds of progressive pundits and activists from all sides, who diligently discussed both the needs and the means for achieving democracy, reforms, and renaissance in the Muslim world. And, as expected, there was hardly a Muslim speaker who did not stress the pivotal importance of seeing progress toward settling the Israeli-Palestinian conflict.

The emir of Qatar, Sheikh Hamad bin Khalifa al-Thani, kicked off the discussion by stressing that hot conflicts in the Arab-Islamic world had to be resolved if we hoped to make progress on reform issues. He was followed by Palestinian Authority Civil Affairs Minister Mohammed Dahlan, who called on America and the Muslim countries to pressure Prime Minister Ariel Sharon to stop what Dahlan saw as delaying tactics. Indeed, almost every speaker ended his or her speech by arguing that American credibility hinged on resolving the Palestine issue.

Rami Khouri, executive editor of the *Daily Star* in Lebanon, summarized these sentiments, noting: "Democracy is essential, but it is incomplete without full sovereignty, and cannot be promoted credibly under conditions of foreign occupation. Resolving the Palestine issue in this respect is vital for progress and should be addressed alongside movement toward democratic reform."

As a person sensitive to this issue, I was deeply impressed by the civility with which the issue was discussed. The word "occupation" was scarcely mentioned, and the usual accusatory terms "brutal," "racist," and "apartheid" were pleasantly absent from the main discourse.

This stood in sharp contrast to another East-West conference that took place earlier that month in Putrajaya, Malaysia, in which the Malaysian prime minister reportedly stated that Israel should cease to be "an exclusively Jewish racist state," where the leftist Israeli delegation was snubbed for being overly concerned with "Israel's racist needs and wishes." The overwhelming majority of participants at the event stated that Israel was founded on pillars of injustice and must be dismantled (peacefully, of course).

Enticed by this aura of civility in Doha, I was curious to find out what the participants had in mind when they pressed for "progress" on the Palestine issue: progress toward what?

Deep in my heart, I had hoped to find the Doha participants more accommodating of the so-called "two-state solution" and the road map leading to it. If this were not the case, I thought, then we were in big trouble again. Muslims might be nourishing a utopian dream that the U.S. cannot deliver and, sooner or later, the whole dialogue process, and all the goodwill and reforms that depend on it, would blow up in the same conflagration that consumed the Oslo process.

I was not the only American with such concerns. Richard Holbrooke, America's former ambassador to the U.N., who was on the same panel with Dahlan, stated that the Arab world must contribute its share toward meaningful movement of the peace process. He reminded the audience that, by now, two-and-a-half generations of Arabs have been brought up on textbooks that do not show Israel on any map, and that such continued denial, on a grassroots level, is a major hindrance to any peaceful settlement.

I had a friendly conversation on this issue with one of Dahlan's aides, who confessed that "we Palestinians do not believe in a two-state solution, for we can't agree to the notion of 'Jewish state.'" "Judaism is a religion," he added, "and religions should not have states." When I pointed out that Israeli society is 70 percent secular, bonded by history, not religion, and that by "Jewish state" Israelis mean (for lack of a better term) a "national Jewish state," he replied: "Still, Palestine is too small for two states."

This was somewhat disappointing to me, given the official Palestinian Authority endorsement of the road map. "Road map to what?", I thought, "to a Middle East without Israel?" Where was the reform and liberalism among the post-Arafat Palestinian leadership that was expected to breed flexibility and compromise?

I discussed my disappointment with an Egyptian scholar renowned as a champion of liberalism in the Arab context. His answer was even more blunt: "The Jews should build themselves a Vatican," he said, "a spiritual center somewhere near Jerusalem. But there is no place for a Jewish state in Palestine, not even a national Jewish state. The Jews were driven out two thousand years ago, and that should be final, similar to the expulsion of the Moors from Spain five hundred years ago."

The problem with Muslim elites could be seen again, even at the University of California, Irvine, where the Muslim Student Union organized a meeting entitled, "A World Without Israel"—cut and dry. Also in May came a colorful radio confession by the editor of the Egyptian newspaper *Al-Arabi*, Abd al-Halim Qandil: "Those who signed the Camp David agreement...can simply piss on it and drink their own urine, because the Egyptian people will never recognize the legitimacy of the Israeli entity."

Qandil's bald statement drove home a very sobering realization: in 2005, I still cannot name a single Muslim leader (or a journalist, or an intellectual) who has publicly acknowledged the Israeli-Palestinian conflict as a dispute between two legitimate national movements. One side dreams of a world without Israel, the other sees Israel as a major player in the democratization and economic development of the region. Will this clash of expectations burst into another round of bloodshed?

My heart goes out to all the Europeans and Americans who believe they have found a spark of flexibility on Israel's legitimacy in the progressive Muslim camp. But looking ahead at the plentiful attempts to build bridges to the Muslim world, one wonders whether this outpouring of goodwill should not first be harnessed toward hammering out basic common goals and educational campaigns to promote them, rather than glossing over oceans of fundamental disagreement. Failure to address uncomfortable differences has a terrible way of extracting higher costs later on.

4. "Remembrance, Vigilance, and Beyond," Address to the United Nations Non-Governmental Organizations Session, January 26, 2006

On the 2006 Holocaust Remembrance Day at the U.N., I was invited to address the meeting of the U.N. non-governmental organizations. My words, which connected the victims of the Holocaust to modern victims of terrorism, were echoed by Ambassador Dan Gillerman, who commented harshly on how unfairly Israel was treated in the U.N. I'm glad I reminded the U.N. audience of another intended genocide, from which I escaped: the 1948 Arab war of extermination.

On this solemn day of remembrance for the victims of the Holocaust, I am grateful for the opportunity to highlight the memory of my grandparents, who perished in Auschwitz in 1942, and that of my son, Daniel Pearl, who was murdered sixty years later in Karachi, Pakistan. Situated thousands of miles apart, and executed under different circumstances by people of a different faith, language, and purpose, the two murders nevertheless illuminate each other as well as the topic under discussion.

Four years ago, almost to the day, in a desolate dungeon in Karachi, Pakistan, my son Danny was looking in the eye of evil and proclaiming his identity. Forced to appear before his captors' video camera, he said with pride: "My name is Daniel Pearl. I am a Jewish-American from Encino, California...My father is Jewish, my mother is Jewish, I am Jewish."

I doubt whether my grandparents were ever asked to state their Jewishness—the Nazis did not need such confirmation. Yet Danny, I am sure, had a special message to convey in those words. I know that when Danny said, "I am Jewish," what he was trying to tell his captors was: "I respect Islam precisely because I am Jewish, and I expect you to respect me and my faith precisely because you are, or claim to be, 'good Muslims.'" In other words, "I come from a place where one's heritage is the source of one's strength, and strength is measured by one's capacity to accommodate diversity, because it is only through diversity that we recognize our common humanity."

"I am Jewish" was his way of saying: "I understand suffering because the suffering of my ancestors is etched on my consciousness, and I understand Muslims' suffering, as well, for I have seen your people in Kosovo, I have worked with your carpet weavers in Iran, and I have sung with your pearl divers in Qatar." Indeed, he was a journalist who gave voice to millions of voiceless Muslims, from Iran to Yemen, from Sudan to Pakistan, and gave Western readers a glimpse of the human face behind the news.

He walked, laughed, and cried with those he met—at home in the world. So, I believe that when Danny uttered his final words, "I am Jewish," he was telling the world: "I am reminding you of the challenge of understanding others."

"I am Jewish" means I proclaim my right to be who I am, and I remind you, as did my ancestors for three millennia, of the shining dignity of being different.

"I am Jewish" means I am the litmus test of your faith and the fire test of your strength. Let's come to our senses.

And as he stood there, demanding sanity in the face of madness, that dark dungeon in Karachi turned into a localized microcosmos that both personified and magnified the age-old struggle between inclusiveness and exclusiveness, humanity and savagery, between his great-grandparents and their Nazi executioners, civilization and barbarity, between Abel and Cain.

The goodness of Danny's smile, the principles by which he lived, and the sound of his last words then became an icon that awakened millions of people around the world who realized that the hatred that took his life threatens the very fabric of civilized society and that, political correctness aside, we are in the midst of a profound clash of cultures—a clash not along conventional East-West divides, nor along national or religious boundaries, but between those who pride themselves on killing innocents to transmit political messages and those who are appalled by such acts.

Danny's last words, "I am Jewish," thus assume a universal dimension and have come to symbolize the freedom of every individual to assert his faith, heritage, and identity. Like the diary of Anne Frank in the 1950s, these three simple words have inspired young people of all denominations to re-study the anatomy of antisemitism, to take pride in their heritage, to reflect on the consequences of fanaticism, and to stand up for tolerance and humanity everywhere. These words ring today as a majestic poem to the freedom of the human spirit and its amazing capacity to weave together the dignity of being different with the awareness that we are *one*.

I believe I was invited to speak in this forum because it is generally recognized that the forces that killed Danny are of the same species as those that killed my grandparents in the Holocaust. Both are products of the same disease: the dehumanization of the "other." And both were fueled by unabated incitement, thriving on the silence of the enlightened world. Danny's tragedy reminds us that these forces did not die in 1945; they are dangerously active today and must be fought by education, dialogue, vigilance, and timely response.

To this end, the Daniel Pearl Foundation was created to promote cross-cultural understanding using Danny's three major vocations: journalism, music, and dialogue. The Foundation brings Muslim journalists on fellowships to work at U.S. newspapers; it trains hundreds of high-school students in the art of balanced and objective international reporting; it brings together hundreds of musical concerts worldwide to promote intercultural respect; and it sponsors public dialogues between Jews and Muslims to explore common ground and air grievances.

Our power lies not in resources but in a symbol, a face of a person who earned respect on both sides of the East-West divide, a face that is instantly recognized the world over as an icon of peace. What makes such a humble symbol so powerful is that, unfortunately, the world is in dire need of an icon of peace.

It is a symbol that reminds Jews of the rise of postmodern antisemitism. It is a symbol that reminds Muslims of their own struggle against terrorism and fanaticism, a symbol that reminds Jews of their heritage, pride, and identity, a symbol that reminds Americans of good old-fashioned American and Western values and journalists of their commitment to truth and fairness. Danny speaks to all of us. He is a symbol that reminds people all over the world of their common humanity. The Foundation's activities are inspired by this symbol.

However, are these activities enough? Can these concerts, projects, and dialogues prevent another murder, another atrocity, or another genocide?

As I stand here before you, I represent three generations scarred by hate-based murders. My grandparents perished in a genocide that *was*. I narrowly escaped a genocide that was *meant to be* (and failed in 1948), and Danny, my son, fell victim to the murderous terrorism the world faces today, which targets people for what they represent, not what they are.

Remembrance is a call for vigilance. But remembrance in silence, even a vigilant one, betrays those who we remember, for it permits genocidal forces to advance and strengthen their position to launch another yet deadlier assault. Remembrance is a safeguard only if accompanied by vigilance and timely action.

For example, today the president of Iran, Mahmoud Ahmadinejad, is both building a nuclear arsenal and proclaiming he wants to wipe Israel off the map. Many around the world treat his words as much more than simply the wild statements of a politician, but as a very real threat of a new genocide that may exceed earlier ones. Here the United Nations has a crucial role to play by addressing the root cause of anti-Israel sentiments.

It might come as a surprise to some of you, but after a century of bloodshed, several peace agreements, many negotiations and interfaith dialogues, and countless U.N.-funded cultural programs, the majority of Muslims today still reject the idea that Jews deserve a state in some part of Palestine. Instead, Muslims perceive Israel to be a temporary outpost of Western colonialism, hastily created out of guilt or greed. No Arab leader has dared affirm that Israel is the historical homeland of the Jewish people. This rejectionist ideology, which I have dubbed "Zionophobia" to mirror the popular term "Islamophobia," has paralyzed the peace camps in Israel and Palestine and has provided the fuel and intellectual basis for a constant stream of violence and genocidal plans such as those announced by Ahmadinejad.

Current U.N. educational programs aiming to combat intolerance, religious prejudice, bigotry, and antisemitism should also address the problem of Zionophobia, which condemns 5.5 million human beings to eternal statelessness, if not genocide. Current outreach programs deal exclusively with the right of an individual to live as an equal member of society, but neglect the right of a society (in this case, the State of Israel) to live as an equal member in the family of nations.

If the U.N. is to lend its moral weight and educational resources to the prevention of genocide, it must devote serious efforts toward reversing the Zionophobic culture that is rampant in the Muslim world—just as it must do more to curb all forms of racism, including xenophobia and Islamophobia. The theme of our DPI-NGO briefing is "promoting tolerance and cross-cultural communication to help prevent future acts of genocide." Yet the very descendants and relatives of the victims of the Holocaust we honor here at the U.N. today are now being threatened with genocide. They deserve protection of a special kind: tolerance and respect for their ties to the birthplace of their history, the same tolerance and respect we should extend to the Palestinians. The U.N. should lead the way toward providing this protection. The memory of six million Jewish victims of the Holocaust, abandoned by the international community and denied this protection, cries out to us to take this lead.

And the murder of one man, my son, by the same forces of intolerance demonstrates the challenges we face as we strive for a society based on mutual respect and love of all peoples.

5. "Remembering Ilan Halimi," YNetNews.com, March 19, 2006

On January 21, 2006, an atrocity occurred in Paris when a group of Muslims calling itself the Gang of Barbarians kidnapped Ilan Halimi, a twenty-three-year-old Jewish man who worked as a cellphone salesman. For the next twenty-four days, Halimi's abductors tortured him as they bargained with his desperate mother for a ransom for his release. On February 13, he was discovered bound, maimed, and nearly dead at a Paris train station. He died on the way to the hospital. I wrote this eulogy for him in protest, as an indictment of French society for the climate of antisemitism and Zionophobia they allowed to fester, which led to Halimi's savage murder.

"Pour Ilan"—this is what the sign says, held by demonstrators in a quiet march, in Paris, in your memory.

Pour Ilan, Ilan Halimi, my newly fallen son.

When I weep for you, I weep for my son Daniel, too—your brother in pain—two treasures crushed in the claws of history.

When I weep for you, I weep with my burned face, with my hands tied behind my back, with my screaming mind—my sanity that was shattered when the doors of the heavens slammed on your life.

They rush to your memorial, the politicians, the dignitaries, Jewish leaders, too. They talk about joblessness, crime, jealousy, and greed. "They believe, and I quote, that 'Jews have money,'" said Interior Minister Sarkozy.

They always talk about "them"—the criminals, the barbarians—rarely about *themselves.*

How could it be?

They do not talk about the silence and tacit encouragement that have created this climate in France, where a gang of youngsters would choose to target Jews over other prey. A climate in which torturing a Jew is considered a lesser form of cruelty than the unimaginable. "We tortured him because he was a Jew," said one of the abductors last week.

How did this climate of inhumanity infiltrate a country that gave the world liberty, equality, and brotherhood? Ilan did not ask his captors this question—he knew the answer.

He understood that empathy emanates from the dignity and respect that society extends to its members. And he knew firsthand that while some members of the French Jewish community have risen to prominence, Jews, as a collective, have not enjoyed standard dignity and respect—they have been villainized and dehumanized in all strata of French society as no other group has.

Israelis, not Jews

Of course, only Israelis are dehumanized today in the French media, not all Jews—France is a modern country, and it knows the rules of post-WWII discourse. Likewise, French Jews are no longer accused of killing God's son or Christian boys. They are now villainized for one and only one crime: loving and caring for that "shitty little country," as French Ambassador Bernard called Israel, a country that, according to a 2005 survey, a majority of Europeans consider "the greatest threat to world peace."

Ilan's misfortune was that the gangsters of Bagneux were quick to discover what every child in Europe knew all along—who causes the troubles in the world and who can be bashed with impunity.

It is safe for us to talk about the gangsters of Bagneux, not so safe to talk about the French media. But if the death of Ilan Halimi is to have a meaningful and permanent mark on our consciousness, it is vital that we examine all sacred pillars of society. By licensing unrestrained assaults against Israel and Zionism—two cherished symbols of French Jewry—and denying the Jewish community a fair opportunity to make the case for Israel, the media has effectively turned French Jewry into social outcasts.

Classic antisemitism

This, coupled with classical antisemitic broadcasts pouring over from Middle East channels, offers some explanation for the barbaric and inexplicable inhumanity of Ilan's abductors.

Indeed, how can the residents of Bagneux be expected to respect the life of Ilan if he cherishes the Magen David—the most despised symbol in all of Europe, barring the swastika. A symbol that, for more than a decade, French media has refused to associate with any praiseworthy quality. What empathy could Ilan expect from his abductors when the symbol of his identity evoked nothing but revulsion in their Pavlovian brains? How could they remain deaf for twenty long days to his infinite screams, blended with his mother's pleas over the phone?

Video incitement

Unless they convinced themselves that this young man deserved subhuman treatment, either by virtue of belonging to the "despised," or as a cousin to those "monstrous Israeli soldiers" they repeatedly saw on TV, intentionally killing Palestinian children.

Or perhaps they were reminded of that video (now suspected of being a forgery) of the dying Palestinian child Mohammed al-Dura that France 2 was so eager to air on September 2000. Not one time, but day after day, night after night, with stubbornness and perseverance that only bigotry can sustain. So eager, in fact, that it found its way to the hands of Daniel Pearl's murderers in Pakistan and was used in their gruesome video to justify the murder—a grim reminder of the consequences of irresponsible journalism.

Deeper down

But let us dig a bit deeper.

How can the good citizens of Bagneux be expected to muster the courage to tell their gangster-neighbors, "Stop!", when they see around them a culture of capitulation, deceit, and herd pressure? A culture where frightened teachers yield to students refusing Holocaust classes, where police do not see what the government does not want to admit, where politicians vie with each other to proclaim what most Frenchmen know to be false, that is, that the Paris riots were void of religious or cultural undercurrents, and where the one writer who suggests otherwise is harshly rebuked by his peers as racist?

A culture where the darling of European philosophers, Tariq Ramadan, defines sympathy for a beleaguered Israel as betrayal of universal values, and where that same philosopher proclaims the West "morally bankrupt" to the mesmerized admiration of his Western colleagues.

True legacy

Oh, Ilan and Daniel, two beautiful sons of the West, intellectuals and barbarians have gathered again to challenge the vitality of your moral heritage. Remind them who you are.

You, two principled disciples of Abraham, Socrates, and Jeremiah, two proud emissaries of Aquinas, Rashi, and Galileo, two burning torches of Rousseau and Jefferson, Herzl and Einstein. Tell them what they refuse to see on your charred bodies: that Western civilization ain't ready to surrender, that youngsters like you attest to its strength and vitality, that "bankruptcy" is not in your vocabulary. And, finally, that your legacy will witness the downfall of your murderers. It will!

Danny and Ilan, my two fallen sons, it was not the barbarians alone who killed you. Twisted intellectuals were there all along, spreading the fuel while watching the barbarians light the fuse. They killed you because you are the soul of Western civilization, a soul they chose to disown.

Let there be no silence on your grave, Ilan, no rest nor learned discussion, until the racist climate of your murder stands trial in the court of history. Until another Zola rises with a louder "J'accuse" and this culture of deceit goes down in infamy, as did the Dreyfus Affair and the Munich Treaty.

Yitgadal Ve'Yitkadash Shmai Rabah

6. "The Postage Stamp Question: A Key to Peace in Palestine," *Nasseeb Vibes*, April 9, 2006

Nasseeb Vibes *is published out of Riyadh, Saudi Arabia. I was happy that its editors gave me an opportunity to directly address readers in the Muslim world. I presented them with the whole story of the Israeli-Palestinian conflict in two words: "postage stamp." The editors followed my piece with a rebuttal from a Palestinian who insisted that peace is secondary to justice—justice, of course, for one side only. Anytime someone wants an elevator pitch encapsulating the entire conflict, I still use these two words: "postage stamp."*

Assalamu Alaikum, *Shalom Aleichem*, dear friends on *Vibes*.

I am flattered by the large number of viewers who clicked on my *Vibes* interview last September, and I am honored by this opportunity to address your candid comments.

Naturally, some of my answers in that interview were deemed unsatisfactory to some viewers. For example, my characterization of the root cause of the current wave of violence as an "ideology of tantrum" was criticized for ignoring the political injustices suffered by Muslims (to which I am not oblivious), and my insistence on differentiating acts of deliberate cruelty from other forms of violence was not deemed essential by some readers. But I believe the main source of disagreement can safely be attributed to the Israeli-Palestinian conflict, which some commentators felt I have not treated with due attention to the Palestinian side. I have decided, therefore, to devote this conversation to that painful conflict and, moreover, to deviate from conventional analyses and go directly to what I consider the core of the core of the conflict, an issue that I call: The Postage Stamp Question.

I will begin with some background material. Much of it derives from my own experience as a native of Tel Aviv.

Imagine yourself waking up one morning to find a newspaper headline: "Majority of Palestinians Support the Zionist Dream of Theodor Herzl and David Ben-Gurion." Surely you would rub your eyes in disbelief, glance at Abu Mazen's latest speeches, and conclude that it must be April Fools' Day.

It is not. The headline of the January 19, 2005, article in the *Palestine Chronicle* reads loud and clear: "Majority of Palestinians Support Two

States," followed by, "Some 54 percent of the Palestinians support a two-state solution on the basis of the 1967 lines, with border corrections and no massive return of refugees, confirming that there has been a change in Palestinian public opinion since the death of Yasser Arafat."

True, the article does not mention Zionism or Zionist dreams, but from everything I know about the history of Zionism—and I grew up in an avid Zionist family—an independent Jewish state within some recognized and friendly boundaries is precisely what Zionism has been aiming to achieve since 1896, when Herzl wrote his booklet "Der Judenstaat" ("The State-of-the-Jews"). Therefore, anyone who endorses the now fashionable two-state solution also endorses the aims of Zionism and might as well be called a "Zionist at heart."

Indeed, since neither Herzl nor the Balfour Declaration, of 1917, outlined any specific borders for the intended Jewish state, the struggle in the first half of the twentieth century was not over borders, but over the very idea of creating a national home for the Jewish people in *any* part of Palestine. The Arabs viewed such an idea as a dangerous reincarnation of European colonialism, while Jews viewed it as a legitimate move of repatriation to their historical homeland.

Readers whose sentiments toward Zionism were shaped by slogans such as, "Zionism Is Racism" (U.N., 1975), "Zionism Is Not Racism" (U.N., 1991), "Zionism Is a Cancer" (Opinion, Al Jazeera, May 2004), and "Zionism Is a Disease" (speakers at the 2004 pro-Palestinian conference at Duke University) would naturally wonder whether Zionists' aspirations were indeed as modest and innocuous as described above and whether Arab objections were aimed against those modest aspirations. Most Israelis believe this to be the case, and they cite the following sequence of historical events as evidence.

Ze'ev Jabotinsky, by far the most ambitious hardliner of all Zionist leaders, wrote in 1937, "we beg merely for a small fraction of this vast piece of land."[1] That same year, when the British-appointed Peel Commission proposed a two-state solution, with a Jewish state on approximately 25 percent of the current area of Israel, the Zionist leadership accepted (after a fierce debate), while the Arabs retorted with the famous: "Not even the size of a postage stamp."

In November 1947, when the U.N. General Assembly voted for a

1 Ze'ev Jabotinsky, *Medinah Ivrit* (Tel Aviv: T. Kopp, 1937), 79.

partition plan with an independent Palestinian state on about double the size of the West Bank and Gaza (it included the entire Galilee and big chunks of the Negev), the Zionist leadership accepted (this time enthusiastically) and the Arabs rejected. (A five-army attack followed in May 1948, when the State of Israel was established). The fact that this rejection took place before the emergence of the Palestinian refugee problem is seen by Israelis as a proof that the core of the conflict lies not in settlements, refugees, borders, or resource disputes, but in the "postage stamp" ideology.

The next indicative development took place three years prior to the 1967 war at the first Arab League summit meeting in Cairo, January 1964. At that time, Jordan controlled the West Bank and Egypt governed Gaza; both regions were entirely free of Jewish presence. A peace agreement with Israel would have created a Palestinian state which, according to the *Palestine Chronicle*, would satisfy most Palestinians today. Yet the Arab League collectively called for "the final liquidation of Israel"[2] and formed the PLO a few months later.

The Arab Summit conference in Khartoum, August 1967, sheds additional light on sentiments toward the fundamental Zionist idea. Now Israel controlled the West Bank and Gaza, and started radiating land-for-peace overtures toward Egyptian President Gamal Abdel Nasser and King Hussain of Jordan.[3] These overtures were rejected by the Khartoum conference with the famous "Three Nos:" "No recognition, no negotiation, no peace."[4] Israelis took an especially sober notice of the "no negotiation" phrase and interpreted it to mean: "Not even the size of a postage stamp. Your very presence in the Middle East is unacceptable and will remain so till the end of days." It was this unfortunate phrase that gave a misguided ideological legitimacy to the settlement movement: "If we are destined to live by the sword till the end of days, we might as well do it from a position of strength."

In 1988, Arafat recognized Israel's existence and the Oslo process began. To many Israelis, that recognition signaled the end of the "postage stamp" ideology and brought Yitzhak Rabin and the peace camp to power. However, in the aftermath of the Oslo breakdown, leaders of the shattered

2 Avi Shlaim, *The Iron Wall: Israel and the Arab World* (New York: W.W. Norton and Company, Inc., 2001), 230.

3 Shlaim, *The Iron Wall*, 256.

4 Shlaim, *The Iron Wall*, 258.

Israeli peace camp confessed in public that they had been fooled all along.[5] Their major complaints were that Arafat's recognition of Israel was kept out of the collective consciousness of the Palestinian people, compromises were not discussed in public, incitement continued unabated, and the PLO charter, explicitly calling for the destruction of Israel, remained unaltered (as Farouq Kadoumi, head of the PLO political department, stated in 2004). Arafat's formal recognition of Israel, as well as the whole Oslo exercise, were perceived by ordinary Palestinians as a "Trojan Horse" in a grand scheme aiming toward a Palestinian state "from the river to the sea."[6]

Indeed, to this very day, not a single Arab leader has publicly acknowledged Zionism as a legitimate national movement.

In view of this history, my Israeli friends are monitoring with great optimism the poll cited in the *Palestine Chronicle* and are asking themselves: "Could this be a signal of a true change in attitude?" I would now like to explain why this question is so pivotal to peace in the Middle East and why all other issues—suicide bombing, refugees, rockets, separation wall, settlements, holy places, etc.—are but surface manifestations of that key question.

To understand the significance of this question we must recall that Israeli society is secular—70 percent of Israelis do not practice Judaic rituals and do not believe in the afterlife or divine supervision of one's actions and thoughts. The cement of Israeli society is not Judaic religion but Jewish history, and that history is intimately tied to the land of the Bible—the birthplace of the Jewish nation.

Denying Israelis the right for sovereignty over some part of this land would amount to denying the essence of their national identity which, in turn, would commit their collective memory to images of homelessness, persecution, and genocide. Thus, while world attention is focused on terrorism, occupation, border corrections, separation walls, and other newsmaking items, Israelis' attention is attuned to one and only one indicator: their postage stamp, namely, whether Palestinians accept their right

---

5 See Judea Pearl, "Oslo Failed Because It Never Started," *Jewish Journal*, September 20, 2023, p. 140.

6 Faisal Husseini, in The Middle East Media Research Institute (MEMRI), "Faysál al-Husseini in His Last Interview: The Oslo Accords Were a Trojan Horse; the Strategic Goal Is the Liberation of Palestine from the [Jordan] River to the [Mediterranean] Sea," https://www.memri.org/reports/faysal-al-husseini-his-last-interview-oslo-accords-were-trojan-horse-strategic-goal#_edn1.

of repatriation, in sovereignty, to some part of their ancestral land. It is for this reason that Arafat's remark to President Clinton that Jews never had a Temple in Jerusalem did more damage to the peace process than all terrorist acts put together. It signaled to Israelis that the "postage stamp" ideology is not dead after all, and it warned them that no matter what agreement they sign, it can easily be broken by some incident and burst into an all-out "just war" against the colonial postage stamp.

All analysts understand that a prerequisite to any peace process in the Middle East is the revitalization of the Israeli peace camp—the same camp that brought Rabin to power and got shattered at the breakdown of the Oslo process. It is only this camp that can give an Israeli government the political backing to dismantle settlements and provide resources to ensure a viable Palestinian state. And, as I have explained before, Israelis would flock to the peace camp if and only if it can pave the way to the Zionist dream of a legitimate postage stamp. Public opinion polls like the one reported in the *Palestine Chronicle* are therefore extremely encouraging, especially if they are echoed in the Palestinian media and the Palestinian school curriculum.

This is, my friends, my postage stamp narrative of the Israeli-Palestinian conflict, and I welcome your comments. Critics of my analysis can fall into one of two categories:

1. Arabs do not really object to Zionism on a postage stamp scale.

2. Jews do not deserve a sovereign postage stamp because they are a religion, not a nation.

I would be curious to see which of the two categories receives more votes on *Vibes*, and I would be glad to pursue the discussion accordingly.

One request, though. If your comment falls into the first category, please back it with an explicit statement: "Zionism is a legitimate national movement!" I will advertise your statement among my Israeli friends and, *inshallah*, we will thus be making a meaningful contribution to world peace.

7. "Shoah Denial Conference: Damage Assessment," *Jewish Journal*, December 28, 2006

On December 11, 2006, Iranian President Mahmoud Ahmadinejad opened the "International Conference to Review the Global Vision of the Holocaust," a two-day gathering in Tehran of Holocaust-deniers from around the world. He cynically asserted that if the world trusted that the Holocaust actually happened, then it should have no problem with an open discussion of its veracity. Ahmadinejad and the likeminded will never forgive the Jewish people for bringing to world consciousness the existential imperative of the State of Israel for our continued survival. In this piece, I tried to touch on the psychopathy and obsessiveness of the Holocaust-denial industry.

While world Jewry recovers from the shock of Iranian President Mahmoud Ahmadinejad's Holocaust Conference in Tehran, emotions are slowly giving way to analysis. Why is Ahmadinejad pursuing this foolish crusade against the Holocaust? After all, even he must know that the Holocaust is one of the most documented events in human history and, hence, that denying its reality or even questioning its magnitude and significance is likely to end up in embarrassment. Why, then, is he so insistent?

The three main reasons analysts cite for Ahmadinejad's obsession with the Holocaust are themselves questionable. We understand, of course, that by questioning the Holocaust, Ahmadinejad hopes to undermine what he believes was the main justification for the creation of the State of Israel in 1948. We also accept *Newsweek*'s Fareed Zakaria's explanation that "Iran is seeking leadership in the Middle East, and what better way to do so than by appropriating the core grievance of the Sunni Arabs: Israel." Finally, Ahmadinejad clearly enjoys ridiculing what he sees as a European double-standard—criminalizing Holocaust deniers on the one hand and advocating free speech on the other.

But these reasons, if they are the real reasons, entail heavy risks for Ahmadinejad. First, a serious risk exists that, driven by all the media attention, curious, bright youngsters in Iran and Arab countries will venture to dig into the vast evidence for the Holocaust and, upon realizing its magnitude and veracity, begin to ask what other parts of history were purged from their state-controlled education. Second, promoting the Palestinian cause through Holocaust denial tarnishes the former with all the absurdities of the latter, in much the same way that post-September 11 conspiracy theories have discredited Muslims and weakened their claims. Lastly, using Holocaust denial as an instrument for delegitimizing Israel may actually backfire. Columbia professor Joseph Massad argued (*Al Ahram*, 2004) that Arabs' preoccupation with Holocaust denial creates the impression that the Holocaust, if it were true, suffices to justify the establishment of Israel. This, according to Massad, serves the Zionist agenda, hence, "All those in the Arab world who deny the Jewish Holocaust are in my opinion Zionists."

My concerns lie elsewhere. I fear that as the buzz winds down and the dust settles, there will be only one thing remembered from the Holocaust Conference in Tehran: Israel and the Holocaust are one. That is, Israel owes its existence to one and only one factor: European guilt over the crime of the Holocaust. Once this is established, the next obvious question is: Why should the Palestinians pay for Europe's crime?

We, of course, do not see things that way. For us, the State of Israel is the culmination of a long historical process of collective homecoming, not a rescue boat from the claws of Germany. While the Nazi genocide definitely accelerated that process, it did not initiate or redirect it. The concepts of "Holy Land," "Shivat Zion," "Kibbutz Galuyot"—the ingathering of the exiles—three vital engines of Jewish history, are as old as Judaism itself. The majority of the six hundred thousand Jews who immigrated to Palestine prior to 1940 did not flee the Holocaust, nor did the five hundred eighty thousand Jews who came to Israel from Arab countries in the early 1950s. Jews are generally aware of the immutable connection between Eretz Israel and Jewishness. We know deep down that Shimon Peres is not less indigenous to the Land of Canaan than, say, Mahmoud Abbas. Yet we seem unwilling to openly assert it.

Take the movie *Munich*, for example, written and produced by two educated Jewish artists. While a Palestinian terrorist in the movie is shown yearning for his father's orchard, you will be wasting your time combing the script for a hint that Israeli society has any clue why they are in Israel and not, say, in Uganda. Tony Kushner knows why; he also knows that every Israeli knows why, yet he apparently did not feel comfortable enough to articulate it anywhere in his script.

I see a similar pattern in the criticism of the Holocaust Conference in Tehran. I hear tons of well-deserved condemnations of Ahmadinejad for orchestrating such an offensive conference, but not one voice saying: "Hey man! What a waste of time. We don't need a Shoah to justify a Jewish state on that sliver of land. Our history was born there, and our collective consciousness has remained there."

The main danger that I see emerging from Ahmadinejad's conference is that the international community, busy to rectify his misconceptions about the Holocaust, would ignore, and in fact mimic, his wanton disregard of the historical, national, and religious ties that bind the Jewish people to their ancient land. They ought to be reminded, and Ahmadinejad has given us a stage to do so.

8. "A Meaningful Peace Plan," *Jewish Journal*, February 8, 2007

The idea of revitalizing the 2002 Saudi peace plan continues to come up, sporadically, but has never led anywhere. Here I identify the plan's Achilles heel and propose a concrete and realizable solution to overcome this weakness: monitored investment in permanent housing for Palestinian refugees in the West Bank.

While attending the U.S.-Islamic World Forum in Doha, Qatar, in 2005, an Arab leader asked me at the dinner table: "Tell me, why didn't Israelis accept the Saudi peace proposal of 2002? In fact, they did not even respond to it. Did it not offer them everything that they ever wished for: peace, recognition, security, you name it?" I looked at him with amusement.

"Do you know what Israelis see when they read a peace proposal in the newspaper?" I asked. "They skip the text about peace, recognition, and security and seek the one word that counts: 'refugees.' The rest is trivial. If that word is embedded in 'right of return' or 'a just solution' or 'Resolution 194' or some other euphemism for dismantling Israel, the proposal is automatically deemed a nonstarter."

"What did the Saudi proposal say about the refugee problem?" he asked.

"Like you, I don't have the precise language," I said. "But like most Israelis, I distinctly recall the words 'just solution,' which should settle your question right there."

"Interesting," my Arab colleague said. "I have always assumed that if we build trust and solve the land problem, some solution will eventually be found for the refugee problem."

"Yes, many Israelis made this assumption during the Oslo period," I said. "But no more."

I was reminded of this conversation last week, when I read President Jimmy Carter's book, *Palestine: Peace Not Apartheid*, and found the following passage on page 211: "The Delphic wording of this statement [the Saudi proposal] was deliberate, in Arabic as well as in Hebrew and English, but the Arabs defend it by saying it is there to be explored by the Israelis and others and that, in any case, it is a more positive and clear commitment to international law than anything now coming from Israel."

I recalled how the Delphic wording of the Oslo agreement was deliberate, too, and how, in the aftermath of the Oslo breakdown, leaders of the shattered Israeli peace camp confessed in public that they had been fooled and betrayed by their Palestinian comrades. Specifically, sworn promises to prepare the Palestinian public for compromises on the refugee problem were never acted on (Haim Shur, *Maariv*, June 6, 2001). This inaction, according to Israeli analysts, was the main reason for the outbreak of the Second Intifada. Yasser Arafat simply could not face his people with "an end to the conflict" after decades of promising them a return to Haifa and Jaffa. But more than six years have passed since the breakdown of the Oslo process, and memory is short. People tend to forget that leaving the hard problems to resolve themselves exacts a heavy toll.

Last month saw renewed calls from both Israelis and Palestinians to revitalize the Saudi proposal (e.g., Collett Avital, *Jerusalem Post*, January 23, 2007), and I was a bit concerned that another case of "hard problems later" would be looming in front of our eyes. I was pleasantly mistaken. Israeli peace activists seem to remember the Oslo lesson vividly and painfully. In his third exchange with Palestinian analyst Salameh Nematt, published simultaneously in Hebrew, Arabic, and English, Israeli peace activist Akiva Eldar wrote: "We, the Israelis, need to be convinced that there is a solution to the refugee problem. Nothing is more likely to deter Israelis than the expression 'right of return.' In their eyes, these words are a synonym for the destruction of the Jewish state.

"Politicians on both sides know that it is inconceivable to strip a sovereign state, such as Israel, from its authority to decide whom to accept as its citizens. New cities have been built on the villages in which the refugees lived. Children and grandchildren of Jewish refugees from Europe were born in houses that remained standing.

"Anyone in his right mind knows that the solution to the Palestinian refugee problem is not to create a Jewish refugee problem. The solution can be found in a peace process that is based on two states and the absorption of most of the Palestinian refugees in their new state."

But suppose the Palestinians do sign a peace agreement with the provision that most refugees will be absorbed into their new state. How does one ensure that after Israel withdraws from most of the territories and makes room for a Palestinian state, Palestinian refugees will not continue to be kept in their wretched camps as a source of anger and uncontrolled militancy against Israel? After all, Israel cannot be asked to make irrevocable concessions in land and security while the Arabs are merely signing reversible promises to settle the refugees.

Here comes my humble suggestion, resting again on Saudi wisdom and goodwill. Instead of drawing fancy peace proposals, the Saudis, together with other oil-rich countries, should immediately launch a "Palestinian Marshall Plan" to build permanent housing for Palestinian refugees in the West Bank. Israel would monitor the plan and lift the embargo on foreign aid in stages. Each month's allotment would be proportional to the number of housing units completed.

We are constantly being told that the ball of peace lies entirely in Israel's court, because Palestinians have no control over their destiny and Israel's economy is so much stronger. It ain't necessarily so. Here is a peace proposal that depends entirely on Arab goodwill and peaceful Palestinian intentions. It should start today.

9. "Why Do Homo Sapiens Recognize Israel's Right to Exist?" *Los Angeles Times*, March 27, 2007

Saree Makdisi is a professor in UCLA's English department with whom I have sparred a number of times over the years, including once in a campus debate over the racist nature of the Boycott, Divestment, and Sanctions (BDS) movement (see "Debating the BDS Movement's Immorality" for my opening argument, p. 91). This op-ed was motivated by a question that Makdisi asked: Why should Israel demand the right *to exist and not be satisfied with recognition of the fact of its existence? It's a fair question and one that is still being asked by many well-meaning people, who think that it's unreasonable for Israel to be so particular. Here I argue that such insistence is absolutely essential for any peace agreement to be credible.*

Saree Makdisi's recent "Outside the Tent" column, "In the War of Words, The Times Is Israel's Ally" (published in the *Los Angeles Times*, March 11, 2007), raises interesting questions regarding the international community's insistence that Palestinians recognize Israel's right to exist. Recognition, says Makdisi, takes place simultaneously between sovereign states, not as a condition for attaining sovereignty. Moreover, countries merely recognize each other's polities, while Palestinians are unfairly requested to recognize Israel's "right to exist," which is a much deeper commitment, accepting not merely a political reality but also an ideological paradigm that morally justifies that reality.

These demands are indeed unique, but they adequately reflect the unique, unprecedented nature of the Middle East conflict. Never in the history of nations has a society defined itself on the ruins of a neighboring democracy and never has such a society sought sovereignty and international legitimacy while admitting its intent. Makdisi, for example, is not a bit embarrassed to argue for a Palestinian state on Israel's tomb while quoting from Orwell on language and morality.

The unique demand to recognize Israel's "right," not merely its "existence," reflects the general understanding among students of history that the core of the conflict and its resulting sufferings lies not in resource or border disputes, but in a deep ideological resistance by Palestinian Arabs to accommodate any form of a Jewish homeland in any part of Palestine since the end of World War I, accompanied by a persistent denial of any historical connection between the Jewish people and their national birthplace. For the record, Jews have accepted Palestinian Arabs as equally indigenous to the land and equally entitled to independent sovereignty, while Palestinian Arabs, and their Arab neighbors, have rejected any two-state solution offered since the 1920s, including the Peel Commission recommendation of 1937, the United Nations 1947 decision, and the Camp David offer in 2000.

Noting that the first and second rejections took place prior to the emergence of the refugee problem, and that the territories rejected in those cases were vastly broader than the West Bank and Gaza, it is only reasonable to assume that a deeper, ideological resistance propels Arab hostility toward Israel, a resistance that transcends borders or refugee problems. It is therefore perfectly reasonable that the international community verifies, prior to giving its blessing, whether this deeper resistance still stands in the way of future attempts to reach a lasting peace. The failure of the Oslo process was costly to all sides.

Makdisi is right; Israel's demand that its "right to exist" be recognized has become the norm of civilized discourse. However, this demand reflects a genuine universal anxiety, not about Israel's existence but about its neighbors' readiness to work toward a lasting, conciliatory peace. Absent such readiness, formal recognitions of existence are mere invitations to a bloodier conflict.

10. "Science and Human Freedom," University of Toronto Commencement Address, June 21, 2007

When I was selected as a commencement speaker for the University of Toronto and to receive my first honorary doctorate, some professors warned me not to provoke the Muslim students and faculty by dwelling on the Holocaust in my address. I chose to talk about the relationship between science and human freedom, and to set up my argument I discussed the differences between Muslim and Western cultures as it is reflected in the progress of science. I later heard from the university president that I had offended some Muslim students who revered two major figures that I criticized, Professor Tariq Ramadan and Sheikh Yusuf al-Qaradawi. I believed that I did not need to apologize for my position. The university president agreed with me.

It is a great honor for me to receive this doctorate degree from your esteemed university, and it is also a timely honor—I've been waiting more than forty years for an opportunity to consummate my PhD degree in an official graduation ceremony, because, and this is a difficult confession for me to make, I skipped my other graduation ceremonies, all three of them.

When my bachelor's degree was awarded, I was on board a ship heading to America. And when the time came to get my PhD degree, I had a tough dilemma. The ceremony fell on the very same day that I was to receive a master's degree in physics from a different university, and I could not make up my mind between the two. At the end of the day, I stayed home and had the two diplomas delivered by mail. This was my teenage rebellion, very fashionable in the 1960s: "Who cares for ceremonies and symbols, caps, gowns, and speeches? It is the knowledge that counts, right?"

Wrong!

I have another confession to make today, a secret that I've kept even from my wife. I truly regret not having gone to my graduation in 1965, which, in some strange sense, caused me to feel that my degree is somewhat fake or improperly earned, even though the diploma itself is properly signed and well encased, I am sure, in a very safe place at home.

And I should have known better. Coming from computer science, the science of symbols, I should have known the importance of symbols to the workings of the mind and to the workings of society. I should have known that in all primitive societies initiations into adulthood are consummated not by signing documents, not even by passing a test, but by a ritual communal dance with feather hats and dragon masks, and all the tribal chiefs, and the village elderly, and women and children present. And I should have known that the neural architecture of modern man is not much different from that of the hunting caveman.

I know better now. I know that it is not the signature on your diploma that counts but the statement of deservedness that you will be making by stepping up to this stage and receiving your degree in the presence of your teachers, families, and peers, who will bear witness to and cheerfully approve of your claim for accomplishment. That is what counts, and that is what you will remember. And that is why we put on these funny caps and gowns, so you will retain a visual memory of this tribal dance.

Why?

Because it is only through a communal testimony that your accomplishments become embedded in a relevant and meaningful context, larger than yourself, and it is through this context of an extended tribal community that you will be able to apply what you have learned in a way that would make it meaningful and rewarding to you for the rest of your life.

What is this tribal community that you are joining today? The cap and gown that I wear unveil its identity; it is the tribe of "scientific freedom fighters."

This cap and gown were first worn at the University of Padua, Italy, in the thirteenth–fourteenth centuries, the place where Galileo later taught and where he invented the telescope (1608) and discovered the amazing fact that physics listens to the language of algebra (1632). Galileo is one of my heroes, because, to me, he represents the essence of scientific pursuit. Just to have the illusion that I am emulating Galileo in his funny outfit sends a thrill down my spine.

Galileo always reminds me of the inextricable connection between science and freedom.

How?

Because Galileo showed that to be a scientist you must have both respect for the truth and the audacity to believe that you can find it. This might sound trivial. Science, by definition, is about truth, so what's all this talk about freedom? It is not so trivial. Truth can be elusive, even in our times, covered by the heavy fog of fear and hidden agenda. It is only after the murder of my son, Danny, that I came to appreciate how hard it is, even in the age of the internet, to stay the course of truth.

Just two weeks ago, Abdurrahman Wahid, the former president of Indonesia, and Israel Lau, the former chief rabbi of Israel, made an interesting observation, published in the *Wall Street Journal*: "the countries in which Holocaust denial is most rampant also tend to be the ones that are most economically backward and politically repressive."

Now, what is the connection, you might ask, between Holocaust denial and repressiveness? Is lack of freedom the cause of truth denial, or the other way around? The idea is, said Wahid and Lau, that "those who are dishonest when it comes to the truth of the past are hardly in a position to reckon honestly with the problems of the present."

What Galileo showed us is that you cannot have one honesty without the other; scientific truth demands scientific honesty, and scientific honesty demands intellectual honesty overall. We all remember the one thousand years of zero scientific progress through the Middle Ages—what caused this? The conventional answer is that the Church was repressive of scientific discourse. But this could not be the whole story. There was no repressive Church in the Muslim world. And Muslim scientists had access to the richest libraries of the time, well-funded astronomical observatories, and all the writings of the Greek and Roman philosophers. So, why didn't a genius like Galileo emerge in Cordoba or Alexandria or Baghdad in the eighth or ninth century? Why was science held back in almost total stagnation for one thousand years until, as though by miracle, the genius of Copernicus, Vieta, and Galileo emerged in Dark Age Europe of all places? Can you imagine where mankind would be today had the Renaissance and the Scientific Revolution taken place in the fifth century instead of the fifteenth?

What Galileo taught us is that permission to read, translate, observe, and use fancy equipment is not enough; the development of science requires a restless and rebellious spirit, a spirit that puts the individual at the center of the universe and proclaims: "I don't care about Aristotle and his fancy books. I want to see these two rocks dropped from the Tower of Pisa, and I want to see them with my own two eyes."

In other words, what Galileo showed us is that you cannot truly search for the truth unless you are free to rebel against the detractors of truth: conventional wisdom, peer pressure, sacred cows, wishful thinking, revered authority, and hidden agenda. In short, free to perceive yourself as an *agent* in control of your destiny, not an *object* at the mercy of destiny.

Remarkably, this Western perception of man as a free agent, sometimes called the "scientific philosophy," is not always taken for granted, even today. "The West is morally bankrupt," declares Professor Tariq Ramadan, the darling star of European intellectuals. "Take from the West all its science and technology," says Sheikh Yusuf al-Qaradawi to his Al Jazeera listeners, "but you must reject Western philosophy, because it is corrupted at its roots by the pagan philosophies of Greece and Rome."

Sorry to disappoint you, Sheikh Yusuf al-Qaradawi, but you can't have science and technology without Western philosophy of freedom, honesty, and individual *agency*. It has been tried before, for one thousand years in your own courtyard, and failed. And sorry to disappoint you, Professor Ramadan, but Western civilization is mighty proud of its ethics, values, and achievements, and "bankruptcy" is not in its lexicon—far from it.

The spirit of the West shines brightly today through the work of hundreds of humble yet courageous and principled young scientists and engineers, who are graduating from this great university. This spirit is rooted indeed in the skeptical inquiry of the pagan Socrates, and the moral clarity of the biblical Jeremiah, and the rebellious spirit of Galileo. But, behold, it shows no sign of bankruptcy or decline. It is, in fact, the only beacon of hope and moral courage for humanity today.

So, I congratulate you all today on joining the extended family of Socrates, Galileo, and Einstein, and I welcome you to the tribal dance of science, the dance of freedom and humanity.

11. "Moral Relativism and A Mighty Heart," *The New Republic*, July 3, 2007

I wrote this op-ed in reaction to the movie A Mighty Heart, *directed by Michael Winterbottom and based on the book by Danny's widow, Mariane Pearl. I objected to several parts of the movie, primarily the anti-American sentiments Winterbottom expresses in certain scenes. He takes the position that America and, more broadly, the West are imperialist entities that mistreat non-Westerners. I felt that this was contrary to Danny's worldview.*

I used to believe that the world essentially divided into two types of people: those who were broadly tolerant and those who felt threatened by differences. If only the forces of tolerance could win out over the forces of intolerance, I reasoned, the world might finally know some measure of peace.

But there was a problem with my theory, and it was never clearer than in a conversation I once had with a Pakistani friend who told me that he loathed people like President Bush, who insisted on dividing the world into "us" and "them." My friend, of course, was taking an innocent stand against intolerance and did not realize that, in so doing, he was in fact dividing the world into "us" and "them," falling straight into the camp of people he loathed.

This is a political version of a famous paradox formulated by Bertrand Russell in 1901, which shook the logical foundations of mathematics. Any person who claims to be tolerant naturally defines himself in opposition to those who are intolerant. But that makes him intolerant of certain people—which invalidates his claim to be tolerant. The political lesson of Russell's paradox is that there is no such thing as unqualified tolerance. Ultimately, one must be able to expound intolerance of certain groups or ideologies without surrendering the moral high ground normally linked to tolerance and inclusivity. One should, in fact, condemn and resist political doctrines that advocate the murder of innocents, that undermine the basic norms of civilization, or that seek to make pluralism impossible. There can be no moral equivalence between those who seek—however clumsily—to build a more liberal, tolerant world and those who advocate the annihilation of other faiths, cultures, or states.

Which brings me to my son, Daniel Pearl. Thanks to the release of *A Mighty Heart*, the movie based on Mariane Pearl's book of the same title, Danny's legacy is once again receiving attention. Of course, no movie could ever capture exactly what made Danny special—his humor, his integrity, his love of humanity—or why he was admired by so many. For journalists, Danny represents the courage and nobility inherent in their profession. For Americans, Danny is a symbol of one of our very best national instincts: the desire to extend a warm hand of friendship and dialogue to faraway lands and peoples. And for anyone who is proud of their heritage or faith, Danny's last words, "I am Jewish," showed that it is possible to find dignity in one's identity even in the darkest of moments. Traces of these ideas are certainly evident in *A Mighty Heart*, and I hope viewers will leave the theater inspired by them.

At the same time, I am worried that *A Mighty Heart* falls into a trap Bertrand Russell would have recognized: the paradox of moral equivalence, of seeking to extend the logic of tolerance a step too far. You can see traces of this logic in the film's comparison of Danny's abduction with Guantanamo—it opens with pictures from the prison—and its comparison of al-Qaeda militants with CIA agents. You can also see it in the comments of the movie's director, Michael Winterbottom, who wrote on the *Washington Post*'s website that *A Mighty Heart* and his previous film, *The Road to Guantanamo*, "are very similar. Both are stories about people who are victims of increasing violence on both sides. There are extremists on both sides who want to ratchet up the levels of violence, and hundreds of thousands of people have died because of this."

Drawing a comparison between Danny's murder and the detainment of suspects in Guantanamo is precisely what the killers wanted, as expressed in both their emails and the murder video. Obviously, Winterbottom did not mean to echo their sentiments and certainly not to justify their demands or actions. Still, I am concerned that aspects of his movie will play into the hands of professional obscurers of moral clarity.

Indeed, following an advance screening of *A Mighty Heart*, a panelist representing the Council on American-Islamic Relations reportedly said: "We need to end the culture of bombs, torture, occupation, and violence. This is the message to take from the film." The message that angry youngsters are hearing is unfortunate: All forms of violence are equally evil; therefore, as long as one persists, others should not be ruled out. This is precisely the logic used by Mohammad Sidique Khan, one of the London suicide bombers, in his videotape on Al Jazeera. "Your democratically elected government," he told his British countrymen, "continues to perpetrate atrocities against my people....[W]e will not stop."

Danny's tragedy demands an end to this logic. There can be no comparison between those who take pride in the killing of an unarmed journalist and those who vow to end such acts—no ifs, ands, or buts. Moral relativism died with Daniel Pearl, in Karachi, on January 31, 2002.

There was a time when drawing moral symmetries between two sides of every conflict was a mark of original thinking. Today, with Western intellectuals overextending two-sidedness to reckless absurdities, it reflects nothing but lazy conformity. What is needed now is for intellectuals, filmmakers, and the rest of us to resist this dangerous trend and draw legitimate distinctions where such distinctions are warranted.

My son Danny had the courage to examine all sides. He was a genuine listener and a champion of dialogue. Yet he also had principles and red lines. He was tolerant but not mindlessly so. I hope viewers will remember this when they see *A Mighty Heart*.

12. "You Have the Right to Feel Offended," *Jewish Journal*, August 17, 2007

The title speaks for itself. However, when it comes to Zionophobia, we Jews refrain from expressing offense. We don't like making people feel guilty, especially over Zionism, the part of ourselves that we have given people license to abuse with impunity. I maintain that even in today's climate, where most cultural values have been cheapened by victimhood rhetoric, an expression of genuine offense still has a powerful role to play.

A conference organized by the Jewish People Policy Planning Institute in Jerusalem last month dealt with anti-Israel attacks in the United States that constitute, according to organizers, a "long-term threat" to Israel's standing. Brandeis University President Jehuda Reinharz told *Ha'aretz* that American academics are at the forefront of those denying Israel's right to exist as a Jewish state and admitted: "I see no combined effort to fight this by the Jewish organizations, and, in truth, I myself don't know how this could be done."

I doubt whether organizational efforts could stop anti-Israel attacks, but two incidents in the past few weeks have suggested for me a grassroots approach that, if pursued vigorously, might well slow down their growth. The approach calls for exercising honesty, moral assertiveness, and personal indignation against attacks on Israel's legitimacy.

The incidents I am talking about started with a rather routine scenario. In fact, it has probably happened to you so many times that it did not leave a memorable mark. Like many of us, I am on the email lists of friends and colleagues who occasionally call my attention to an article worth reading. So it was that on one of these bright California mornings, I received a message from a colleague with an article and a comment: "Palestinians, with all their suffering under the Israeli apartheid regime, have never been Holocaust deniers." It is, by today's standards, a rather commonplace remark, one that could have been written by any of my friends from the far-Left or the Muslim community. I would normally either brush it off with a head shake, "There he goes again, the same old rhetoric," or start an argument on whether the comparison to apartheid South Africa is appropriate.

I do not exactly know what it was that morning that compelled me to do neither of the two, but resort, instead, to what I normally refuse to do—take offense. It may have been the recent vote in the U.N. Human Rights Commission, calling for a ban on "religious insults," or it may have been the latest press blitz on the moral ills of Islamophobia. Whatever the cause, somehow an invisible force jolted me into writing my colleague thus: "The word 'apartheid' is offensive to me. In fact, it is very, very offensive. And since I am not situated on the extreme end of the political spectrum, I venture to suspect that there are others on your email list who were offended by it and who may wish to tell you that this word is not conducive to peace and understanding. It conveys anger, carelessness, and a desire to hurt and defame. Hence, it shuts off the ears of the very people you are attempting to reach."

After a short exchange of polite messages, in which my colleague explained that, echoing his idols, President Jimmy Carter and journalist Amira Hass, he used this word not to offend but to evoke a sense of justice among his Jewish friends, I realized that I handled it correctly.

I realized that taking offense is a statement of conscience that shifts attention from the accused to the legitimacy of the accusation. It calls into question the accuser's choice of words, his assumptions, his worldview, as well as his intentions, and, thus, turns the accuser into a defendant, at least for a short moment of reflection. For a split second, I even ventured to imagine how powerful it could be if each one of us were to implant a moment of reflection into the mind of an anti-Israel colleague, but I soon forgot about the incident, and I received no further messages from this colleague. Evidently, he had either deleted my name from his mailing list or had taken note of our exchange and become more conscientious of what he sent and to whom.

A few weeks later, a similar incident occurred. This time, harsh anti-Zionist slurs were scattered throughout an essay authored by the sender, a history professor at an American university. Essentially, the author blamed Zionism for being the evil force that drives Bernard Lewis's "anti-Muslim diatribes." Emboldened by my previous experience, I sat down and wrote this man—let's call him Mahmoud—a message, this time a little longer. I explained that I had found his contempt of Zionism deeply offensive and that, given that I consider myself progressive and open-minded, others may share my feeling but were too polite to say so. "I hope," I said, "that as a writer who spends pages describing how offensive Orientalism and Islamophobia are to Muslims and Arabs, you will be able to understand other people's sensitivities and accommodate them in the future." I then went further and explained to Mahmoud that, for me, Zionism is the realization of a millennia-old belief in the right of the Jewish people to a national home in the birthplace of their history, a right that is no less sacred than that of the Palestinians or the Saudis. Additionally, I wrote, it pains me to see my hopes for peace being spat upon. Such hopes require that all sides accept a two-state arrangement as a historically just solution, and anti-Zionist rhetoric, by negating the legitimacy of this solution, acts as an oppressor of peace.

Mahmoud explained that he did not mean to delegitimize Zionism or the two-state solution. His portrayal of Lewis's Zionism as the mother of all evils was apparently triggered by a speech delivered at the American Enterprise Institute (AEI) in March of 2007, in which Lewis pitted Europe and Islam against each other, coupled with AEI (and Lewis's) one-sided support of Israel. Personally, I have never understood why a one-sided support of Israel, which to me is tantamount to a one-sided support of a quest for coexistence, would be considered a crime, but this takes us away from our main story.

The point of my story is that, again, I felt invigorated by exercising an almost forgotten right—the right to be offended.

13. "The Daniel Pearl Standard," *The Wall Street Journal*, January 30, 2008

The question of what constitutes genuine journalism and what differentiates a journalist from a propagandist, especially when journalists are getting injured or killed, has been around since a free press was first conceptualized. Today, when increasing segments of the mainstream media are introducing propaganda into their news reporting, this question becomes doubly acute. Here I propose to define the difference between a journalist and a propagandist in no uncertain terms: just choose any media outlet and "ask yourself when was the last time it ran a picture of a child, a grandmother, or any empathy-evoking scene from the 'other side' of a conflict." You can then assess journalistic bias by comparing the frequencies at which such scenes are shown.

This week marks the sixth anniversary of the murder of my son Daniel Pearl, a reporter for this newspaper. It is a fitting occasion to step back and reflect on what this tragedy has taught us.

I am often asked why Danny's death has touched so many people and why he, of all victims of terror, is so often singled out as an icon of the troubled journey of the twenty-first century. My first answer is that he was a journalist, and journalists, more than any other professionals, represent the strength, beauty, and vulnerability of an open society. When an unarmed journalist is killed, we are reminded of both the freedoms that we treasure in our society and how vulnerable we all are to forces that threaten those freedoms. But this still does not explain the attention given to Danny's tragedy. After all, thirty other journalists were killed in 2002, and one hundred eighteen journalists have been killed in Iraq alone since that war began.

The shocking element in Danny's murder was that he was killed not for what he wrote or planned to write, but for what he represented—America, modernity, openness, pluralism, curiosity, dialogue, fairness, objectivity, freedom of inquiry, truth, and respect for all people. In short, each and every one of us was targeted in Karachi in January of 2002.

This new twist of killing journalists for what they represent has changed the course of journalism as well as the rest of society. It was through Danny's face that people came to grasp the depth of cruelty and inhumanity into which this planet of ours has been allowed to sink in the past two decades. His murder proved that 9/11 was not an isolated event, and helped resurrect the age-old ideas of right and wrong, good and evil. Moral relativism died with Daniel Pearl in January 2002.

And unarmed journalists in regions of conflict became many times more vulnerable. They are no longer perceived as neutral, information-gathering agents, but rather as representing political or ideological entities. The press and media has indeed become more polarized and agenda-driven. Journalists today are pressured to serve the ideologies of those who pay their salaries or those who supply them with sources of information. CNN's admission, in 2003, that it concealed information about the Iraqi regime in order to keep its office in Baghdad is a perfect example of this pressure. In the recent Gaza chaos, Western news agencies have willingly reported Hamas propaganda stunts as truth.

One of the things that saddens me most is that the press and media have had an active, perhaps even major role in fermenting hate and inhumanity. It was not religious fanaticism alone. This was first brought to my attention by the Pakistani consul general who came to offer condolences at our home in California. When we spoke about the antisemitic element in Danny's murder, she said: "What can you expect of these people who never saw a Jew in their lives and who have been exposed, day and night, to televised images of Israeli soldiers targeting and killing Palestinian children." At the time, it was not clear whether she was trying to exonerate Pakistan from responsibility for Danny's murder, or to pass on the responsibility to European and Arab media for their persistent dehumanization of Jews, Americans, and Israelis. The answer was unveiled in 2004, when a friend told me that photos of Mohammed al-Dura were used as background in the videotape of Danny's murder.

Al-Dura, readers may recall, is the twelve-year-old Palestinian boy who allegedly died from Israeli bullets in Gaza in September of 2001. As we now know, the whole scene is very likely to have been a fraud, choreographed by stringers and cameramen of France 2, the official news channel of France. France 2 aired the tape repeatedly and distributed it all over the world to anyone who needed an excuse to ratchet up anger or violence, among them Danny's killers. The Pakistani consul was right. The media cannot be totally exonerated from responsibility for Danny's murder, as well as for the "tsunami of hate" that has swept the world and continues to rise.

Ironically, the increase of independent news channels in the Arab world, a process which is generally considered a positive step forward, has contributed significantly to this spread of hatred and violence. On the one hand, this process has led to the democratization of the media, for it allows viewers to examine alternative viewpoints, occasionally opposing the official party line. On the other hand, democratization has led to vulgarization. Competition has forced news channels to echo, rather than inform, viewers' sentiments—to reinforce, rather than examine, long-held prejudices. Eager to satisfy their customers' appetite for self-righteousness, these channels have not thought through the harmful, in fact lethal, long-term effects of choreographing victim-victimizer narratives as news coverage. Surely they have an obligation to expose villainy and excess. This is what journalism is all about. But in a world infected with fanatics who run around with lit matches, journalists cannot simply pour gasoline into the street and pretend they bear no responsibility for the inevitable explosion.

In one memorial service for Danny, a Catholic priest made an interesting observation that, serving as a mediator of reality, the modern journalist can be likened to the biblical prophet. My first reaction was that the comparison is too far-fetched. Yet on further reflection I came to understand his point. Who serves today as the moral compass of society, and, like the ancient prophets, risks his or her life by exposing corruption, institutional injustice, terrorism, and fanaticism? The journalist.

But the Bible also offers us a foolproof test for discerning false prophets from true ones. The test is not based on the nature of the reported facts, but on the method and principles invoked in the message. Translated into secular, modern vocabulary, the true journalist will never compromise on universal principles of ethics and humanity and will never allow us to forget that all people, including our adversaries, need be portrayed with dignity and respect as children of one God. Accordingly, to distinguish true from false journalism, just choose any newspaper or TV channel and ask yourself when was the last time it ran a picture of a child, a grandmother, or any empathy-evoking scene from the "other side" of a conflict.

I propose this simple test as the "Daniel Pearl standard of responsible journalism." Anyone who reads Danny's stories today and examines the way he reported the human story behind the news, would agree that adopting the proposed standard for the profession would be a fitting tribute to his legacy.

14. "Israel, Starting from Scratch," *Los Angeles Times*, May 12, 2008

In May 2008, the Los Angeles Times *hosted a five-part debate in its pages between me and law professor George E. Bisharat of the University of California College of the Law, San Francisco. This is the fifth debate in the series, prompted by the following question from the* Times*: "Could Arabs and Israelis have done anything differently before 1948 that would have laid a better foundation for the Middle East?" This gave me the opportunity to articulate my formula for peace for the first time: Two states for two peoples, equally legitimate and equally indigenous.*

Point: Judea Pearl

Until fairly recently, I believed that the Zionist movement ignored signs of national awakening among Palestinians in the early twentieth century. I believed that if only it had done more to acknowledge and accommodate that awakening, much of the animosity between the two peoples could have been avoided. Yet a short journey through the worn and dusty pages on my history bookshelf unveiled a different story, evidently unavailable to English readers. Zionists were both aware and respectful of Palestinian aspirations and made persistent attempts to reach reciprocal recognition and accommodation.

For example, David Ben-Gurion, Israel's first prime minister, wrote in the Yiddish newspaper *Yidisher Kemfer* in 1918: "The Land of Israel is not an empty country....West of Jordan alone houses three-quarters of a million people. On no account must we injure the rights of the inhabitants." The next year, Chaim Weizmann wrote in *Ha'aretz* (December 15, 1919): "If indeed there is among the Arabs a national movement, we must relate to it with the utmost seriousness." Most revealing yet was a fiery speech given by Ben-Gurion in November 1930, in which he said,

> We ought not to diminish the Arabs' freedom for self-determination for fear that it would present difficulties to our own mission. The entire moral core encapsulated in the Zionist idea is the notion that a nation—every nation—is its own purpose and not a tool for the purposes of other nations. And in the same way that we want the Jewish people to be master of its own affairs, capable of determining its historical destiny without dependence on the will—even goodwill—of other nations, so too we must seek for the Arabs.

The Middle East would look significantly different today had Arab leadership been able to reciprocate Ben-Gurion's offer with some recognition, however mild, of the Jewish right for self-determination. Unfortunately, the idea of Jews returning to rebuild their ancient homeland, a notion that inspired worldwide Zionists with infinite energies of sacrifice and creative development, was dismissed by the Arabs as a fabrication designed to serve European imperialism.

This clash of paradigms came to a juncture in July 1937, when the British Peel Commission recommended the partition of Palestine into two separate states, leaving Jews about 20 percent of the land. The Arabs flatly rejected the partition plan, arguing that they should not be turned into a minority in any part of Palestine, however slender the margin. Had this plan been accepted, much of European Jewry could have been saved, and Israel would have become a thriving Hong Kong-type enclave, home to ten million Jews and neighbor to an equally thriving Palestinian state four times its size.

A second juncture presented itself in 1947, when the United Nations

General Assembly voted thirty-three to thirteen in favor of a partition plan that allotted 55 percent of the land for a Jewish state side by side with a Palestinian state twice the size of the present-day West Bank and Gaza Strip. Arab leaders rejected this plan as unfair, citing 1947 demographic figures that did not factor in the millions of Jews in Europe and Arab countries who were waiting to emigrate.

Had the partition plan been accepted, the humiliating defeat of the five Arab armies that attacked Israel in May 1948 would have been avoided, fears of Arabs' genocidal designs would not have settled into the Israeli mindset, the Palestinian refugee problem would not have emerged, and efforts toward reconciliation and collaboration would have moved the region to a new era of dignity and prosperity.

Sixty years later, the world, the region, and two bleeding nations are still awaiting the first Arab leader, intellectual, or spokesperson to publicly accept Jews as a nation, equally indigenous to the land and equally deserving a sovereign homeland..

Counterpoint: George E. Bisharat

Judea,

You imply that if Palestinians had packed up and abandoned their homes, fields, and communities to make room for a Jewish state in Palestine, then conflict would have been avoided and much of European Jewry might have been saved. That is quite a moral responsibility to shift to Palestinians—and it is unfair.

Imagine that a foreign government were granted authority over California against our expressed will. With its aid, a persecuted people from elsewhere immigrated here in great numbers. Imagine further that these immigrants aspired not to live among us as equals, but to displace us and establish a state to serve their interests but not ours. Finally, an international organization endorsed this plan. Wouldn't we respond with outrage? That is exactly how Palestinians responded. Their efforts to defend their independence have been sometimes valiant and sometimes crude. But they follow a tradition of struggles for freedom against foreign domination that we must respect.

No one has ever answered satisfactorily why Palestinians should have paid the moral debt that Christian Europe incurred for its centuries of persecution of Jews. In fact, no answer is possible. When the British, and later the United Nations, proposed awarding part of Palestine to Jews, they and other Western nations that dominated the organization at the time let themselves off cheaply. In the name of justice for Jews, a great injustice was perpetrated against the Palestinians.

Judea, you also overlook the expansionist ambitions of political Zionism (the movement to create a Jewish state in Palestine). Long ago, Zionists determined to take the entire country "goat by goat, dunum by dunum" (a dunum is the local measure of land). But Zionist—and later Israeli—leaders have been careful to admit only what political traffic would bear. They accepted partition of Palestine as a tactical advance, as it provided them previously lacking international legitimacy. Ben-Gurion knew that force would be necessary to clear the land of Palestinians for Jewish settlement. He confided to his diary in 1937: "The compulsory transfer of the Arabs from the valleys of the proposed Jewish state could give us something which we never had...a Galilee free from Arab population....We must uproot from our hearts the assumption that the thing is not possible. It can be done." Later, in July 1948, Ben-Gurion ordered the forcible expulsion of the Palestinian residents of Lydda and Ramla.

In short, conflict was inevitable once Zionists sought a Jewish state in a land with an Arab majority. Ethnic separatism cannot be imposed on a multicultural society except through violence. Palestinians were bound to oppose a movement that would either displace them or reduce them to a powerless minority where their ancestors had lived for centuries. Had Jews come to live with Palestinian Arabs as equals, not usurpers, they might have been welcomed. Yet Zionism's terrible mistake can still be rectified by establishing equal rights for everyone in Israel and Palestine, regardless of religion or race.

Response from Judea Pearl

Dear George,

Before we go further into the discussion, I must correct a terrible misconception that seems to be the basis of your counterpoint. For the record, the two-state solution that was proposed to the Arabs in 1937 and 1947 did not imply, as you state, that Palestinians must "pack up, abandon their homes, fields, and communities, and make room for a Jewish state in Palestine." It implied that Palestinians will continue to live in their villages but allow Jewish immigration to areas designated as a Jewish state (20 percent of the land in the 1937 proposal), where Palestinians will enjoy full rights similar to the rights that French nationals enjoy in Montreal. Conversely, indigenous Jews will become a minority with full rights in the areas designated as a Palestinian state.

Moving Palestinians from their land was rejected by every Zionist leader from 1918 until bloody hostilities broke out in 1936. Even then, with the exception of a few anecdotes, removing Palestinians was never policy. Ben-Gurion said in 1918: "Dispossessing the current inhabitants of the country is not the mission of Zionism. Had Zionism to aspire to inherit the place of these inhabitants—it would be nothing but a dangerous utopia and an empty, damaging, and reactionary dream."

Chaim Weizmann wrote in *Ha'aretz* in 1919,

> If indeed there is among the Arabs a national movement, we must relate to it with the utmost seriousness....The Arabs are concerned about two issues: 1. The Jews will soon come in their millions and conquer the country and chase out the Arabs....Responsible Zionists never said and never wished such things. 2. There is no place in Eretz Israel for a large number of inhabitants. This is total ignorance. It is enough to notice what is happening now in Tunis, Tangier, and California to realize that there is a vast space here for a great work of many Jews, without touching even one Arab.

Moreover, Palestinians knew perfectly well that Zionists had no such intentions whatsoever. The Arab newspaper *Carmel* wrote in an editorial in the 1920s: "The Arabs never doubt that the potential absorption capacity of Eretz Israel is enormous and, therefore, that it is possible to settle here enough Jews without dispossessing or constraining even a single Arab. It is obvious that 'this is all' the Zionists want. But it is also obvious that this is precisely what the Arabs do not want."

The Arab concern was that—as I stated in my point—Arabs who remain in the Jewish state will turn into a minority. This was indeed a price that some Arabs were asked to pay, and for three reasons: First, the Jews, though not (visibly) physically present in their historical homeland, are no less indigenous to that land, having maintained spiritual and historical ties to it since their second century expulsion by the Roman Empire. Second, the idea that the homeless must forever remain homeless is morally unacceptable. Third, in 1930, the Jews were under obvious threat of physical annihilation in Europe.

Note that I placed the Holocaust as the third point. The important point is the first one. My grandfather, who came to Israel in 1924 to rebuild the ancient town of Bnei Brak, was no less indigenous to the land than the peasants in the neighboring village of Jamusin, who could not and wished not to cultivate the arid land that he bought from them in hard cash. He and his ancestors prayed three times a day, "And thou shall walk us in sovereignty back to our country." The people of Jamusin, you must admit, though they were strongly attached to their village and land, never heard the word "sovereignty" in their lives. Thus, the 1920s saw a clash between two legitimate, yet deficient national movements: Zionism, deficient in physical presence, but strong in historical bonds; and Palestinian nationalism, weak in historical bonds (e.g., no national holidays), and strong in physical presence.

It is time that we admit, recognize, and forgive each other's weaknesses, and proclaim loud and clear: "Two states for two peoples, equally indigenous and equally legitimate."

15. "Early Zionists and Arabs," *Middle East Quarterly*, Fall 2008

Here I address a major misconception, even among Israelis, that early Zionists did not appreciate the size of the Arab population residing in Eretz Israel. Primary sources from the time tell a different story and prove that early Zionists had a detailed plan that aimed at understanding, accommodating, and benefitting their Arab neighbors. For example, in my own private collection I have an original letter written by David Ben-Gurion in 1917, in which he presents a village-by-village count of the Arab population in the land. Two years later, he argued that they should be seen as our brethren.

Ben-Gurion: Our Arab Brethren

During World War I, Israel's future first prime minister, David Ben-Gurion, spent three years in New York, exiled from Palestine "for conspiring against Ottoman rule." He devoted most of his time to organizing the He-Halutz youth movement with Yitzhak Ben-Zvi, but he also published, a few months before issuance of the Balfour Declaration, an interesting treatise: "On the Origin of the *Falahin*,"[1] the Arab peasants in Palestine. In this work, Ben-Gurion, the scholar and historian, argued that the *falahin* are descendants of Jews who remained in Palestine after the Roman expulsion and who later converted to Islam:

> The logical, self-evident conclusion of all the above is as follows: The agricultural community that the Arabs found in Eretz Israel in the seventh century was none other than the Hebrew farmers that remained on their land despite all the persecution and oppression of the Roman and Byzantine emperors. Some of them accepted Christianity, at least on the surface, but many held on to their ancestral faith and occasionally revolted against their Christian oppressors. After the Arab conquest, the Arabic language and Muslim religion spread gradually among the countrymen. In his essay, "Ancient Names in Palestine and Syria in Our Times," Dr. George Kampmeyer proves, based on historico-linguistic analysis, that for a certain period of time, both Aramaic and Arabic were in use and only slowly did the former give way to the latter. The greater majority and main structures of the Muslim *falahin* in western Eretz Israel present to us one racial strand and a whole ethnic unit, and there is no doubt that much Jewish blood flows in their veins—the blood of those Jewish farmers, "lay persons," who chose in the travesty of times to abandon their faith in order to remain on their land.

Ben-Gurion's theory may not withstand modern DNA analysis, but his essay reveals a genuine attempt to establish an ancestral kinship with the Arab population and to bridge cultural and religious divides.

1 David Ben-Gurion, "Leberur Motsa Ha'Falahim," *Der Yidisher Kemfer*, January 22, 1918, reprinted in David Ben-Gurion, *Anachnu U'Shcheneinu* (Tel Aviv: Davar, 1931), 13–25.

Ben-Gurion: Palestinian Arab Rights

In 1918, Israel Zangwill, an on-again, off-again member of the Zionist movement and author of the influential novel, *Children of the Ghetto* (1892), wrote an article suggesting that the Arabs should be persuaded to "trek" from Palestine.[2] Ben-Gurion was quick to distance the Zionist movement from any such notion. In an article published that year in the Yiddish-language newspaper *Yidisher Kemfer*, Ben-Gurion ridiculed Zangwill:

> Eretz Israel is not an empty country....West of Jordan alone houses three-quarters of a million people. On no account must we injure the rights of the inhabitants. Only "Ghetto Dreamers" like Zangwill can imagine that Eretz Israel will be given to the Jews with the added right of dispossessing the current inhabitants of the country. This is not the mission of Zionism. Had Zionism to aspire to inherit the place of these inhabitants—it would be nothing but a dangerous utopia and an empty, damaging, and reactionary dream....Not to take from others—but to build the ruins. [We claim] no rights on our past—but on our future. Not the preservation of historic inheritance—but the creation of new national assets—this is the core claim and right of the Hebrew nation in its country.[3]

Weizmann: Arab Glory and Arab Rights

In 1918, the British government sent Chaim Weizmann, the future first president of Israel and a key player behind the Balfour Declaration, to Palestine to advise on the future development of the country. There, he met with Arab and Armenian representatives and delivered the following speech in the house of the High Commissioner in Jerusalem,

> With heartfelt admiration and great interest we are viewing today the current war of liberation conducted by the ancient Arabic nation. We

2 Diana Muir, "A Land without a People for a People without a Land," *Middle East Quarterly* 15, no. 2 (Spring 2008): 55–62.

3 David Ben-Gurion, "Zechuyot Ha'Yehudim Ve'Zulatam B'Eretz Yisrael," *Der Yidisher Kemfer*, January, 23, 1918, reprinted in David Ben-Gurion, *Anachnu U'Shcheneinu* (Tel Aviv: Davar, 1931), 31.

> see how the scattered Arab forces are being united under the goodwill of Western governments and other peace-loving nations, and how, from the mist of war there emerge new and immense political possibilities. We see again the formation of a strong and united Arab political body, freshly renovated and aiming to renovate the great tradition of Arab science and literature that are so close to our heart. This kinship found its glorious expression particularly in the Spanish period of the Hebrew-Arabic development when our greatest authors wrote and thought in the Arabic language, as well as in Hebrew.[4]

Perhaps anticipating future criticism that Zionism, while promising Palestinians human and civil rights, denied them national rights, Weizmann wrote in the newspaper *Ha'aretz*,

> If indeed there is among the Arabs a national movement, we must relate to it with the utmost seriousness....The Arabs are concerned about two issues: 1. The Jews will soon come in their millions and conquer the country and chase out the Arabs....Responsible Zionists never said and never wished such things. 2. There is no place in Eretz Israel for a large number of inhabitants. This is total ignorance. It is enough to notice what is happening now in Tunis, Tangier, and California to realize that there is a vast space here for a great work of many Jews, without touching even one Arab.[5]

Ben-Gurion: Palestinian Self-Determination

In November 1930, about a year after the Arab riots that led to the Hebron massacre, Ben-Gurion addressed the First Congress of Hebrew Workers and delivered a lecture entitled, "The Foreign Policy of the Hebrew Nation." In this lecture, later published in Ben-Gurion's first book, *We and Our Neighbors*, he not only acknowledged the national aspirations of the Palestinian Arabs but also recognized Arab self-determination as an inalienable right, regardless of its impact on the Zionist plan:

---

4 Chaim Weizmann, *Devarim* (Tel Aviv: Mizpah Publishers, 1936), 1:99.

5 Weizmann, *Devarim*, 1:129.

There is in the world a principle called "the right for self-determination." We have always and everywhere been its worshipers and champions. We have defended that right for every nation, every part of a nation, and every collective of people. There is no doubt whatsoever that the Arab people in Eretz Israel have this right. And this right is not limited by or conditional upon the result of its influence on us and our interests. We ought not to diminish the Arabs' freedom for self-determination for fear that it would present difficulties to our own mission. The entire moral core encapsulated in the Zionist idea is the notion that a nation—every nation—is its own purpose and not a tool for the purposes of other nations. And in the same way that we want the Jewish people to be master of its own affairs, capable of determining its historical destiny without being dependent on the will—even goodwill—of other nations, so, too, we must seek for the Arabs....

The characteristic feature of a political movement is its ability to rally the masses behind it. In this sense, there is no doubt that we are witnessing a political movement. And we should not dismiss it, our way should not be through the [British] government....

We should not attempt to turn the Arabs into Zionists. I do not see why an Arab need be a Zionist. But we must explain to him what Zionism is, what it aspires to achieve, on what it rests, what its power and promises are, and what its attitude is toward the Arabs in this land and the Arab nation in our neighborhood. It is imperative that the Arab knows that we have not come here to dispossess him, to subjugate him, or to worsen his condition. The Arab must know that Zionism is not an accidental, temporary phenomenon but a historical imperative, that it relies on the needs and strength of the entire Jewish nation, and that it is impossible to dismiss or silence it....

In much the same way that we need to educate the Arab public to understand our interest, so also we need to educate our public to understand the Arabs and work toward decent neighborly relations...mutual recognition is prerequisite to mutual understanding.[6]

6 Ben-Gurion, *Anachnu U'Shcheneinu*, 257.

The total Arab rejection of his overtures, followed by the bloody riots of 1936–39, eroded Ben-Gurion's confidence in achieving Arab understanding through education and cooperation. It remains an interesting exercise, though, to imagine what the Middle East would be like today had Arab leadership reciprocated with some recognition, however mild, of the Jewish right to self-determination.

Jabotinsky before the Holocaust

Ze'ev Jabotinsky, Ben-Gurion's rival, garnered a reputation as an advocate of an "iron wall" approach toward the Arabs. Yet even he expressed respect for Arab nationalism and explained Arab fears of reciprocating Ben-Gurion's offer. Not only does Jabotinsky's article, "The Arabs of Eretz Israel," dispel the myth of Zionist denial and naïveté, but it also disproves the popular notion that Arabs feared dispossession by Jewish immigrants:

> There is no point talking about the possibility that the Arabs in Eretz Israel would consent to the Zionist plan while we are a minority here. I express it with such confidence not because I enjoy disappointing decent people but, simply, to save them disappointments: All these decent people, except those blind from birth, have understood already that this is something that is utterly illogical—to obtain the Arabs' consent and goodwill to turn Eretz Israel from an Arabic country to a country with Jewish majority.
>
> Every indigenous people, regardless of whether it is primitive or advanced, views its country as a national home and aspires to be and remain its sole and eternal landlord; it does not voluntarily agree to accommodate, not only new landlords, but even new partners or new participants. And our most misleading argument would be if we rely on the fact that our agricultural settlements bring them economical advantages; though this is an undisputed truth, there is no nation in the world that sold its national aspirations for bread and butter.
>
> Many of us still think in full honesty that a terrible misunderstanding has occurred, that the Arabs did not understand us, and that this is the reason why they oppose us; but if only we could explain to them how

> benevolent our intentions, they would stretch their hands back to us. This is a mistake that has been proven so again and again. I will bring one such incident. Several years ago, when the late Nahum Sokolow visited Eretz Israel, and he was one of the most moderate and diplomatic Zionists at that time, he delivered an elaborate speech on this misunderstanding. He explained clearly how mistaken Arabs are in thinking that we wish to steal their property or dispossess them or oppress them. "We do not even want to have a Jewish government; we want merely a government representing the League of Nations." Sokolow's speech received an immediate response in the main editorial of the Arab newspaper *Carmel*, the content of which I convey here from memory:
>
> "The Zionists"—so wrote the Arab editor—"are tormenting their nerves unnecessarily. There is no misunderstanding here whatsoever. The Arabs never doubted that the potential absorption capacity of Eretz Israel is enormous and, therefore, that it is possible to settle here enough Jews without dispossessing or constraining even a single Arab. It is obvious that 'this is all' the Zionists want. But it is also obvious that this is precisely what the Arabs do not want; for, then, the Jews will turn into a majority and, from the nature of things, a Jewish government will be established and the fate of the Arab minority will depend on Jewish goodwill; Jews know perfectly well what minority existence is like. There is no misunderstanding here whatsoever."[7]

The Arab editor's argument is rather compelling, but Jabotinsky confronts it with a moral dilemma that is no less compelling:

> Whoever thinks that our arguments [for Jewish immigration] are immoral, I would beg him to address the following question: If this [Jewish immigration] is immoral, what should the Jewish people do…?
>
> Our planet is no longer blessed with uninhabited islands. Take any oasis in any desert, it is already taken by the native who inhabits that place from time immemorial and rejects the coming of new settlers that will become a majority, or just come in great numbers. In short—if there is a homeless nation in the world, its very yearning for a homeland is

7 Ze'ev Jabotinsky, *Medinah Ivrit* (Tel Aviv: T. Kopp, 1937), 73–75.

> immoral. The homeless must forever remain homeless; all the land in the universe has already been divided—that's it. These are the conclusions of "morality...."
>
> This sort of morality has a place among cannibals, not in the civilized world. The land belongs not to those who have too much land but to those who have none. If we appropriate one parcel of land from the owners of mega-estates and give it to an exiled nation—it is a just deed.[8]

New Historians often cite anecdotal and secondhand evidence or diary entries lacking in context that depict an exaggerated, hostile attitude of early Zionist leaders toward the Arabs. In contrast, the quotations cited above were articulated in prominent and open public forums and published widely for Hebrew readers in Palestine and the Diaspora. It is these quotations, therefore, that are true representations of the dominant attitude of the Yishuv, the pre-1948 Jewish community in Palestine. They were annunciated broadly with the aim of shaping public opinion, educational norms, and cultural molds, which no doubt contributed to the culture of accommodation that governs the Israeli mindset today.

16. "It's Time for Words to Lead the Peace Process," *Jewish Journal*, November 20, 2008

This piece is about mutual apologies: an Israeli apology to the Palestinians and a Palestinian apology to the Israelis. It was inspired by journalist Uri Avnery's position that Israel should apologize to the Palestinians for their displacement during the War of Independence. He further envisioned the exact wording of the Israeli apology to be delivered to the Knesset. I followed Avnery's piece with this article, in which I take up his theme and envision what a reciprocal Palestinian apology should look like.

It is now clear that no peace agreement, not even on principles, will be signed by the Israeli-Palestinian negotiating team before some time in 2009,

8 Jabotinsky, *Medinah Ivrit*, 77–79.

after the new American administration takes charge, the Israeli election runs its course, and the fate of Mahmoud Abbas's presidency is decided. Analysts who have been urging the two sides to expedite matters for all the many reasons that made the window of opportunities narrower by the day are now urging them to "keep the momentum going," lest the window, which I doubt ever existed, becomes too narrow to reopen. But how do you keep momentum going when the two sides are locked in a fundamentally immobile stalemate?

Israel is physically unable to accommodate a sovereign neighbor a rocket range away from its vital airports, one whose youngsters openly vow to destroy it. And Palestinians, on their part, cannot change their youngsters' vows after having nourished them for decades, especially under occupation, while Iran is promising to turn those vows into reality. Yet there is a way. If we cannot move on the ground, we should move above it—in the metaphysical sphere of words, metaphors, and paradigms—to create a movement that not only would maintain the perception of "keeping the momentum going," but could actually be the key to any future movement on the ground.

Let us be frank: The current stalemate is ideological, not physical, and it hangs on two major contentions: "historical right" and "justice," which must be wrestled with in words before we can expect any substantive movement on the ground. Starting with "historical right," we recall that a year ago the Annapolis process was on the verge of collapse on account of two words: "Jewish state." In the week preceding Annapolis, Palestinian Authority chief negotiator Saeb Erekat proclaimed, "The PA would never acknowledge Israel's Jewish identity," to which Prime Minister Ehud Olmert reacted angrily with: "We won't hold negotiations on our existence as a Jewish state....Whoever does not accept this cannot hold any negotiations with me."

Clearly, to the secular Israeli society, the insistence on a Jewish state has nothing to do with kosher food or wearing yarmulkes; it has to do with historical claims of co-ownership and legitimacy, which are prerequisites for any lasting peace, regardless of its shape. Olmert's reaction, which is shared by the vast majority of Israelis, translates into: "Whoever refuses to tell his children that Jews are here by moral and historical imperative has no intention of honoring his agreements in the long run." In other words, recognizing Israel as a "Jewish state" is seen by Israelis as a litmus test for

Arabs' intentions to take peace agreements as permanent. Unfortunately, for the Arabs, the words "Jewish state" signal the legitimization of a theocratic society and the exclusion of non-Jews from co-ownership in the state.

Can these two views be reconciled?

Of course they can. If the PA agrees to recognize Israel's "historical right" to exist (instead of just "right to exist" or "exist as a Jewish state"), fears connected with religious exclusion will not be awakened and Israel's demand for a proof of intention will simultaneously be satisfied: You do not teach your children of your neighbor's "historical right" unless you intend to make the final status agreement truly final—education is an irreversible investment. But would the PA ever agree to grant Israel such recognition?

This brings us to the second magical word: "justice." One of the main impediments to Palestinians' recognition of Israel's "right to exist," be it historical or de facto, is their fear that such recognition would delegitimize the Arabs' struggle against the Zionist program throughout the first half of the twentieth century, thus contextualizing the entire conflict as a whimsical Arab aggression and weakening their claims to the "right of return." All analysts agree that Palestinians would never agree to give up, tarnish, or weaken this right. They might, however, accept a symbolic recognition that would satisfy, neutralize, and perhaps even substitute for the literal right of return. Palestinian columnist Daoud Kuttab wrote in the *Washington Post* (May 12): "The basic demand is not the physical return of all refugees but for Israel to take responsibility for causing this decades-long tragedy."

Similar to Jewish refugees from Arab countries, Palestinian refugees demand their place in history through recognition that their suffering was not a senseless dust storm but part of a manmade historical process, for which someone bears responsibility and is prepared to amend the injustice. Journalist Uri Avnery, an Israeli peace activist and former member of the Knesset, believes that this deep sense of injustice can be satisfied through an open and frank Israeli apology. "I believe that peace between us and the Palestinian people—a real peace, based on real conciliation—starts with an apology," he wrote in Arabic Media Internet Network (June 14). "In my mind's eye," he writes, "I see the president of the state or the prime minister addressing an extraordinary session of the Knesset and making an historic speech of apology:"

> Madam Speaker, honorable Knesset,
>
> On behalf of the State of Israel and all its citizens, I address today the sons and daughters of the Palestinian people, wherever they are. We recognize the fact that we have committed against you an historic injustice, and we humbly ask your forgiveness. The burning desire of the founding fathers of the Zionist movement was to save the Jews of Europe, where the dark clouds of hatred for the Jews were gathering. In Eastern Europe, pogroms were raging, and all over Europe there were signs of the process that would eventually lead to the terrible Holocaust, in which six million Jews perished.
>
> All this does not justify what happened afterwards. The creation of the Jewish national home in this country has involved a profound injustice to you, the people who lived here for generations. We cannot ignore anymore the fact that in the war of 1948—which is the War of Independence for us and the Nakba for you—some seven hundred fifty thousand Palestinians were compelled to leave their homes and lands. As for the precise circumstances of this tragedy, I propose the establishment of a Committee for Truth and Reconciliation composed of experts from your and from our side, whose conclusions will from then on be incorporated in the schoolbooks, yours and ours.

Is Israeli society ready to make such an apology and assume such responsibility? Not a chance.

For an Israeli, admitting guilt for creating the refugee problem is tantamount to embedding Israel's birth in sin, thus undermining the legitimacy of its existence and encouraging those who threaten that existence. The dominant attitude is: They started the war, wars have painful consequences; they fled on their own, despite our official calls to stay put. We are clean. Can this attitude be reconciled with Palestinians' demands for official recognition of their suffering? I believe it can.

Whereas Israelis refuse to assume full responsibility for the consequences of the 1948 war, they are certainly prepared to assume part of that responsibility. After all, Israelis are not unaware of stories about field commanders in the 1948 war who initiated private campaigns to scare Arab villagers and, on some occasions, to force them out. So, how do we find words to express reciprocal responsibility? Here I take author's liberty and, following Avnery, appeal to my mind's eye and envision the continuation of that extraordinary Knesset session at the end of the Israeli president's speech. I see Abbas waiting for the applause to subside, stepping to the podium, and saying,

> Madam Speaker, honorable Knesset,
>
> On behalf of the Palestinian people and the future state of Palestine, I address today the sons and daughters of the Jewish nation, wherever they are. We recognize the fact that we have committed against you an historic injustice, and we humbly ask your forgiveness. The burning desire of the founding fathers of the Palestinian national movement was to liberate Palestine from colonial powers, first the Ottoman Empire and then the British Mandate Authorities. In their zeal to achieve independence, they have treated the creation of a Jewish national home in this country as a form of colonial occupation, rather than a homecoming endeavor of a potentially friendly neighbor, a partner to liberation, whose historical attachment to this landscape was not weaker than ours.
>
> We cannot ignore anymore the fact that the Great Arab Revolt, of 1936–1939, resulted in the British White Paper, which prevented thousands, if not millions, of European Jews from escaping the Nazi extermination plan. Nor can we ignore the fact that when survivors of Nazi concentration camps sought refuge in Palestine, we were instrumental in denying them safety, and, when they finally established their historical homeland, we called the armies of our Arab brethren to wipe out their newly created state. Subsequently, for the past sixty years, in our zeal to rectify the injustice done to us, we have taught our children that only your demise can bring about the justice and liberty they so badly deserve. They took our teachings rather seriously, and some of them resorted to terror wars that killed, maimed, and injured thousands of your citizens.

Admittedly, this scenario is utopian. The idea of Palestinians apologizing to Israel is so heretical in prevailing political consciousness that only six Google entries mention such a gesture, compared with six hundred fifteen entries citing "Israel must apologize." Yet, peace begins with ideas, and ideas are shaped by words. And the utopian scenario I painted above gives a feasible frame to reciprocal words that must be said, in one form or another, for a lasting peace to set in.

And if not now, when? Recall, we must keep the momentum going.

17. "The Forgotten Miracle: Nov. 29, 1947," *Jewish Journal*, December 18, 2008

The miracle of the November 29, 1947, U.N. vote to partition Palestine into a state for the Jews and a state for the Arabs is the subject of many of my op-eds. In this first piece on the topic, I urged the Jewish community to appreciate the magnitude of this historic event and called for instituting an annual thanksgiving celebration. Four years later, on November 29, 2012, the Israeli Leadership Council (now the Israeli American Council), Los Angeles organized just such a celebration. While it has not become annual, as I hoped and expected, November 29 celebrations continue to be held by enlightened communities, including in Los Angeles in 2023.

I originally planned to write a column about the flood of condemnations that Muslim leaders issued following the massacre in Mumbai and how disappointed I was not to find a single fatwa in those texts, nor a mention of any religious offense: no "sin," no "hell," nor "apostasy." I was also tempted to write about liberated Western TV anchors finally shaking off those funny adjectives: "activists," "militants," and "fighters" and returning to good old-fashioned "terrorists"—a glorious triumph of the English language over years of politically correct oppression.

But I had to suspend those plans and pay my dues first to the gods of history, which, for us Jews, must take precedence over all other gods. This obligation is pounded into us by the first commandment: "I am the Lord your God who brought you out of Egypt, out of the land of slavery. Thou shall not have any other god before me." In other words, to recognize me, says God, you must acknowledge your past, for I am revealing myself to you through the movements of history, or, put in modern vocabulary: If you forget your past, gone is your Jewish identity.

Why dwell on lost history? Because last month saw the anniversary of one of the most significant events in Jewish history, perhaps the most significant since the Exodus from Egypt—November 29, 1947—the day the U.N. General Assembly voted thirty-three to thirteen to partition Palestine into a Jewish state and an Arab state. Believe it or not, but this momentous event, which changed so dramatically the physical, spiritual, and political life of every Jew in our generation, as well as the course of history in general, passed virtually unnoticed in our community, including in the pages of this paper.

I felt compelled, therefore, to amend this thankless rebuff of history and do what I can to compensate for the loss of opportunity. Imagine if the Jewish community in Los Angeles invited the consuls general of the thirty-three countries who voted yes on that fateful day to thank them publicly for listening to their conscience and, defying the pressures of the time (and there were millions of such pressures), voting to grant the Jewish nation what other nations take for granted—a state of its own. I can see thirty-three flags hanging from the Jewish Federation building, thirty-three bands representing their respective countries, and the word "yes" repeated in thirty-three different languages in a staged reenactment of that miraculous and fateful vote in 1947.

Too theatrical? Extravagant?

Let's face it. It's not very often that we can honestly thank thirty-three countries for their governments' decisions, especially not these days. And it's not very often that we can forge a network of friendships with thirty-three local ethnic communities representing: Australia, Belgium, Bolivia, Brazil, Byelorussian SSR, Canada, Costa Rica, Czechoslovakia, Denmark, Dominican Republic, Ecuador, France, Guatemala, Haiti, Iceland, Liberia, Luxembourg, Netherlands, New Zealand, Nicaragua, Norway, Panama, Paraguay, Peru, Philippines, Poland, Sweden, Ukrainian SSR, Union of South Africa, United States, Union of Soviet Socialist Republics, Uruguay, and Venezuela. I purposely spell out the names of these countries, in case anyone wonders who they ought to thank for that spectacular turn that Jewish history took in November 1947, and for the dignity, pride, and self-image world Jewry has enjoyed since.

Each of these names harbors an intriguing story behind its "yes" vote. Some voted yes out of moral conviction (e.g., Brazil, Guatemala), some through diplomatic arm-twisting (e.g., Philippines, Haiti), and others as a result of personal pleadings of ordinary, courageous Jews who understood the collective responsibility that history bestowed upon them in 1947. A brief, yet fascinating account of some of these stories can be found in Benny Morris's new book, \ (Yale University Press, 2008, 51–61). Others have yet to be unearthed and are patiently awaiting a creative historian, novelist, or filmmaker to be lifted from oblivion and added to the crown of Jewish lore and world history.

The story behind the pivotal U.S. vote is perhaps the best known and highlights the courage of Eddie Jacobson, President Harry S. Truman's friend and former business partner from Kansas City, Missouri, who risked that friendship and wrote to Truman on October 3, 1947: "Harry, my people need help and I am appealing to you to help them." To which Truman answered evasively: "When I see you I'll tell you just what the difficulties are." Still, Jacobson did not give up. He did not mind being called "pushy Jew" and pleaded with Truman to grant one more audience to Chaim Weizmann, the engine behind the Zionist effort, who was not happy at all with the way the State Department was dragging its feet.

Weizmann had good reason to be nervous, for the outcome remained uncertain until literally minutes before the actual vote. In a preliminary vote taken on November 25, six Latin American countries abstained, and the required two-thirds majority was not obtained. And while the fate of one whole nation was hanging in the balance, the Arabs were lobbying aggressively, promising money, oil, and bloodshed. Yet, at the end of the day, the miracle did happen: thirty-three ayes, thirteen nays, and ten abstains—a brand-new chapter in world history.

The no and abstaining votes unfold heroic stories of their own. One of those tells us of a letter exchange between Albert Einstein and Jawaharlal Nehru, then the prime minister of India, which was discovered in Israeli archives (*Guardian*, February 16, 2005). In his plea, which Nehru politely declined, Einstein wrote: "The Jewish people alone has for centuries been in the anomalous position of being victimized and hounded as a people, though bereft of all the rights and protections which even the smallest people normally has....Zionism offered the means of ending this discrimination. Through the return to the land to which they were bound by close historic ties...Jews sought to abolish their pariah status among peoples." And concerning the Arabs' demands to own all of Palestine, Einstein wrote: "In the august scale of justice, which weighs need against need, there is no doubt as to whose [need] is more heavy."

I find Einstein's letter heroic, not because of any risk he took in this exchange, but because he agreed to forgo personal hesitations and harness his worldwide reputation and friendly relations with Nehru to his people's calling. Einstein was a lukewarm Zionist, constantly torn between his belief that Zionism is the only just solution and his deep concern about potential misuse of power by the ensuing Jewish state. On one occasion, in 1938, he even expressed preference for a binational one-state solution. He could have easily told his "mobilizers" from the Jewish Agency executive: "Sorry, I am not your guy;" "I can't get involved in politics right now;" "I don't know Nehru well enough;" or "I myself am often critical of the course the Zionist movement has taken." (Sound familiar?) Yet when he heard the bells of history ringing his name, he knew exactly what was to be done. He put aside those personal hesitations and stood firmly with his people.

We owe it to the gods of history to mention Einstein and Jacobson and thirty-two other heroic stories that heralded the greatest gift history has given us: A state that contributes to humanity more than all the countries in the United Nations that mourn its birth (paraphrasing U.N. Ambassador Dan Gillerman). We owe it because the offerings we give to the gods of history today will strengthen the spines of our children and grandchildren tomorrow. Indeed, on campuses ruled by Noam Chomsky's disciples and "New Marranos" (Jewish faculty peer-pressured into silence), where will Jewish students find the courage to stand up to anti-Israel slurs in the cafeteria, library, or the classroom, if they have not heard about November 29, Eddie Jacobson, or any of the other thirty-two heroic stories that led to the U.N. vote of 1947? Where would they gather the courage to lift their eyes from the salad plate and tell their abuser: "Accuse me; I am Albert Einstein's kin, and what you just said offends everything I cherish and stand for. If you value our friendship, read first about November 29, 1947."

Speaking of college campuses, imagine Hillel students at UCLA or UC Irvine inviting student organizations representing all the thirty-three yes-voting countries to a "thanksgiving get-together" on November 29. This could include a multicultural talent show, a reenactment of the U.N. vote, or a reading of U.N. Resolution 181. Imagine what it would do to Israel's image and Jewish posture on campus. It is for this reason that I decided to devote this column to the gift of history: The miracle of November 29, 1947.

Finally, to compensate for overlooking the November miracle in 2008, I am including a poem that Natan Alterman wrote on December 19, 1947, soon after the U.N. decision to partition Palestine, which reflects his understanding of the sacrifices that everyone knew would have to be made for independence. It is Alterman's most popular poem and is often read in school assemblies and at public gatherings in Israel.

The Silver Platter
By Natan Alterman
(Translated from the Hebrew by David P. Stern)

"No state is served to a nation on a silver platter."
(Chaim Weizmann, December 15, 1947)

...And the land will grow still
Crimson skies dimming, misting
Slowly paling again
Over smoking frontiers

As the nation stands up
Torn at heart but existing
To receive its first wonder
In two thousand years

As the moment draws near
It will rise, darkness facing
Stand straight in the moonlight
In terror and joy

...When across from it step out
Toward it slowly pacing
In plain sight of all
A young girl and a boy

Dressed in battle gear, dirty
Shoes heavy with grime
On the path they will climb up
While their lips remain sealed

To change garb, to wipe brow
They have not yet found time
Still bone weary from days
And from nights in the field

Full of endless fatigue
And all drained of emotion
Yet the dew of their youth
Is still seen on their head

Thus like statues they stand
Stiff and still with no motion
And no sign that will show
If they live or are dead

Then a nation in tears
And amazed at this matter
Will ask: Who are you?
And the two will then say

With soft voice: We—
Are the silver platter
On which the Jews' state
Was presented today

Then they fall back in darkness
As the dazed nation looks
And the rest can be found
In the history books.

18. "Daniel Pearl and the Normalization of Evil," *The Wall Street Journal*, February 3, 2009

Here I express my frustration with journalists and others who speak in terms of a "cycle of violence" and cannot see terrorism as a distinct threat to civilized society. My definition of terrorism at the time was, "the ideological license to elevate one's grievances above the norms of civilized society." It still is.

This week marks the seventh anniversary of the murder of our son, former *Wall Street Journal* reporter Daniel Pearl. My wife Ruth and I wonder: Would Danny have believed that today's world emerged after his tragedy?

The answer does not come easily. Danny was an optimist, a true believer in the goodness of mankind. Yet he was also a realist, and would not let idealism bend the harshness of facts. Neither he, nor the millions who were shocked by his murder, could have possibly predicted that seven years later his abductor, Omar Saeed Sheikh, according to several South Asian reports, would be planning terror acts from the safety of a Pakistani jail. Or that his murderer, Khalid Sheikh Mohammed, now in Guantanamo, would proudly boast of his murder in a military tribunal in March 2007 to the cheers of sympathetic jihadi supporters. Or that this ideology of barbarism would be celebrated in European and American universities, fueling rally after rally for Hamas, Hezbollah, and other heroes of "the resistance." Or that another kidnapped young man, Israeli Gilad Shalit, would spend his nine hundred fiftieth day of captivity with no Red Cross visitation, while world leaders seriously debate whether his kidnappers deserve international recognition.

No. Those around the world who mourned for Danny in 2002 genuinely hoped that Danny's murder would be a turning point in the history of man's inhumanity to man and that the targeting of innocents to transmit political messages would quickly become, like slavery and human sacrifice, an embarrassing relic of a bygone era. But, somehow, barbarism, often cloaked in the language of "resistance," has gained acceptance in the most elite circles of our society. The words "war on terror" cannot be uttered today without fear of offense. Civilized society, so it seems, is so numbed by violence that it has lost its gift to be disgusted by evil.

I believe it all started with well-meaning analysts, who in their zeal to find creative solutions to terror decided that terror is not a real enemy, but a tactic. Thus the basic engine that propels acts of terrorism—the ideological license to elevate one's grievances above the norms of civilized society—was wished away in favor of seemingly more manageable "tactical" considerations. This mentality of surrender then worked its way through politicians like the former mayor of London, Ken Livingstone. In July 2005, he told Sky News that suicide bombing is almost man's second nature. "In an unfair balance, that's what people use," explained Mr. Livingstone.

But the clearest endorsement of terror as a legitimate instrument of political bargaining came from former President Jimmy Carter. In his book, *Palestine: Peace Not Apartheid*, Mr. Carter appeals to the sponsors of suicide bombing. "It is imperative that the general Arab community and all significant Palestinian groups make it clear that they will end the suicide bombings and other acts of terrorism when international laws and the ultimate goals of the Roadmap for Peace are accepted by Israel." Acts of terror, according to Mr. Carter, are no longer taboo, but effective tools for terrorists to address perceived injustices. Mr. Carter's logic has become the dominant paradigm in rationalizing terror. When asked what Israel should do to stop Hamas's rockets aimed at innocent civilians, the Syrian first lady, Asma al-Assad, did not hesitate for a moment in her response: "They should end the occupation." In other words, terror must earn a dividend before it is stopped.

The media have played a major role in handing terrorism this victory of acceptability. Qatari-based Al Jazeera television, for example, is still providing Sheikh Yusuf al-Qaradawi hours of free air time each week to spew his hateful interpretation of the Koran, authorize suicide bombing, and call for jihad against Jews and Americans. Then came the August 2008 birthday of Samir Kuntar, the unrepentant killer who, in 1979, smashed the head of a four-year-old Israeli girl with his rifle after killing her father before her eyes. Al Jazeera elevated Kuntar to heroic heights with orchestras, fireworks, and sword dances, presenting him to fifty million viewers as Arab society's role model. No mainstream Western media outlet dared to expose Al Jazeera's efforts to warp its young viewers into the likes of Kuntar. Al Jazeera's management continues to receive royal treatment in all major press clubs.

Some American pundits and TV anchors didn't seem much different from Al Jazeera in their analysis of the recent war in Gaza. Bill Moyers was quick to lend Hamas legitimacy as a "resistance" movement, together with honorary membership in PBS's imaginary "cycle of violence." In his January 9 TV show, Mr. Moyers explained to his viewers that "each [side] greases the cycle of violence, as one man's terrorism becomes another's resistance to oppression." He then stated—without blushing—that for readers of the Hebrew Bible "God-soaked violence became genetically coded." The "cycle of violence" platitude allows analysts to empower terror with the guise of reciprocity, and, amazingly, indict terror's victims for violence as immutable as DNA.

When we ask ourselves what it is about the American psyche that enables genocidal organizations like Hamas—the charter of which would offend every neuron in our brains—to become tolerated in public discourse, we should take a hard look at our universities and the way they are currently being manipulated by terrorist sympathizers. At my own university, UCLA, a symposium last week on human rights turned into a Hamas recruitment rally by a clever academic gimmick. The director of the Center for Near Eastern Studies carefully selected only Israel-bashers for the panel, each of whom concluded that the Jewish state is the greatest criminal in human history. The primary purpose of the event was evident the morning after, when unsuspecting, uninvolved students read an article in the campus newspaper titled, "Scholars Say: Israel Is in Violation of Human Rights in Gaza," to which the good name of the University of California was attached. This is where Hamas scored its main triumph—another inch of academic respectability, another inroad into Western minds.

Danny's picture is hanging just in front of me, his warm smile as reassuring as ever. But I find it hard to look him straight in the eyes and say: You did not die in vain.

19. "Is Anti-Zionism Hate?" *Los Angeles Times*, March 15, 2009

The nauseating mantra, "anti-Zionism is not antisemitism," has long been used by many intellectuals to justify unrestrained attacks on the core of Jewish peoplehood in the belief that the former is less despicable than the latter. In this op-ed, I attempt to argue for the opposite, citing three reasons why anti-Zionism is more dangerous than antisemitism.

In January, at a symposium at UCLA (choreographed by the Center for Near Eastern Studies), four longtime Israel-bashers were invited to analyze the human rights conditions in Gaza, and used the stage to attack the legitimacy of Zionism and its vision of a two-state solution for Israel and the Palestinians. They criminalized Israel's existence, distorted its motives, and maligned its character, its birth, even its conception. At one point, the excited audience reportedly chanted "Zionism is Nazism" and worse.

Jewish leaders condemned this hate-fest as a dangerous invitation to antisemitic hysteria and pointed to the chilling effect it had on UCLA students and faculty on a campus known for its open and civil atmosphere. The organizers, some of them Jewish, took refuge in "academic freedom" and the argument that anti-Zionism is not antisemitism.

I fully support this mantra, not because it exonerates anti-Zionists from charges of antisemitism, but because the distinction helps us focus attention on the discriminatory, immoral, and more dangerous character of anti-Zionism. Anti-Zionism rejects the very notion that Jews are a nation—a collective bonded by a common history—and, accordingly, denies Jews the right to self-determination in their historical birthplace. It seeks the dismantling of the Jewish nation-state: Israel. Anti-Zionism earns its discriminatory character by denying the Jewish people what it grants to other historically bonded collectives (e.g., French, Spanish, Palestinians), namely, the right to nationhood, self-determination, and legitimate coexistence with other indigenous claimants. Antisemitism rejects Jews as equal members of the human race; anti-Zionism rejects Israel as an equal member in the family of nations.

Are Jews a nation? Some philosophers would argue that Jews are a nation first and religion second. Indeed, the narrative of Exodus and the vision of the impending journey to the Land of Canaan were etched in the minds of the Jewish people before they received the Torah at Mt. Sinai. But, philosophy aside, the unshaken conviction in their eventual repatriation to the birthplace of their history has been the engine behind Jewish endurance and hopes throughout their turbulent journey that started with the Roman expulsion in 70 CE. More importantly, shared history, not religion, is today the primary uniting force behind the secular, multiethnic society of Israel. The majority of its members do not practice religious laws and do not believe in divine supervision or the afterlife. The same applies to American Jewry, which is likewise largely secular. Identification with a common historical ethos, culminating in the reestablishment of the State of Israel, is the central bond of Jewish collectivity in America.

There are, of course, Jews who are non-Zionists and even anti-Zionists. The ultra-Orthodox cult of Neturei Karta and the Leftist cult of Noam Chomsky are notable examples. The former rejects any earthly attempt to interfere with God's messianic plan, while the latter abhors all forms of nationalism, especially successful ones. There are also Jews who find it difficult to defend their identity against the growing viciousness of anti-Israel propaganda, and eventually hide, disown, or denounce their historical roots in favor of social acceptance and other expediencies. But these are marginal minorities at best; the vital tissues of Jewish identity today feed on Jewish history and its natural derivatives: the State of Israel, its struggle for survival, its cultural and scientific achievements, and its relentless drive for peace.

Given this understanding of Jewish nationhood, anti-Zionism is in many ways more dangerous than antisemitism. First, anti-Zionism targets the most vulnerable part of the Jewish people, namely, the Jewish population of Israel, whose physical safety and personal dignity depend crucially on maintaining Israel's sovereignty. Put bluntly, the anti-Zionist plan to do away with Israel condemns 5.5 million human beings, mostly refugees or children of refugees, to eternal defenselessness in a region where genocidal designs are not uncommon. Secondly, modern society has developed antibodies against antisemitism but not against anti-Zionism. Today, antisemitic stereotypes evoke revulsion in most people of conscience, while anti-Zionist rhetoric has become a mark of academic sophistication and social acceptance in certain extreme yet vocal circles of U.S. academia and media elite. Anti-Zionism disguises itself in the cloak of political debate, exempt from sensitivities and rules of civility that govern interreligious discourse, to attack the most cherished symbol of Jewish identity.

Finally, anti-Zionist rhetoric is a stab in the back to the Israeli peace camp, which overwhelmingly stands for a two-state solution. It also gives credence to enemies of coexistence who claim that the eventual elimination of Israel is the hidden agenda of every Palestinian. It is anti-Zionism, then, not antisemitism that poses a more dangerous threat to lives, historical justice, and the prospects of peace in the Middle East.

20. "Our New Marranos," *Jewish Journal*, March 18, 2009

I wrote this piece in reaction to two articles: one in the Los Angeles Times *claiming that South African apartheid was charitable compared to Israel's relation with the Palestinians, and the other, in UCLA's* Daily Bruin, *complaining that my equation of anti-Zionism with racism somehow limits the right of anti-Zionists to express and define themselves. Anti-Zionists are extremely delicate organisms. They are so used to seeing themselves as being on the vanguard of morality that they cannot take even mild criticism, let alone criticism that indicts them as racist.*

Four years ago, in a column in this journal, I argued for the formula, "Anti-Zionism = Racism," instead of the standard claim that anti-Zionism is a cover for antisemitism. My aim was to empower pro-Israel students with a more potent intellectual weapon to fight back the rising anti-Israel campaign on college campuses. The logic in the new formula was based on three simple axioms: Anti-Zionists deny Jews what they grant to other historically bonded collectives—the right for sovereignty; anti-Zionists and their drive to dismantle Israel commit the most vulnerable part of the Jewish people to a dangerous, potentially genocidal experiment; and, finally, anti-Zionism attacks with impunity the most cherished symbol of Jewish identity—Israel.

While the logic was impeccable, the verdict was harsh. Having positioned themselves as the righteous guardians of the oppressed, anti-Zionists are not used to assuming responsibility for their words and actions. A formula that reminds them that ideologies have consequences, that consequences may endanger lives, and that those lives deserve a moment of reflection, can be a traumatic experience for any self-righteous activist. Additionally, anti-Zionists are used to accusing others of racism, oppression, brutality, discrimination, and other moral misdeeds. A formula that burdens them with guilt, let alone the guilt of racism, is hard to accept.

Jewish anti-Zionists took special offense at the idea that their ideology can be criticized on a moral ground, since they have come to believe that they are the true carriers of prophetic Judaism. Any criticism of their anti-Israel mission is decried as erecting a moral barrier between them and mainstream Judaism. I would like to refer to these Jews as our "new Marranos" because, like the Jews who were coerced into conversion by the Spanish Inquisition, many anti-Zionist Jews have abandoned and denounced their historical identity to gain social acceptance after facing a vicious wave of anti-Israel propaganda. Keeping this in mind, I have always felt a warm spot for our new Marranos, regardless of how painful their rhetoric and deeds, for I know how hard it must be to resist the harshness of peer pressure and the tempting comfort of intellectual surrender.

However, these lost brethren of ours now demand equal voice in mainstream Jewish life, and, accordingly, they feel offended, muzzled, and marginalized by any characterization that points to the consequences of their actions. "They [Zionists] seek to limit the discourse, to erect walls that delineate what can and can't be said," Ben Ehrenreich complained in the *Los Angeles Times* ("Zionism Is the Problem," March 12) after stating that South African apartheid was charitable compared to Israel's. "In insisting that anti-Zionism is pernicious," Rachel Roberts, an active anti-Zionist student at UCLA, wrote in the *Daily Bruin*, "Pearl denies Jews who disagree with his view the right to define ourselves according to our own beliefs and circumstances" ("Professor's Opinion Offensive to Both Jews and Palestinians," March 12).

I have no qualms with the dishonesty of these complaints. Blinded by wishful victimhood and self-righteousness, these writers probably do believe that the abusive language they have been hurling at Zionists in the past few decades has been a friendly invitation to enlightened discourse. Some idealists have infinite capacity for self-delusion, and idealists are badly needed in our world. The qualms I do have concern their demand to be treated as mainstream Jews who just happen to have a minor disagreement with the community at large and merely wish to define themselves according to their "beliefs and circumstances." This juxtaposition of Jews who wish to define themselves one way or another, and anti-Zionists who insist on telling everyone else how they ought to define themselves, was what caught my attention in their writings.

I first asked myself: Why not? Why not treat anti-Zionist Jews like a new brand of Judaism? After all, our history has known many fierce debates before: Chasidim and Mitnagdim, Karaim and Shabtaim, Prushim and Tsdokim, Conservative and Reform Jews. Why not embrace anti-Zionist Jews as another brand of Judaism? Asked in this way, the answer was immediate: Zionism does not deny any segment of the Jewish people the right to engage in a debate about how they should express their Jewishness, whether they wish to do so in the land of the Maccabees or in the land of George Washington—it is up to the individual to decide. It is, however, pernicious for any group, Jews and non-Jews, to deny another group the right to sovereignty in their historical homeland, especially when this sovereignty is embedded in a secular, democratic, inclusive, multiethnic, and peace-seeking state like Israel.

Moreover, it is pernicious, if not plain racist, for any group to join forces with organizations committed to the destruction of another people's homeland, be it through verbal defamation, boycotts, divestment, or direct physical violence. Anti-Zionists do engage in these activities, and this is what distinguishes them from other Jews, both Zionist and non-Zionist, who merely try to redefine themselves.

To the best of my recollection, and my history books are truly dusty, I do not believe the old Marranos demanded acceptance as equal players in Jewish education and the Jewish community life of sixteenth-century Europe. They could have easily argued that their newly acquired religion was the true carrier of the spirit of biblical Judaism, hence they should be equal partners in the ongoing debate on Jewish identity. But they did not. Instead, they spent their energy pretending that they were better Christians than their Christian neighbors and concealing any association with Judaism that might raise suspicion of infidelity. In concealing their identity our new Marranos excel, indeed. Their anti-Israel diatribes, loaded with comparisons to Nazi Germany and South Africa, are second only to Hamas's. Yet, contrary to the old Marranos, they now demand a seat in the modern-day synagogue—our universities.

To obtain academic credentials, anti-Zionist Jews attempt to position themselves as continuing a long historical debate about the role of Eretz Israel in Jewish life, supposedly an important question that Jews have been debating for centuries and which continues to this very day. There was indeed such a debate, a short-lived one: For two millennia, our ancestors prayed three times a day, "And He shall walk us in sovereignty back to our country" (Birchat Hamazon), and felt no need for debate. The debate started in the late nineteenth century and ended with clear winners and clear losers. The Balfour Declaration, the Shoah, the establishment of the State of Israel, and the refocusing of Jewish education in the Diaspora around Israel's culture, needs, and accomplishments have turned the old debate into an irrelevant wrinkle in the dustbin of history.

Still, there are probably some Jewish professors who are excavating that dustbin with great hopes of discovering a shred of an idea that would be relevant today. Such discoveries would empower our new Marranos with an illusion of academic continuity and embolden their demands for equal voice in Jewish education. I do not believe we should yield to those demands as long as Israel is dear to our heart.

21. "The Crucible of UC Irvine," *Jewish Journal*, May 27, 2009

The problem of Zionophobia in academia is more than well known by now. UC Irvine has been a pioneering laboratory for the development of this pathology, with the approval of its administration. It became a role model for other universities, whose students mimicked the Zionophobic slander they witnessed there. In 2021, I was on a panel with Douglas Haynes, the vice chancellor of student affairs at UC Irvine. I confronted him with these allegations. He skillfully dodged all of my questions. I remember the last question he dodged. I asked him: "Are you prepared to make a public statement saying that Zionist students are welcome at UC Irvine?" He could not say "yes." The violent clashes that broke out in 2024 are a result of this institutionalized dereliction of moral norms.

Universities, like religions, are often judged not by what they preach but by what they tolerate. This painful truth came to mind upon reading Neelie Genya Milstein's op-ed article in these pages, "Protecting Hate at UC Irvine" (May 22, 2009), in which she describes the atmosphere at the University of California at Irvine (UCI), where the Muslim Student Union (MSU) celebrated a weeklong lynching of Jewish identity under the banner, "Israel: The Politics of Genocide."

"At UCI," Milstein wrote, "hate is a yearly event that lasts for a week. It isn't just any hatred. It is hatred directed at me, my friends, my community, and my history."

"You are a Jew; a proud Jew, a proud supporter of Israel. Now you are seen as nothing but a racist murderer on your own campus," she wrote. Milstein is not alone. Her frustration is shared by many students and faculty at Irvine. What is happening at UCI is part of a coordinated assault on Jewish identity at campuses across the nation, an assault that threatens to erode the dignity, values, and peoplehood of all Jewish students in the generation to come. We must understand its anatomy, for universities hold the key to our future.

UCI has long been a proving ground for a nationally orchestrated Israel-defamation campaign. The combination of a large and highly motivated Muslim student organization, an affluent and supportive Muslim community, a non-confrontational university administration, and a divided (what's new?) Jewish leadership has turned the UCI campus into a veritable petri dish to test the limits of hate, bigotry, and intimidation. Pro-Israel students, with the help of organizations like Hillel, StandWithUs, and others, have mobilized to reach out to the MSU, but have been unable to temper the rising intensity of their assault. Many Orwellian hyperboles were first tested at UCI, among them: "Genocide in Jenin," "Zionism Is Cancer," "The World without Israel," "Ethnic Cleansing in Palestine," "Holocaust in The Holy Land," "Israel: The Fourth Reich." This year, the masters of absurdity upped the ante with mental deformities such as: "Allah is a terrorist," "The Zionist-Jew is a party of Satan," along with images of Anne Frank in a Palestinian kaffiyeh, blood-drenched Israeli flags, and heroic Hamas fighters advancing the cause of peace—all in the prime location on campus, near the flagpoles and the administration building, giving the hate-fest the appearance of a university-sponsored event.

Naturally, despite their tireless and honest efforts, university administrators have been powerless to prevent UCI from becoming a national focus of anxieties and expectations. Indeed, on the day the official UCI marquee at the entrance to campus displayed the "Israel-Genocide" sign, I received messages from colleagues as far away as Indiana asking whether California Education Code allows such use of the University of California name. "What next for us?" they asked.

On the other side of the fault line, anti-Israel propagandists have been watching UCI performances thirsting for new ideas and new opportunities for upcoming hate-fests on other campuses. I wonder, for example, whether Susan Slyomovics, the director of UCLA Center for Near Eastern Studies, would have mustered the imagination to choreograph her famous Gaza

Symposium last January 22, had she not been emboldened by Irvine's 2005 workshop, "A World Without Israel." For readers who missed Slyomovics's show, it was described by a foreign diplomat (not Israeli) in the audience as "the dirtiest Israel-bashing and indeed full-fledged antisemitic hate fest I have experienced in my two-and-a-half years in this city."

Likewise, I would speculate that UCLA Chancellor Gene Block is keenly tuned to the happenings at UCI, for he is facing a similar dilemma: How long can a university refrain from confronting obsessed Israel bashers/deniers—bent on stifling debate and trampling campus norms of civil discourse—and still convince the public that students should feel safe and welcome, and their sensitivities respected?

In 2005, in response to faculty complaints over the hate speeches by MSU's speaker Malik Ali, UCI Vice Chancellor Manuel Gomez wrote that the administration is "legally prohibited from either proscribing or prescribing the content of speech, as long as speakers conform to campus policies and applicable laws." This is no longer the current stance of the university. In a recent letter, UCI Chancellor Michael Drake wrote: "We must reject disrespectful and hateful slurs, particularly those based on race, religion, ethnicity, sexuality, or any other fundamental aspect of identity.... We reject antisemitism. We reject anti-Islamic rhetoric. We reject dehumanizing stereotypes. We embrace dialogue and mutual understanding." Theoretically, this is precisely what Milstein requested: "I am not asking the UCI administration to censor the hate speech. I am asking them to denounce this style of rhetoric and displays just as they would denounce campaigns for white supremacy, sexism, or Islamophobia."

But there is a catch that lies at the core of the issue, which only a few bold university administrators have thus far dared to address. Does the content of "Israel: The Politics of Genocide" fall within Drake's categories of what "we reject," or is it deemed to be a commendable model of academic free speech? Unfortunately, the declarative "we reject antisemitism" does not get us closer to answering this question. Iranian President Mahmoud Ahmadinejad and UCI's MSU have learned to absolve themselves skillfully of charges of antisemitism; behold, it is only the "Zionist Jew" who is the Satan, not all Jews. (Imagine Dutch politician Geert Wilders saying: "It is only Sunni Muslims who are morally inferior, not all Muslims.")

I believe that one of the greatest mistakes Jewish advocacy has made in the past decade has been to argue that anti-Zionism is dangerous because it is a thin cover for antisemitism. We should have exposed the immoral character of anti-Zionism in itself and insisted that Israel's statehood be recognized for what it is, a "fundamental aspect of Jewish identity." As Drake implied in his letter, religion has no monopoly on human sensitivity or group identity.

Drake's letter does not identify code-breakers, nor does he specify any offenses. It reminds me of the vague anti-terrorism fatwa that American Muslim organizations issued in 2005, a week after the London bombing, which went through a great linguistic effort not to name bin Laden or al-Qaeda as offenders, and which rendered the fatwa nonbinding. Thus, even if anti-Zionism rhetoric is explicitly recognized as offensive activity at UCI, the MSU will not see itself even remotely involved—naming the offender is essential for reversing the climb in campus temperature.

In 2007, Vice Chancellor Gomez wrote to complaining UCI faculty: "In all honesty, I get dismayed at the fact that even though we have been deeply engaged in creating a safe and dynamic campus community, the attention that continues to be focused on UCI is both distorted and negative." In fairness to Gomez, the UCI administration has indeed invested a tremendous amount of time, resources, and goodwill in efforts to restore civility to the UCI campus. However, the latest MSU carnival proves that there are fundamental limits to what non-confrontational policies can achieve in an academic environment that finds itself attacked by professional, well-funded hate crusaders aiming to test the patience of that environment.

The 2009 spectacle made a blatant mockery of everything the administration has labored to develop, including, I worry, the Daniel Pearl Muslim-Jewish dialogue that UCI hosted in May 2005. It is time for the university to reassess the way it tolerates the intolerant. Its legal obligation to tolerate that which is wrong does not diminish its moral obligation to point to that which is right.

22. "Moment Asks 35 American Jews Two Big Questions: What Does It Mean to Be a Jew Today? What Do Jews Bring to the World?" *Moment Magazine*, May/June 2010

The punchline of my response to these questions from Moment Magazine *is the sentence: "Empowered by Israel, we offer the world an unprecedented role model of a society that was blighted by oppression and managed to lift itself from the margin of history to become a world center of art, business, and science."*

Being Jewish is to see oneself as a member of an extended family, bonded by shared history and shared destiny. Our whole culture is based on the tribal idea that we have a special responsibility to one another and to the world around us. It's not that we aspire to greater ideals than other collectives but that we have found a cognitively compelling way of encoding those aspirations so that they will be pursued effectively, using a unique symbiosis between tribalism and universalism.

God promises Abraham: "I will make you into a great nation and all people on Earth will be blessed through you." Thus, our reward is in the progress of mankind, not in personal redemption; to be Jewish is to be universal in compassion and tribal in responsibility.

In the time of our grandfathers, the prayer shawl was our unifying symbol. Today, Israel is our unifying force, for it is the most powerful symbol of our potential as a collective. Empowered by Israel, we offer the world an unprecedented role model of a society that was blighted by oppression and managed to lift itself from the margin of history to become a world center of art, business, and science. We also provide an example of a society which constantly creates, questions the status quo, innovates, and aspires to improve the lot of mankind.

The strengthening of Israel and peace in the Middle East should be our highest priority as Jewish people, for this will enable us to continue our collective identity and channel all of our cultural charge to the betterment of mankind.

23. "Jews of Discomfort," *Jewish Journal*, July 28, 2010

I use the term "Jews of discomfort" to describe a type of Jew, who emerged at the turn of the century, willing to amputate part of their Jewishness for social acceptance. A Jew of discomfort, e.g., Peter Beinart, blames his people. A Jew of spine, e.g., Bernard-Henri Lévy, confronts his maligners.

What makes fog float in midair, while raindrops fall straight down to Earth? Physics teaches us that it is all a matter of "surface-to-weight ratio"—a simple parameter that determines whether soap bubbles rise or fall and how many passengers a jet plane can carry. The larger the surface, so the theory goes, the easier it is for an object to lift its weight against gravitational pull. The analogy came to mind this past week, on Tisha B'Av, when I pondered the fate of the Jewish people and tried to assess our collective surface-to-weight ratio.

It was a particularly cogent day to compare the amount of energy we spend at the boundaries of our existence, facing outward to defend our being, vis-à-vis the resources we waste facing inward, on self-congratulation, finger-pointing, and other forms of added weight. Take the protest march on behalf of Gilad Shalit last month. Tens of thousands of Israelis took to the roads, tens of thousands stood by roadsides feeding the marchers, and millions watched the marchers on Israeli TV. I have not seen any of it on CNN, for it was aimed inward, toward the Israeli government. We would have surely seen some of it had this enormous energy been directed outward, say, as a protest against the United Nations or the Red Cross or foreign embassies for not doing their share in stopping the most blatant human rights violation of our generation.

Or take Peter Beinart's much-debated article, "The Failure of the American Jewish Establishment" (*New York Review of Books*, June 10). Judging by the number of invitations I received to attend his lecture in Los Angeles, one would think that this creative intellectual has finally discovered a formula for peace or a new weapon to silence rockets without hurting civilians or, at the very least, an Arab intellectual willing to accept Israel. None of the above. Reading his article again and again, all I hear is how uncomfortable he feels being a Jew at a time when Jews are accused of supporting a nondemocratic entity called Israel, and how we can now extricate ourselves from this discomfort by speaking out, not against the distortions, but against a leadership that places its faith in the solid democratic character of Israeli society. I hear a desperate son coming home screaming: "Mother, the boys at school called you dirty names again. I hate you for causing me to face those bullies, and I hate you for making me feel so inadequate, unable to defend your honor except by joining them in amplifying your blemishes."

Beinart was treated royally in Los Angeles because he is the prophetic voice for many Jews of Discomfort. They love him, because he takes their discomfort and elevates it to a noble feeling of moral purity. They used to feel guilty for Israel's actions while conscious of her problems. No more. Elevated in virtue, they now see every blemish on Israel's face as the "litmus test" for her impure personality—hers, not theirs.

Observe another Jewish intellectual, the French philosopher Bernard-Henri Lévy, who is perhaps further to the left than Beinart. He, too, feels uncomfortable with some of Israel's actions, and he, too, proposed ways to correct them. Yet instead of pointing fingers at the Jewish establishment, he takes to the trenches and, using his column in the *Huffington Post*, he tells his Leftist colleagues: Stop this madness, look at yourself in the mirror. Is your liberalism dead when it comes to Israel? (*Huffington Post*, June 7).

It is all a matter of surface-to-weight ratio, says my physics book: Jews of Spine confront their maligners, Jews of Discomfort blame their leaders. Deep inside, Lévy knows, perhaps, that ours may well be the last generation in which Jews can earn respect in academic and intellectual circles. Pro-coexistence scholars are already pariahs in academia, forced to hide their sentiments from colleagues, and if Israel goes under, Jews of Discomfort will certainly find themselves exorcised by the elite they now seek to appease. They would be remembered not for their discomfort, but for what they really were: members of a people who once supported a mistake called Israel—ruling elites do not easily forgive "mistakes" they labored to undo.

I will end with a request to readers. If you agree with my views or share my concerns, do not simply succumb to the temptation of sending this article to another member of your synagogue. Take to the trenches and face outward. Knock on the door of your gentile neighbor or officemate and say: "Remember, Joe, how I used to go along with all your sarcastic criticism of Israel? Times have changed, Joe. My people are in trouble, and there are things I must do even at the risk of testing our friendship. I want to tell you how strongly I feel about Israel, what is factual and what is malice in what you hear, and why our world will not be the same without that tiny, shining spot called Israel."

24. "Moral Dimension of Palestinian Statehood," *Jewish Journal*, September 28, 2011

Palestinian statehood has been presented as the supreme moral question of our time. Here I deal squarely with the moral conditions on which Palestinian statehood should be contingent, in light of their historical objection to Jewish statehood. The key is in my final paragraph: "In the supreme court of world justice...the Palestinians will earn their right to statehood as soon as they can join Israelis in chanting: 'Two states for two peoples, equally legitimate and equally indigenous.'"

I felt terribly guilty when Palestinian Authority President Mahmoud Abbas told the U.N. General Assembly: "Enough! It is time for the Palestinian people to gain their freedom and independence." How can we deny to others what we claim for ourselves?

Let there be no misunderstanding. I am a daily listener to what Abbas's television is telling his children about the fate of Israel. I, therefore, know what everyone else knows, that when Abbas speaks of "freedom and independence" he is not talking about a two-state solution. He means freedom to demand the return of Tel Aviv to Palestinian hands and independence to pursue that demand from a position of power and legitimacy. Still, the words "freedom and independence" evoked the age-old question of equity and justice: "Can we deny to others what we demand for ourselves?"

I was not the only one to have this reaction to the Palestinian bid for statehood. A recent study by the Pew Research Center found that more than 40 percent of Americans favor the United States recognizing Palestine as a state. True, only 10 percent of the respondents said that they are following the news closely on this issue, but this is exactly what we mean by the "moral dimension"—the level of consciousness that has no patience for sorting out facts, figures, intentions, and consequences, but instead draws meaning from the force of certain words and their deep roots at the heart of human experience. At that level, we must admit, Israel's campaign has been a failure. Say what you will about Israel's need for security or the wisdom of entering direct negotiations before seeking statehood, it simply does not sound "right" to deny a people the right of self-determination. David Ben-Gurion expressed it quite clearly in 1931, at a time when he saw the Arabs as partners for coexistence: "There is in the world a principle called 'the right for self-determination.' We have always and everywhere been its champions.... We ought not to diminish the Arabs' right for self-determination for fear that it would present difficulties to our own mission."

The public debate preceding the U.N. session revealed a glaring asymmetry between the two sides. The Palestinian side spoke of human rights, historical justice, personal dignity, and moral obligation, while the Israeli side, including its U.S. supporters, debated and agonized over pragmatic considerations: Will statehood truly advance the peace process? Will it change things on the ground? Will it lead to renewed negotiations? Will Hamas overrun or shun the new state, if created? Will the United States use its veto power? What will Abbas's next move be?

This placed the Israeli side at a severe disadvantage. Impartial observers, even if convinced that the Palestinian bid is aimed to intensify, not resolve, the Israeli-Palestinian conflict, preferred to keep silent and let the parties fight it out in the United Nations. No one wishes to appear insensitive to moral arguments or be on the wrong side of justice. For some obscure reason, even the staunchest advocates of the Israeli position were not prepared to address the moral dimension head on and to frame their arguments in a context of universally compelling principles of ethics and justice.

The only one who did so was President Barack Obama in his speech at the General Assembly on September 21. The president said: "The Jewish people have forged a successful state in their historic homeland. Israel deserves recognition. It deserves normal relations with its neighbors." Note how the president speaks in the pre-1948 language of "deservedness" and "historical homeland-ness," not in the post-1967 language of security needs, borders, settlements, and other expediencies. In effect, what the president was doing amounts to a bold repudiation of Palestinian claims for sole ownership of justice and morality.

Here is my translation of Obama's speech into the discourse over

Palestinian statehood. Obama: "A successful state in their historic homeland." Translation: No society, no matter how oppressed, is entitled to what it denies to others. In particular, the Arab denial of a people's homeland for sixty-three years is morally unacceptable.

Obama: "Israel deserves recognition." Translation: Never in the history of nations has a society defined itself on the ruins of its neighbor, and never has such a society sought recognition while admitting its intent.

Obama: "It [Israel] deserves normal relations with its neighbors." Translation: Never in the history of human conflict did anyone ask for statehood while teaching its children of the inevitable demise of its neighbor and making no investment in education for peace.

In short, Obama is telling Abbas in no uncertain terms: "You simply do not deserve a state without first doing some elementary homework." It is not surprising that Obama's speech angered Palestinians and their supporters. They are not accustomed to being challenged in the moral dimension, certainly not in public. "The humiliation of Barack Obama," Robert Grenier called the moment in Al Jazeera (English). "No U.S. embassy will be safe," warned a Muslim Brotherhood spokesman in Cairo. It is also not surprising that Obama angered Jewish radicals on the Left. Fringe organizations such as Jewish Voice for Peace will not forgive him for defining so clearly the immoral character of their anti-Israel activities.

What is surprising to me is that mainstream Jewish organizations did not seize on Obama's speech as the moral manifesto of their objection to Palestinian statehood. Instead, we are hearing the all-too-expected praises of the speech, mixed with arguments on its impact on renewed negotiations and questioning Obama's political motivations. It is all too easy to dismiss Obama's words as part of an election campaign. But, as often happens in our history, it is not what the world means to say that counts, but what one makes of it. The Balfour Declaration, too, could have been dismissed as a campaign speech, or worse. Instead, it was taken seriously by world Jewry and ushered Israel into being.

Let us not forget, most of those who question U.S. support of Israel see Obama as a beacon of moral courage for the twenty-first century. Excerpts from Obama's speech should therefore be quoted and requoted by Israel advocates on television and radio shows. Copies of Obama's words should decorate students' walks on U.S. campuses, including the offices of my academic colleagues at UCLA. In short, Obama's words should become Israel's trust deed of moral justice in the court of world opinion.

I will end with an answer I gave to a friend who asked what I thought about the moral justification for a Palestinian state. "In the supreme court of world justice," I said, "the Palestinians will earn their right to statehood as soon as they can join Israelis in chanting: Two states for two peoples, equally legitimate and equally indigenous."

25. "What Does It Mean to Be Pro-Israel Today?" *Moment Magazine*, January/February 2012

Moment Magazine *asked twenty-four individuals the above question. Here's my key point: "Those who do not see Israel as the central piece of Jewish life are not pro-Israel, and I doubt they are pro-Jewish."*

Jews are a nation bonded by a common history and a common historical narrative. If we forget that narrative, gone is our Jewishness. Throughout our history, the driving engine of survival has been the hope for returning to sovereignty in the birthplace of our history—*Eretz Israel.* The State of Israel is the culmination of this dream and also the crucible in which Jewish heritage attains its full expression and comes to life through the resuscitating touch of normalcy.

What binds American Jews together today? Most of us are secular; the religious bond is gone. Few of us speak Hebrew; the language bond is gone. What remains is the historical narrative of eighty generations and Israel, the realization of that dream and the spiritual and cultural light that radiates to the rest of the world. If we abandon Israel, we abandon our future. If Israel is gone, Jewish life will be gone in one or two generations. Those who do not see Israel as the central piece of Jewish life are not pro-Israel, and I doubt they are pro-Jewish.

26. "Judea Pearl: Boycott Israel? Not on My Campus," *Jewish Journal*, January 3, 2014

Most U.S. academics, as well as campus administrators, object to boycotting Israel—for the wrong reasons. This is my analysis of why my Jewish colleagues in academia are totally misguided and misleading in their approach to fighting the BDS movement.

There are many good reasons to oppose the American Studies Association (ASA) decision to boycott Israeli universities. But there are some bad reasons as well. Many arguments against the boycott play exactly into the hands of the pro-boycott propagandists and give them the ammunition they need to continue their racist campaign with renewed vigor and self-righteousness. The two most dangerous "objections" to the boycott consist of these arguments: 1) There are worse violators of human rights in the world, so why pick on Israel? and 2) Israel is aware of her crimes and is willing to confess and repent with the help of an international team of expert "confessors," who are about to fix all that is broken with Zionism.

I will not comment on the second point, because anyone who has been watching Israel's relentless effort to extricate itself from having to control other people's lives, how her poets, playwrights, educators, philosophers, journalists, jurors, and political leaders have been struggling for the past sixty-six years to redefine Zionism to fit the changing dynamics of society and circumstances, would laugh at the idea that what Zionism needs at this point is expert confessors from the Diaspora to teach it what it truly stands for.

But the first point deserves a comment or two, because it has been used as a crutch by many commentators, not least among them UCLA professor David Myers, writing in these pages. Admitting, "You caught me stealing, but there are bigger thieves in town," is precisely what the boycott cronies want to hear, and the ASA president's response, "We have to start somewhere," sounds much more compelling and honest than the plea for first chasing after the other thieves in town. After all, once you admit to being part of the Mafia, you have no business telling the police how to go about fighting crime, and you should not be surprised if you are arrested first.

I want to assure our students that the case against academic boycott is not as flimsy as these arguments make it sound and that the majority of faculty on our campuses do recognize both the difficult predicaments of Israel and the non-academic character of the boycott campaign. They recognize that Israel did not choose to occupy another people. Her presence in the West Bank was imposed upon her by neighbors who admit to wishing her disappearance and who make sure she understands that lifting the occupation would only intensify their wishes. They recognize that, obviously, the occupation "has a negative impact on the working conditions of Palestinian researchers and students" (this is a quote from the ASA resolution). But it is also obvious that Israel cannot lift movement restrictions in the West Bank while she is intimidated daily, both rhetorically and physically, with existential threats. Normalcy must be symmetrical.

They recognize that while occupation is ugly and unsustainable, the Arab side shares (at least) equal responsibility for prolonging this conflict by nourishing a culture in which coexistence is nonexistent. In particular, Palestinian educators, researchers, students, and academic institutions who now call for boycotting Israel are greatly responsible for perpetuating this culture of anti-coexistence, hence no less deserving of a boycott than their Israeli counterparts. Most ASA members should agree that denying peoplehood to a people for more than sixty-five years is no less a crime than causing students at Nablus University to be late to class.

ASA members should be concerned about the reputation of their organization if allowed to be hijacked by the rhetoric of the BDS (Boycott, Divestment, and Sanctions) movement and its radical supporters. While the resolution itself may sound benign, ASA members should take a hard look at the purpose for which this document will be used in the future, given the radical agenda of its supporters. The leaders of the BDS movement do not hide that purpose: In every conversation with them, they make it crystal clear that their ultimate goal is not to end the occupation, nor is it to achieve a peaceful solution in the Middle East, but rather to defame Israel in the public eye, to choreograph an arena where Israel's criminality is debated, to intimidate pro-coexistence voices into silence, if not shame, and eventually bring about Israel's isolation, if not her demise. Omar Barghouti, a key ideologist of BDS, stated publicly (September 29, 2013): "Colonizers [read: Zionists] are not entitled to self-determination, by any definition of self-determination."

ASA members should also take a hard look at what the passing of this resolution would do to campus climate, how it would isolate faculty members who choose to collaborate with Israeli universities, and what it would mean to the posture of Jewish students on campus once BDS supporters sense the smell of victory, however mild. The commentary by UCLA professor Robin Kelley, who wrote in support of the boycott in these pages, was a perfect reflection of this BDS mentality. We are witnessing a "professor of history" who is as quick to desecrate the word "apartheid" as he is to ignore the historical context of the Israeli-Palestinian conflict and the responsibility of the Arab side in sustaining that conflict. Some "professors of history" can preach for hours and hours on the moral right of the Palestinian people to self-determination and, at the same time, ignore or deny the historical right of their neighbors to the same self-determination. In the old days, we used to label such professors "racists," but nowadays that label is reserved strictly for Islamophobes and "white settlers' colonial societies," so, on a technicality, Kelley is exonerated.

One of Israel's painful misfortunes is that professors like Kelley formed their worldview at a time when the only villains in town were "white settlers." Today, when there are no such settlers in existence (except perhaps the British settlers in the Falkland Islands), history professors must invent them, no matter how absurd the resemblance. And you can guess who they chose for the honor—the only functioning society in the Middle East that speaks the language of its historical birthplace.

On the positive side, we should not forget that despite its symbolic victory in the ASA case, the BDS movement has given the Jewish people two important gifts. First, support of BDS has become a crisp and unmistakable litmus test by which to distinguish potential discussants from hopeless bigots, and by which to determine who to include and who to exclude from the broad tent of "Jewish conversation." Drawing such red lines was one of the smartest things our sages enforced to preserve Jewish identity. At times it involved painful decisions, which left the Karaites, the early Christians, the Shabtaim, the Spanish Conversos, and "Jews for Jesus" out of the community. But these were necessary, lifesaving decisions. Today, as if by divine supervision, BDS supporters find themselves excluded from the Jewish conversation—a lifesaving demarcation line has been drawn and a stronger, more united community has emerged.

The second blessing has been a miraculous awakening and an unprecedented galvanization of Jewish students and faculty to confront the dangers of the BDS assault. It is still too early to assess, but I would nevertheless venture to predict that next year will not be an easy one for Israel's enemies on campus.

27. "Judea Pearl: Standing Up for Israel on Campus," *Jewish Journal*, August 13, 2014

Concerned by the growing anti-Israel sentiment on campus, I have always felt that we underestimate our ability to stand up for Israel. If only we were to display who we are, I thought, by wearing a small pin of commitment depicting, say, the Israeli and American flags, we would evoke in others reciprocal sentiments and collegial respect. Symbols have more power than most people realize, as we see today in the yellow ribbon worn on behalf of the hostages held by Hamas.

It's going to be a tough year on campus. Anti-Israel rallies nationwide indicate that the atmosphere has turned toxic for all of us who love and support Israel. But from many conversations with my university colleagues, I know that despite what we see and read in the media, there is tremendous passion and affinity for Israel throughout our educational institutions, perhaps suppressed for the moment, but still strong.

The open hostility on the other side makes it difficult, even frightening, for us to find a way to project our pro-coexistence voices back into the mix. Many of us may be hesitant to speak up, and our silence further emboldens our detractors and demoralizes our students. I recently had an experience that may reflect on how we can end this silence, clearly and elegantly, without uttering a single word, and in so doing, influence others to do the same.

At a recent scientific conference in Quebec, I decided to wear a simple U.S.-Israel Friendship flag lapel pin, which pairs the Israeli and American flags. For me, it just felt good to make a statement of support for a tiny country fighting for the safety of her citizens. What I did not anticipate was the reaction I received from people around me. From passengers at the airport, hotel receptionists, colleagues at the conference, students and professors, known and unknown, Jews and gentiles, I was amazed and delighted to hear things like, "I love the pin you are wearing!"

"Do you have one for me?"

"I have a friend on a kibbutz!" and so on.

That was a surprise! And all it took was a simple gesture to release those bottled-up feelings awaiting an excuse to get out. Imagine what could happen if a few of us, then a few more, and a few more, started sporting those pins on campus. Could we actually begin to change that toxic campus atmosphere?

I believe we can. Let's display the pin proudly. Let's wear it to classes, to lectures, to the cafeteria, to meetings with students and administrators, everywhere. Let's show our colleagues exactly where we stand. Even more important, let's make sure our Jewish students know they're not alone, that they have a safe place to go, role models they can talk to, mentors with whom they can share their love for Israel, their passion for democracy and justice. As for those with opposing views, they, too, need to know which side common sense is on.

Wearing friendship pins does not represent "advocacy" or "having all the answers" or "imposing an answer" or "taking a definite public stand" or "an issue"—concerns I have heard, verbatim, from other professors. It represents personal support of universal values, no less so than a pin of the International Campaign to Ban Landmines or the Wildlife Conservation Society. The preposterous idea that any mention of Israel should be "controversial" or "political" or "taking sides" or "an issue" is precisely the kind of intellectual terror that the Boycott, Divestment, and Sanctions (BDS) movement attempts to create on our campuses. I refuse to bend to this terror. Israel's being and friendship are as normative as Diet Coke and French wine, and perhaps a bit more noble.

As to wearing a pin with Israeli-Palestinian flags as a statement of peace and reconciliation, I would have considered it a year ago, but not today—not after seeing the faces and hearing the slogans of those who waved Palestinian flags in the anti-Israel demonstrations of the past few months. Too bad, but those faces transformed the flag they were waving into a symbol of death.

Let's not shy away from engagement. Let's welcome it. The stature we have earned through our dedication to research and education commands more weight than all the BDS forces put together, all the anti-Israel resolutions that student unions can draft or pass. I believe this non-imposing statement of identity and concern, heralded by that little pin, will portray us as people of principle and earn us respect in both camps: those who agree with us and those who don't.

So simple an act. So powerful the message. I hope you'll join me in making our sentiments visible, empowering our students to action, and, we hope, restoring sanity to campus life.

28. "The UC's New Dilemma: To Name or Not to Name," *Jewish Journal*, November 4, 2015

The word "Zionism" is avoided like the plague in all official University of California documents. This delinquent avoidance is the root of the campus turmoil and mayhem post-October 7. No matter how loudly Israeli and Zionist students complain about the discrimination, intimidation, and exclusion they experience as Zionists, the administrations continue to sing "antisemitism," appoint taskforces to combat antisemitism, request funding to study the philosophical dimension of antisemitism, but won't spell "Zionism." In this piece, I argue that "you can't cure a problem unless you name it!"

Dozens of speakers representing a variety of views testified last week at UCLA before a university committee tasked with crafting a University of California systemwide policy to combat antisemitism on campuses. Many of the speakers favored adoption of the U.S. State Department's definition of antisemitism, which includes the demonizing of Israel and denial of its right to exist. They argued that because the ultimate goal of anti-Jewish assaults on campus is to intimidate Israel's supporters into silence, adopting the State Department's definition would somehow temper the venom of those assaults. Opponents, mostly from the anti-Israel camp, cited "freedom of speech" as a reason for ambiguity over clarity. I believe both camps are missing the point.

The issue is not how to define antisemitism, but whether to name the problem at hand, thus contributing to its solution, or to let the problem linger in ambiguity until incitements and hostilities get out of hand. As I have argued previously in these pages, among the phobias that currently drive campus racism, Zionophobia trumps antisemitism, and, therefore, treating anti-Zionism as the lesser of the two evils gives racist forces the legitimacy to continue their assaults unabated, under the cover of a "political debate," exempt from norms of discourse that protect other campus groups from similar attacks. I believe not only UCLA, but also the University of California Regents, must explicitly name "anti-Zionism" as a major contributor to campus intolerance and a major threat to the academic climate. When my turn came to speak before the committee, I said the following in an attempt to make this clear,

My name is Judea Pearl. I am a professor of engineering and applied science at UCLA, and I have served on the faculty since fall of 1969.

I came to speak here today because, after laboring my entire career to make this campus a center of academic excellence, I find that I am not exactly welcome here. I was awakened one day to discover that the university I knew was hijacked by proxies of a racist movement called BDS (Boycott, Divestment, and Sanctions), who turned our public square and many of our classrooms into a stage for incriminating me, my colleagues, my students, my scientific collaboration with Israel, and my identity as a Jew with one fabricated crime after another. It has been part of their relentless and obsessive crusade to defame Israel, deny her right to exist, intimidate her supporters, and thus weaken her chances for survival. As a Jew, I am one with my people through the bonds of common history. Israel, the culmination of that history, is the central symbol of our identity as a people.

I submit to you that campus events such as "The World Without Israel," "Anti-Zionist Week," or "Israel Apartheid Week," organized by publicly funded student organizations and tolerated by the administration, are direct assaults on the identity of every Jew on this campus. If you are serious about restoring academic reputation to this university, you must be *explicit* about the root cause of campus intolerance, which is not classical antisemitism but anti-Zionism, anti-Israelism, or Zionophobia. I prefer the term Zionophobia, because it rhymes with Islamophobia and thus reminds us that all forms of racism should be equally deplored and all identity-forming symbols should be equally respected. Religion has no monopoly on human sensitivity.

Two words about free speech:

First, you will not be curtailing anyone's right to free speech by recognizing "the denial of a Jewish homeland" as an unacceptable topic for public discourse on campus, no less unacceptable than "the denial of human rights to blacks, women, or Arabs." Rather, you will merely be affirming the right of the Jewish people to a homeland—which is what Zionism is all about—no more, no less.

Second, no one expects the regents to police speech on campus. We ask only that you set the norms of civil discourse. This, I believe, is both your charter and responsibility: *explicitly* labeling anti-Zionism speeches as obstacles to a respectful academic climate is a necessary first step toward that goal. Not to silence such speeches, but to mark them as unbecoming.

Readers may ask why I emphasize the word "explicit" when it comes to Zionism or Zionophobia. The reason is obvious. The UC Regents know that Zionophobia is the main source of campus intolerance and hostility, and yet the word "Zionism"—a people's quest for self-determination—has never been identified as a moral imperative by those in charge of campus climate.

You can't cure a problem unless you name it! The effectiveness of any recommendation or report summing up the regents' deliberations hinges upon one simple word: Zionism. Any attempt to circumvent this word through ambiguous, roundabout surrogates would mean abandoning the campus to amplified BDS megaphones and intensified anti-Jewish hostilities.

29. "Debating the BDS Movement's Immorality," *Jewish Journal*, May 31, 2017

When I was invited by the UCLA Debate Union to participate in this debate, I agreed on the condition that the motion's title makes it unmistakably clear: it is BDS (Boycott, Divestment, and Sanctions), not Israel, on trial for immorality. My condition was accepted.

If the Jewish people ever needed an icon for their sworn enemies, a litmus test that distinguishes those who oppose the core of Israel's existence from those who have other reasons to criticize the Jewish state, the Boycott,

Divestment, and Sanctions (BDS) movement has given it to us. It has managed to galvanize the Jewish community into an unprecedented wave of unity in opposition to this threat.

A May 22 debate sponsored by the UCLA Debate Union was unique, in that the issue was not the effects of BDS actions but the morality of their aims. I took part in this debate, and I would like to share with readers a summary of my arguments. What follows is an edited version of my remarks:

Dear Friends,

I have not spoken to this debate club before, and I am glad to do so on this occasion because I see it as a historic moment. For more than ten years now, we have been witnessing BDS supporters roaming the campus with their megaphones and slander machines accusing Israel of every imaginable crime, from apartheid to child molesting—accusing, accusing, and accusing. Today, for the first time in the history of UCLA, we see BDS itself on the accused bench, with its deceitful tactics, immoral ideology, and anti-peace stance brought to trial. It is a historic moment.

BDS is not a new phenomenon. It is a brainchild of the Grand Mufti of Jerusalem Haj Amin al-Husseini, who, in April 1936, started the Arab Rejectionist movement (under the auspices of the Arab Higher Committee), and the first thing he did was to launch a boycott of Jewish agricultural products and a general strike against Jewish immigration to Mandatory Palestine from war-bound Europe. The 1936 manifesto of the Rejectionist movement was very similar to what BDS co-founder Omar Barghouti presented here at UCLA on January 15, 2014. It was brutal in its simplicity: Jews are not entitled to any form of self-determination in any part of Palestine, not even the size of a postage stamp—end of discussion!

Here is where BDS earns its distinct immoral character: denying one people rights to a homeland, rights that are granted to all others. This amounts to discrimination based on national identity, which in standard English vocabulary would be labeled "bigotry," if not "racism." This rejectionist ideology has dominated the Arab mindset from 1936 to this very day. BDS is only its latest symptom. It explains why Palestinian Authority President Mahmoud Abbas spends so much time at UNESCO trying to erase Jewish history, why Palestinian children sing, "there is no such thing as Israel," and why their hosts and educators on official Palestinian TV applaud them with "Bravo! Bravo!" It also explains why the Israeli peace camp has such a hard time convincing the majority of Israelis that despite what they see without end in Palestinian schools, there are still some partners for peace among the Palestinians.

The mufti's boycott of 1936 scored one major "victory" for the Palestinians. The British government succumbed to mass Arab unrest and prevented European Jewish refugees from entering Palestine. My grandparents were among those seeking refuge. They perished in Auschwitz in 1942. This, ironically, was the last victory of Arab rejectionism. For eight decades, rejectionism has led the Palestinian people from one disaster to another. It led them to reject a Palestinian state in 1937 and 1947; it drove them to attack Israel in 1948, with the Nakba ("disaster" in Arabic) as a consequence; it led them to reject land-for-peace proposals in Khartoum in 1967, which gave rise to the settlement movement; and it prevented them from accepting any of the peace offers made since. Rejectionism negates the very notion of "end of conflict." Today, rejectionism is the number one obstacle to Palestinian statehood. The total absence of peace education in Palestinian schools and media gives Israelis fairly good reasons to question the ability of Palestinian leadership to honor any peace agreement, however favorable. No country can come to life that openly seeks the elimination of its neighbor.

Back to the moral side of rejectionism. In 2014, BDS's Barghouti stood here at UCLA and proclaimed, "Jews are not a people, and the U.N. principle to self-determination does not apply to them." Barghouti made no effort to hide the racist foundations of BDS ideology, but we should keep them in mind as we consider the question before us tonight: Is BDS moral?

I would like to move now from the history of Zionophobic rejectionism to its current aims and tactics. The leaders of the BDS movement do not hide their real purpose. In every conversation with them, they admit that their ultimate goal is not to end the occupation, and surely not to promote peace or coexistence, but to delegitimize Israel in the international arena, isolate her, and eventually bring about her collapse. What most people fail to realize is that BDS is not interested in boycotting, either, because it knows a boycott cannot achieve any meaningful level of success. Show me one respectable university that would go along with this childish, anti-academic idea. Indeed, one hundred fifty university presidents came out immediately in opposition to boycott. And just last week, we saw all fifty U.S. governors deploring BDS as "incompatible with American values." Not just "academic values" but "American values."

So, if not boycott, what are they trying to achieve on campus? The idea is to bombard university campuses with an endless stream of proposals for anti-Israel resolutions. The charges may vary from season to season, the authors may rotate, and it matters not whether a resolution passes or fails nor whether it is condemned or hailed. The victory lies in having a stage, a microphone, and a finger pointing at Israel, saying: "On trial." It is only a matter of time before innocent students, mostly the gullible and uninformed, start chanting, "On trial." The effect will be felt when these students graduate and become the next generation of American policymakers. A more immediate goal, of course, is bullying pro-coexistence voices into silence.

A common hypocrisy among BDS advocates is to present themselves to new audiences as seekers of universal justice, while whitewashing or downplaying their ultimate goal of putting an end to Israel. They even coined fancy names for that end: "one-state solution" or "a state for all its citizens," a delusional setting of wolves protecting sheep to the sound of progressive slogans, totally oblivious to Middle East realities. Noam Chomsky, a staunch critic of Israel, called this strategy of BDS "hypocrisy crying to Heaven." And Norman Finkelstein, not a warmer friend of Israel, called it "a hypocritical dishonest cult led by dishonest gurus."

Maintaining this dishonesty, however, is crucial for BDS survival. Any attempt to distance itself from the goal of eliminating Israel would cost BDS its vital support base among Palestinians. I believe everyone would like to find out from BDS supporters how peace can emerge between two partners, one insisting on seeing the other dead and the other insisting on staying alive, no matter how glamorous the coffin. Leaving behind this logical impossibility, I believe we should strive for a more realistic vision of peace: two states for two peoples, equally legitimate and equally indigenous. And we must start with the latter.

30. "Why Linda Sarsour Is a Fake Feminist," *Forward*, June 5, 2017

On October 7, Hamas terrorists raped and tortured women and girls of all ages. Yet major feminist and women's rights organizations worldwide remained silent or questioned the veracity of the accounts in the aftermath of these crimes. This follows a pattern I observed in 2017, in which Women's March on Washington co-chair and Palestinian-American activist Linda Sarsour indicated that Zionism and feminism are incompatible. Rather than stand up against her Zionophobia, very few feminists came forward to counter her position, while a group of "prominent Jewish leaders" wrote an open letter in her defense. I wrote this piece in response. I've cut the first part and begin from my own letter to these "prominent Jewish leaders."

Linda Sarsour is a fake feminist because she excludes important communities of women from her politically-driven definition of womanhood. There are millions of Muslim women who view Sarsour's interpretation of Sharia law as an obstacle to their struggle for equality and as an endorsement of their subjugation under male-dominated authorities. If you have not yet had a chance to speak to progressive representatives of these women, I urge you to do so, as I have done. Please speak to Asra Nomani, Qanta Ahmed, Ayaan Hirsi Ali, or Irshad Manji. It was one of these brave women who taught me the expression "fake feminist" when the name Linda Sarsour came up.

But I have a Jewish reason for labeling Sarsour a "fake feminist"—her exclusion of Israeli women. There are more than three million Jewish women in Israel; some are Left-leaning and some Right-leaning, yet most are uniformly proud Zionists who created an exemplary feminist movement. Sarsour and her anti-Zionist supporters now wish to eject these women from their newly defined, exclusivist vision of the feminist tent.

Let's take a closer look at these women. Despite seventy years of wars and besiegement, living under the shadow of one hundred fifty thousand Hezbollah rockets, and traumatized by the fear of finding their children blown to pieces, Israeli women have scored unprecedented achievements of gender equality. They have, in fact, become a beacon of equality in the Middle East and beyond. Sarsour now questions their compatibility with feminism, and some Jewish leaders rush to her defense in the name of building coalitions "on issues of shared concern." Can we look into the eyes of our Zionist daughters and granddaughters and tell them they have been expelled from their movement on the altar of those more pressing issues?

Certainly, as these Jewish leaders contend, we need to "work as allies on issues of shared concern and respectfully disagree when our views diverge." But we do not trade or bargain with issues that are at the center of our identity as a people. From everything that I have learned, the right of Jews to a homeland is one of those central issues of Jewish identity. Some of our sages even went as far as weighing it higher than other Mitsvot in the Torah ("Shekula Keneged Kol Ha-Mitsvot," Sifrei, Parashat Ree). So it is certainly not a peripheral matter that we can "respectfully disagree" about and then brush aside in order to gain a seat on Sarsour's bandwagon.

If there is one thing I respect in Sarsour, it is her candid, uncompromising stand for tenets that are central to her identity—namely, Zionophobia. We saw it in Chicago on April 2. Speaking side by side with convicted Palestinian terrorist Rasmea Odeh, Sarsour proudly proclaimed, "If what is being asked of me by those who pronounce themselves and call themselves Zionist is that I, as a Palestinian-American, have to somehow leave out a part of my identity so you can be welcomed in a space to work on justice, then that's not going to be the right space for you.

"We, as Palestinian-Americans...will not change who we are to make anybody feel comfortable. If you ain't all in, then this ain't the movement for you," she said (*Jewish Telegraphic Agency*, April 2).

Back to our "leaders," I believe many people in your constituencies would have liked to hear from you, however mildly, that we, too, have values and principles that define who we are, and we, too, do not trade these values just to make anybody feel comfortable. I would even venture to predict that your leadership stature in the coalitions that you aim to create would stand taller if you speak candidly to Sarsour and answer her in her own style:

Dear Linda,

As heirs to a justice-driven Jewish heritage and the teachings of our prophets, we believe that "justice, freedom, and dignity" apply to all people, including Israelis, and including American Zionists. Your Zionophobic stance betrays this heritage and compels us to sadly conclude that you are not qualified to lead a feminist movement. Zionophobia, unfortunately, is incompatible with the kind of feminism as we understand it.

31. "The Basel Congress's Unexpected Result, 120 Years Later," *Jewish Journal*, August 30, 2017

We normally associate the Basel Congress with Theodor Herzl's prophecy: "In Basel I founded the Jewish state." Often forgotten is Herzl's second prophecy: "Zionism is a homecoming to the Jewish fold even before it becomes a homecoming to the Jewish land." This article starts with the former and leads to the latter.

One hundred twenty years ago, on September 3, 1897, a Viennese journalist named Theodor Herzl wrote in his diary: "In Basel I founded the Jewish state." He then added a curious note: "If I were to say this out loud today, everybody would laugh at me. In five years, perhaps, but certainly in fifty, everybody will agree."

This was two days after he returned from Basel, Switzerland, where, against all odds, he managed to put together the First Zionist Congress—the event that symbolizes the Jewish claim to self-determination. Herzl had good reasons to feel elated about Basel: two hundred eight delegates from seventeen countries, the elite of European press, all dressed in solemn tuxedos, packed Basel's casino to discuss his proposed solution to the "Jewish Problem." For three days, delegates listened to fiery speeches, debated, and finally came up with as clear a definition of Zionism as one can possibly articulate: "Zionism seeks to establish for the Jewish people a publicly recognized, legally secured homeland in Palestine."

Sure enough, upon his return to his office at the *Neue Freie Presse* newspaper in Vienna, Herzl's coworkers greeted him with obvious mockery as the "future head of state." But that was the least of the problems Herzl had to face. Skepticism, sarcasm, and opposition loomed all over the world. The Vatican issued a letter protesting the "projected occupation of the Holy Places by the Jews." (Sound familiar?) The Ottoman authorities had their suspicions aroused and began to restrict the manner in which Jews were acquiring land in Palestine, especially near Jerusalem. But the worst opposition came from fellow Jews. Orthodox rabbis condemned Herzl's attempt to hasten God's plan of redemption, while Reform rabbis saw it as interference with their vision of becoming a moral light unto the nations by mingling among those nations.

Baron Edmond de Rothschild, the French philanthropist who supported Jewish agricultural communities in Palestine since the 1880s, was adamantly against efforts to obtain international legitimization of Jewish national claims. He feared (justifiably) that such efforts would lead to tougher Ottoman restrictions and that Jews like him would be subject to charges of dual loyalty. Ahad Ha'am, the most influential Jewish intellectual of the time, wrote about his time in Basel that he felt "like a mourner at a wedding feast." His motto was, "Israel will not be redeemed by diplomats, but by prophets." He could not forgive Herzl for luring the world jury with false hopes of a diplomatic solution.

But the cleavage between Herzl and Ahad Ha'am was much deeper. Ahad Ha'am claimed it is futile, and possibly harmful, to argue the Jewish case in diplomatic courts when the Jewish people are spiritually unprepared for the task. What must be done first, he wrote, is "to liberate our people from its inner slavery, from the meekness of the spirit that assimilation has brought upon us." Herzl, on the other hand, understood that the very act of bringing the Jewish question to the international arena, regardless of its outcome, would change the cultural ills of the Jewish masses and rally them to the cause. In retrospect, he was right. There were several forerunners of Jewish self-determination (for example, Moses Hess, Yehuda Alkalai, Leon Pinsker, Eliezer Ben-Yehuda, and Ahad Ha'am himself), but their writings were directed inward, toward the intellectual cliques in the Jewish shtetl. Their overall impact was therefore meager.

Bringing the Jewish claim to an international court created the cultural transformation that Ahad Ha'am yearned for—the shtetl Jew began to take his own problem seriously, and the Zionist program became one of his viable options. History books make a special point of noting that Herzl's predictions were miraculously accurate. Israel was declared a state on May 14, 1948, fifty years and eight months after Herzl wrote: "In Basel I founded the Jewish state." However, I believe Herzl, in effect, founded the Jewish state much earlier. True, Herzl's specific plan to persuade the Ottoman sultan to allocate land for a Jewish state was sheer lunacy and led to painful disappointments. But transforming Jewish statehood into an item on the international political agenda was a monumental achievement—it maintains this position today.

Moreover, the idea that Jews are reclaiming sovereignty by right, not by favor, completely changed the way Jews began to view their standing in the cosmos. It transformed the Jew from an object of history to a shaper of history. This new self-image was the engine that propelled history toward Jewish statehood already in the early 1900s. The forty thousand Jews who made up the Second Aliyah (1904–1914) were different in spirit and determination from the thirty-five thousand Jews who came earlier with the First Aliyah (1882–1903). At their core, they knew they were building a model sovereign nation and that Zionism is the most just and noble endeavor in human history. They established kibbutzim, formed self-defense organizations, founded the town of Tel Aviv, and turned Hebrew into a practical spoken language. This spirit of hope, purpose, and immediacy emanated from the Basel Congress, not from the utopian "in time to come" Zionism of Ahad Ha'am.

The diplomatic efforts that led to the Balfour Declaration and the subsequent ideological immigration of the Third Aliyah (1919–1923) all were direct products of the Zionist movement and made statehood practically inevitable. The miracle of Israel was planted indeed in 1897.

If I had to choose the single most significant impact that the Basel Congress has had on our lives here, in 2017 Los Angeles, I would name one forgotten statement that Herzl made in his first speech at the Basel Congress. On the morning of August 29, 1897, after fifteen minutes of wild cheering, Herzl took the stage and said, "Zionism is a homecoming to the Jewish fold even before it becomes a homecoming to the Jewish land." As I observe how the miracle of Israel is becoming the most powerful uniting force among our divided communities, and as I witness the excitement of our children, grandchildren, and college students as they internalize the relevance of Israel to their identity as Jews, Herzl's statement about "homecoming to the Jewish fold" stands out perhaps as more visionary than his prediction about Israeli statehood. It was the future of the Jewish people, not just of Israel, that was forged there in Basel one hundred twenty years ago.

32. "The Balfour Declaration at 100 and How It Redefined Indigenous People," *Jewish Journal*, November 3, 2017

"Indigenous" is the modern term we use to articulate a people's innate connection to a place, which pop culture associates with the Palestinians. It is a term that so many Jews outside of Israel don't seem to comprehend or have difficulty using when describing their own claim to Eretz Israel. Former British foreign secretary and prime minister Lord Arthur James Balfour had no such difficulty. His understanding of indigenous people should guide us today.

It has been one hundred years since the Balfour Declaration—issued by the British government on November 2, 1917—offered the first international recognition of Jewish national aspirations. In many ways, its importance is obvious: it encouraged some four hundred thousand European Jews to emigrate to Palestine in the years 1917–1940, and made it possible to lay the groundwork for the State of Israel. But there is another significance that has not been fully recognized among modern historians, even though it tells us more about the current obstacles to peace than any of the usual explanations. I am speaking of the politico-philosophical precedent set by the Balfour Declaration regarding national identity, land ownership, self-determination, and the notion of "indigenous people."

On the surface, the declaration's text touches on none of these issues. Known as "history's most famous letter," this sixty-seven-word text actually reads like a holiday greeting card:

> His Majesty's Government view with favour the establishment in Palestine of a national home for the Jewish people, and will use their best endeavors to facilitate the achievement of this object, it being clearly understood that nothing shall be done which may prejudice the civil and religious rights of existing non-Jewish communities in Palestine or the rights and political status enjoyed by Jews in any other country.

A close examination, however, reveals two asymmetries which by today's standards would probably evoke bitter objections. First, the words "people" and "national" are attached to Jews, not to the non-Jewish inhabitants of Palestine, who are referred to as "communities." Second, the non-Jewish communities are assured "civil and religious" rights, not national rights, let alone a "national home." This asymmetry is probably what infuriated Columbia professor Rashid Khalidi, who, in an emotional lecture on September 25 this year, reportedly pounded the table and blasted the Balfour Declaration as "a declaration of war by the British Empire on the indigenous population of the land it was promising to the Jewish people."

Khalidi's outrage at former British Prime Minister Arthur Balfour and his declaration is hardly justified. First, the idea that the Arab population of Palestine harbors national aspirations would have been news to Balfour, just as it would have been to any political observer in 1917. Khalidi admits as much in his book, *The Iron Cage*, in which he labors to explain why Arabs did not develop a ripe sense of national identity until the late 1920s, when it was too late to "crush the Zionist Movement."

Second, the Balfour Declaration did not preclude the creation of a "national home" for other national groups in the region side by side with the Jewish polity. Ottoman Palestine, as we recall, embraced a huge territory which included Jordan and parts of Syria. Various partitions and coexisting constellations were proposed in the course of time, most notably by the Peel Commission of 1937, and by the United Nations in 1947. While Khalidi's book never mentions these proposals as options, and we understand why, it was, in effect, the Balfour Declaration that opened these opportunities for Palestinian statehood.

Third—and this is critical—the concept of "indigenous population" has undergone a profound transformation since 1917, which Palestinian society refuses to accept to this day. By championing the Jewish plight for a homeland, the Balfour Declaration made it absolutely clear that there are other claimants to the title "indigenous population of the land" and that the arguments of those other claimants are no less defensible and no less supported by hard evidence and trust deeds. The Balfour Declaration overturned the narrow conception of "indigenous people" as a group of tribes or families who happened to own land in a particular geographic location and pass it to their heirs over a number of generations. By focusing on the Jewish narrative, the declaration broadened the concept of indigeneity to include peoples who have maintained vivid collective memories of past civilizations and who shaped their identity through dreams of returning to the cradles of those civilizations.

This shift in the definition of indigeneity was only implicit in the sixty-seven-word declaration. It was made explicit two years later, however, in Balfour's introduction to Nahum Sokolow's book, *History of Zionism, 1600-1919*. "The position of the Jews is unique," Balfour wrote,

> For them race, religion and country are inter-related, as they are inter-related in the case of no other race, no other religion, and no other country on Earth....In the case of no other religion is its past development so intimately bound up with the long political history of a petty territory wedged in between States more powerful far than it could ever be; in the case of no other religion are its aspirations and hopes expressed in language and imagery so utterly dependent for their meaning on the conviction that only from this one land, only through this one history, only by this one people, is full religious knowledge to spread through all the world.

A man of wisdom and character, Balfour considered himself primarily a philosopher, not a historian or a statesman. It is amazing how this multifaceted individual managed to take time off from his duties as Britain's foreign secretary and study carefully the role that the Land of Israel had played in Jewish life through the ages. He captured this essence better than some of our most revered history professors, for whom Zionism is a nineteenth century invention that started with Theodor Herzl in 1896, and ended with the Six-Day War of 1967. Balfour understood that Eretz Israel is an inextricable part of Jewish identity. Accordingly, he also understood that indigeneity is based on intellectual attachment and historical continuity no less than on physical presence or genetic lineage.

In 2014, when peace negotiations seemed somewhat hopeful, Palestinian chief negotiator Saeb Erekat was reported in the *New York Times* as saying: "The Palestinians could never accede to Israel's demand that they recognize it as the nation-state of the Jewish people....I cannot change my narrative." A few months later, when pressed to explain what narrative defines his position, Erekat told the *Times of Israel*: "I am the proud son of the Natufians and the Canaanites. I've been there for five thousand five hundred years before Joshua."

On this centennial celebration of the Balfour Declaration it is worth reminding Erekat and Khalidi that the declaration's most profound imprint on the world's consciousness has been a universal understanding that the essence of indigeneity is cultural and intellectual, not genetic or geographical. Palestinian resistance to accepting their neighbors as equally indigenous to the region has been so obsessive and so counterproductive that it begs to be enlivened through a hypothetical scenario, however imaginary. I can't resist imagining Balfour attending Khalidi's lecture at Columbia, raising his hand, and asking politely: "Professor Khalidi, can you name a Canaanite figure who you are proud of? A Canaanite poem that you enjoy reciting? A Canaanite holiday that you celebrate? A Canaanite leader who is a role model to your children?"

Replace the word "Canaanite" with "biblical," and you will find four questions that every Israeli child can answer half asleep. There is merit and wisdom in hypothetical scenarios. In this case, I would hope it could mitigate the Palestinian claim to exclusive ownership of the title "indigenous people" and, God-willing, usher in a genuine reconciliation effort based on mutual recognition and shared indigeneity.

33. "BDS and Zionophobic Racism," in *Anti-Zionism on Campus: The University, Free Speech, and BDS*, eds. Andrew Pessin and Doron S. Ben-Atar (Bloomington: Indiana University Press, 2018), 224–235

This piece appears as Chapter 16 in a book of collected essays by academics grappling with anti-Zionism on campus. Or, to use my preferred term, Zionophobia. If you want a guide to understanding the origin, purpose, character, and tactics of the BDS movement, this piece is for you. As I write in the Preface: "If the Jewish people ever needed a name for its sworn enemies, a name that negates the core of Israel's existence, free of secondary issues of territories, antisemitism, or political grievances, BDS has given it to us." The chapter ends with my advice to university administrators, which is still applicable today.

Preface

My contribution to this volume builds heavily on an article I wrote for the *Los Angeles Review of Books* (LARB) titled, "BDS, Racism and the New McCarthyism."[1] It was written three years ago, when the Boycott, Divestment, and Sanctions (BDS) movement was still an enigmatic phenomenon and only a handful of writers recognized its hypocritical and downright racist character. Things have changed in the past three years. On the global sphere, BDS has managed to reveal its agenda and to galvanize the Jewish community in an unprecedented wave of unity and determination. If the Jewish people ever needed a name for its sworn enemies, a name that negates the core of Israel's existence, free of secondary issues of territories, antisemitism, or political grievances, BDS has given it to us. In fact, it was BDS and the gullible intellectuals who joined its bandwagon that revealed to the world the persistent and uncompromising nature of Arab rejectionism. Even some of my J Street colleagues, who never miss an opportunity to spoil Jewish consensus, managed to find a reason to oppose BDS.

In the microcosm of my own campus, while BDS cronies continued to harass fellow students and silence pro-coexistence voices, the word *BDS* became synonymous with "toxic nuisance" and essentially disappeared from the public square. Even BDS-controlled groups such as Students for Justice in Palestine (SJP) and the Muslim Students Association (MSA) now try hard to hide any association with their mother ideology, BDS, pretending to be working independently. More revealing yet, Hillel's students at University of California, Los Angeles (UCLA) began urging me not to write anti-BDS op-eds anymore, lest they receive undue attention and wake up from their blissful slumber. The recent defeat of a pro-BDS resolution at the Modern Language Association (MLA), the traditional stronghold of anti-Israel academics, testifies to a movement gone stale, kept alive by its adversaries more than its supporters.

It was not BDS's fictional call for an economic boycott of Israel but

1 See Judea Pearl, "BDS, Racism and the New McCarthyism," *Los Angeles Review of Books*, March 16, 2014, https://lareviewofbooks.org/essay/bds-new-mccarthyism/.

its threat to the Zionist idea itself that galvanized this broad resistance and has helped people discover what values unite them all, liberal and conservative, orthodox and secular, and how central the existence of Israel is to Jews and to people of conscience everywhere. With this context in mind, I here submit a revised version of my earlier article.

Imagine a forum on the spread of Islamophobia. The first thing that comes to mind is: "Yes, we should measure the magnitude of this phenomenon, understand the origins of its ideology, examine what drives its advocates, unearth who funds them, assess the dangers they pose to society, and so on."

Similar expectations came to mind when I was invited to participate in the LARB forum on BDS.

Now, imagine my surprise on discovering that this forum did not intend to investigate the inner workings of the BDS movement but to be a "balanced debate" on the merits of its objective: an academic boycott of Israel. Moreover, some of the contributors to the forum were active leaders in the BDS phenomenon and longtime delegitimizers of Israel.

My thought was: should I bestow academic credibility onto an ideology that accuses me of crimes as ridiculous as ethnic cleansing, apartheid, and colonialism when I do research at my alma mater, the Technion, in Israel?

I further thought: why have the editors chosen to give a stage to advocates of a morally deformed movement that even anti-Israel advocate Noam Chomsky describes as a "hypocrisy rising to Heaven,"[2] and arch Israel-hater Norman Finkelstein characterizes as a "hypocritical, dishonest cult" led by "dishonest gurus"?[3] It would be like hosting a balanced debate between supporters and detractors of the Flat Earth Society (FES), or, God forbid, the Americans for the Restoration of Slavery (ARS). Evidently, the editors of LARB had deemed some of the BDS arguments to be semirational or even debatable.

Despite these misgivings, I accepted their invitation, hoping to prove them wrong on both counts.

2 Dave Markland, "Chomsky on BDS: A Transcript," *Z Blogs*, July 4, 2017, https://zcomm.org/zblogs/chomsky-on-bds-a-transcript/.

3 Marcus Dysch, "Finkelstein Disowns 'Silly' Israel Boycott," *The Jewish Chronicle*, February 16, 2012, https://www.thejc.com/news/uk-news/finkelstein -disowns-silly-israel -boycott-1.31716.

The BDS Arguments and Tactics

The core of the BDS appeal seems compelling in its simplicity.[4]

- The Israeli-Palestinian conflict has been going on for too long; it has caused much suffering and must come to an end.
- Israel is guilty of prolonging the conflict, be it via action, inaction, or by merely continuing to exist.
- Boycotting is a nonviolent way of pressuring Israel to act the way we (BDS) think she should.

As many of us have witnessed, BDS tactics are brilliant. Boycott has never been its aim; what university would go along with such a childish, anti-academic idea? Its aim has always been to bombard campuses with an endless stream of anti-Israel resolutions. The charges may vary from season to season, the authors may rotate, and it matters not whether a resolution passes or fails, nor whether it is condemned or hailed. The victory lies in having a stage, a microphone, and a finger pointing at Israel saying, "On trial!" It is only a matter of time before innocent students, mostly the gullible and uninformed, will start chanting, "On trial!" It worked in Munich, and it has worked on some campuses. The effect will be felt among the next generation of policy makers.

The Facts Behind the Rhetoric

Everyone agrees that the Middle East conflict has inflicted unimaginable suffering on both Palestinians and Israelis, that the status quo is not sustainable, and that it must end through some sort of healing and compromise. However, note a fundamental difference in optics between the BDS spokespersons and their opponents. The former see one and only one type of suffering; the latter see suffering on both sides.[5]

Some human beings are endowed with an amazing capacity to filter reality and see only that which fits their agenda. BDS advocates see the checkpoints, the separation wall, the night raids, and the home demolitions in the West Bank. They do not see the innocent victims of terror.

4 See the official website of the BDS movement: https://bdsmovement.net/what-is-bds.

5 I invite readers to examine the essays in the original *Los Angeles Review of Books* collection and note this glaring asymmetry.

They do not see the innocent babies who owe their lives to the wall. They certainly do not see the anxiety of 7.9 million human beings living under the shadow of hundreds of thousands of deadly rockets, aimed at their civilian populations.

BDS followers possess infinite capacity to remember every horror of the 1948 war that led to the Palestinian refugee problem but zero capacity to remember another refugee problem. Between 1936 and 1940, the British government succumbed to mass Palestinian riots and blockaded Jewish refugees from entering Palestine—thus sealing their fate in Auschwitz. My grandparents were among them. Perhaps it is hard for BDS supporters to acknowledge these refugees because they are not with us to testify. What they should be able to acknowledge, though, and rarely do, is the 1948 Arab attack on the newly created nation of Israel, which, by all historical accounts, was genocidal in intent and left deep scars on the Israeli psyche. I mention these scars because they are deliberately ignored by those who urge one side to undo injustices of the past. Scars on both sides beg for healing; seeing some and not others is seeing none.

The one-way prism worn by BDS advocates is most glaring when it comes to the issue of self-determination. Some of their intellectuals preach for hours and hours on the moral right of Palestinians to self-determination. At the same time, they intentionally forget, wish away, or deny the moral right of their neighbors to that same self-determination. In the old days, we used to label such intellectuals *racists* and shun them from the company of those of goodwill. Nowadays, the label *racist* is reserved primarily for Islamophobes and white settlers, real and imaginary, while the distinct racist character of the BDS ideology is rarely condemned for what it is. It is time to change that.

Israel's Exclusive Guilt of Action and Inaction

It is true that the occupation is an ugly predicament. However, anyone who sees Israel as the sole culprit for this unfortunate entanglement is guilty of blindness or dishonesty. Israel has been pilloried elsewhere in this forum, I am sure, so I am going to focus on the Arab contribution that prolongs this conflict. Often overlooked by Israel's detractors is that the Arab side has taken what should have been a diplomatic negotiation on borders and resources and turned it into an almost unresolvable security issue. How?

By nurturing a culture in which coexistence means defeat and ending the conflict is a cardinal sin.

Of course, settlements present a roadblock to a two-state solution. But how can an honest person fixate on a roadblock and not notice the white elephant ahead—the deeply entrenched, triple-tier, hundred-foot wall of Arab rejectionism that blocks all roads to this or to any other solution?

Assigning guilt to one side only and rushing to issue an indictment, a verdict, and a sentence—as BDS has done—is dishonest, reckless, and probably racist. Most people of conscience understand that Israel derives no pleasure from controlling another people's lives. The current situation is imposed on Israel by neighbors who continue to announce that they wish her dead, and lifting the occupation would only embolden their wishes. BDS's complaints about travel restrictions on students in the West Bank appear grotesque compared to the daily existential threats that Israelis are enduring.

The BDS Agenda: From Slander to Elimination

Some people are of the opinion that supporters of the boycott are "decent people whose main motivation is to create the conditions for genuine intellectual exchange."[6] This is indeed what one may be tempted to conclude from reading the texts of their resolutions and proclamations on campuses and in public—a glorious hymn to human rights, peace, brotherhood, and social justice. However, this is not the purpose for which these proclamations are being used.

The leaders of the BDS movement do not hide their real purpose: In every conversation with them, they admit that their ultimate goal is not to end the occupation, and surely not to promote peace or coexistence, but to choreograph an arena in which the criminality of Israel is debated and her character defamed. In other words, their goal is not to win a debate but to stage one, in which the words *boycott Israel* are repeated time and again to slowly penetrate listeners' minds, thereby tarnishing Israel's image with a stain of criminality. Net effect: bullying pro-coexistence voices into silence.[7]

6 David N. Myers, "U.S. Academics Should Not Boycott Israeli Universities," *Jewish Journal*, December 18, 2013, http://jewishjournal.com/opinion/125482/.

7 Indeed, this LARB "forum" was itself a great achievement for BDS: it provided a public arena where the words *boycott Israel* were repeated many times and, unless taken humorously, helped achieve their subliminal goal on unsuspecting readers.

Omar Barghouti, cofounder and top ideologist of BDS, repeatedly has stated that ending the occupation is not the end of BDS. BDS will continue its struggle until Israel's legitimacy is eroded and its sovereignty dissolved. In a video dated September 29, 2013, for example, he states: "Colonizers [read: Zionists] are not entitled to self-determination by any definition of self-determination."[8] In his lecture at UCLA on January 15, 2014, he stated again that Jews in Israel are not entitled to any form of self-determination, on any piece of land, however slim. "They are not a people," he proclaimed (with a straight face), "and the U.N. principle of the right to self-determination does not apply to them."[9]

Consider the implications of committing 6.4 million human beings to eternal statelessness, stripped of their protective sovereignty, in a neighborhood that is boiling with genocidal designs. In so doing, Barghouti has, in effect, defined BDS as a racist, if not genocidal, movement. His statements were not disavowed by any BDS activist that I know of and certainly not by my esteemed colleague Professor Robin Kelley, who introduced Barghouti at UCLA with reverence befitting a reincarnated Mandela. Kelley is a distinguished professor of history, specializing in social movements, poverty, colonialism/imperialism, and race, and has other noble credentials. To charge such professors with racism or bigotry would normally be considered heresy of the first degree. But should it be? Shouldn't they be reminded that words and actions have consequences, that there are human beings affected by those consequences, and that the cruelty of those consequences can exceed that which is inspired by acknowledged racists and bigots?

Who Is Indigenous, and Who Is a Colonizer?

When a student stood up at Barghouti's UCLA lecture and said that he was a tenth-generation Israeli and therefore indigenous, Barghouti scoffed, "You aren't indigenous just because you say you are." So, what does Barghouti accept as a qualification for indigeneity? You guessed correctly: race! According to Barghouti, that young student could be indigenized at

8 Benjamin Doherty, "Watch: Omar Barghouti on 'Ethical Decolonization' and Moving Beyond Zionist Racism," *The Electronic Intifada*, September 29, 2013, https://electronicintifada.net/blogs/benjamin-doherty/watch-omar-barghouti-ethical-decolonization-and-moving-beyond-zionist-racism.

9 Roberta Seid, "Omar Barghouti at UCLA: A Speaker Who Brings Hate," *Jewish Journal*, January 16, 2014, http://jewishjournal.com/opinion/126186/.

the end of a few generations if his family intermarried with the Arab claimants of the land.[10]

This genetically defined conception of ownership is not uncommon in BDS circles; it is endemic to societies lacking historical narratives and traditions on which to base claims.[11] While modern norms no longer accept racial criteria as a basis for claims, BDS intellectuals are still playing the race card when it comes to Israel. The idea that indigeneity, peoplehood, and nationhood are based on collective memories and continuity of historical narratives, not on genetic lineage, must be as foreign to BDS intellectuals as history itself.

It is not surprising, therefore, that misrepresenting Israel as a "white settlers colonialist society" has become a cornerstone of BDS ideology and propaganda. UCLA's James Gelvin, for example, another history professor turned BDS propagandist, continues to teach this white settlers ideology to unsuspecting students year after year, with full knowledge of his department. Readers are invited to count the number of times these labels are used in essays written by BDS supporters.

And, while counting, readers should ask themselves if they can recall:

- One case of white settlers moving into a country they perceived to be the birthplace of their history.
- One case of white settlers speaking a language spoken in the land before the language spoken by its contemporary residents.
- One case of settlers whose holidays commemorated historical events in the land to which they moved—not in the lands from which they came.
- One case of settlers who did not name towns like New York, New Amsterdam, and New Wales (Israeli towns are not named "New

---

10 Eyewitness report by Roberta Seid in Ryan Torok, "Eritrean Solidarity Rally Underscores Community Divisiveness Over Israel," *Jewish Journal*, January 22, 2014, http://jewishjournal.com/news/los_angeles/126278/.

11 A Columbia professor, George Saliba, became famous for allegedly scolding a green-eyed Jewish student for tracing her ancestry to Semitic roots and biblical times. Saliba claimed that the green-eyed student, as well as most Jews of European origin, are descendants of the medieval Khazars and, therefore, have no claim to Middle Eastern lands. See Aymen Jawad, "Middle Eastern Christians and Antisemitism," *The Jerusalem Post*, August 1, 2011, http://www.jpost.com/Opinion/Op-Ed-Contributors/Middle-Eastern-Christians-and-anti-Semitism.

Warsaw," "New Berlin," and "New Baghdad"), but after names by which those towns were known in ancient times.

- One case of settlers who narrated their homecoming journey for eighty generations in poetry, prose, lore, and daily prayers.

Modern philosophers of political liberalism (like John Stewart Mill in "On Liberty"), after rejecting race as a basis for settling territorial claims, have identified collective memory and historical continuity as far more reasonable bases for defining boundaries between groups and nationalities. Today, these collective states of mind are the strongest forces that tie functional societies together—among them the pluralistic, secular, multiethnic, and multiracial society of Israel. They cannot be replaced by the old glues of common blood, common color, or common place of residence.

Why Pick on Israel?

Some of my colleagues find contradiction in BDS's relentless attacks on tolerant Israel, while obvious violators of human rights, such as Iran, Saudi Arabia, or Palestine, enjoy BDS silence, if not favors. I for one am not surprised. For BDS, human rights is merely a slogan to rally the uninformed around the banner of Israel bashing. What is puzzling to me, however, are the intellectuals who have read a chapter or two in the history of the Middle East yet buy into this deception. I can only conclude that there must be some deeply ingrained animosity that turns such intellectuals against Israel. What is it?

I believe the answer lies in what Israel represents to BDS followers and to the world.

To most of the civilized world, Israel represents the ideas of nation-building, historical continuity, and man's victory over repression and death. Marxist-leaning intellectuals (most BDS followers), on the other hand, see Israel's success as a failure of their ideology. It is a pillar of their belief that nationalism is an evil and anachronistic myth. The success of the Zionist experiment refutes this belief. It has unveiled the infinite energy that can be unleashed through that anachronistic and mythical idea called *peoplehood*, as it emerges from the unifying and creative force called *shared history*. It has demonstrated to the world how scattered tribes of beggars and peddlers can lift themselves from the margins of history and transform themselves into a world center of art, science, and entrepreneurship. Marxist intellectuals will never forgive Israel for proving their textbooks wrong.

The entire neural architecture of BDS intellectuals is wired around the hated image of white settlers who have long disappeared from the earth (not counting the Falkland Islands). Israel is hated because the white settler must be reinvented to fit the villain script. These intellectuals cannot stomach Israel's narrative of "a nation rebuilding its historical homeland," which has inspired so many communities to seize control over their destinies and strive for freedom and excellence. They cannot forgive Israel for giving new meaning to man's existence, a meaning that transcends class struggle and racial strife and, instead, unites people and propels them to move forward and dare the impossible. It is no coincidence that despite the daily threats to her existence, Israel is one of the most optimistic nations on Earth.

The Anti-Academic Issue

Some of my colleagues are surprised that BDS has chosen to cross the red line of academic freedom and call for a boycott of Israeli universities. They claim that any university that does not officially denounce the occupation is guilty of a crime and should therefore be punished by boycott. (It is as if any American university that does not officially denounce the Tea Party or abortion clinics deserves punishment).

I am not a bit surprised, because, as we have seen before, it is not the veracity of the charges that matters but their music—in the grand opera of BDS's slander machine, it is not the libretto that matters but the stage and the megaphone. A racist movement that shows no respect for truth or other people's identity can hardly be expected to respect the sanctity of academic freedom.

One academic organization that was lured by the siren song of BDS was the hapless American Studies Association (ASA), which in 2014 passed a resolution calling for an academic boycott of Israel. This turned the whole notion of academic freedom on its head, and naturally, it generated an immediate backlash: over two hundred college and university presidents condemned the ASA for their resolution.

The backlash was, in fact, so profound that, at UCLA, SJP, the campus proxy of BDS, had to change tactics and distance themselves from the BDS movement when they tried to convince the student council to vote for a divestment resolution. They failed—because the tactic was transparently dishonest—and the resolution was defeated seven to five. The important lesson is that, from the students' perspective, affiliation with BDS has finally turned into a liability. One can only hope that this perspective will become the norm on all U.S. campuses. Nevertheless, BDS proxies continue to harass pro-coexistence students and others who do not share the BDS agenda, as we have witnessed in the case of Milan Chatterjee, former president of the Graduate Students Association, who ultimately felt forced to leave UCLA after months of harassment.

What Can University Administrators Do?

My own position on academic boycotts is summarized in an open letter I wrote to John Sexton, president of New York University (NYU):

> January 20, 2014
>
> Dear President Sexton,
>
> I am writing to you as an alumnus of an NYU-affiliated school who is deeply concerned with the recent boycott resolution by the American Studies Association (ASA) and its adverse impact on the reputation of NYU.
>
> I received my PhD in 1965 from the Polytechnic Institute of Brooklyn, which last month became part of NYU. In November 2013, I was awarded the Distinguished Alumnus Award from NYU-Poly, an honor that made my association with NYU stronger and full of pride. I was disappointed therefore to learn that the leadership of the ASA, which pushed through a resolution that threatens the very fabric of academic life, is so intimately connected with NYU, both academically and administratively.
>
> Four ASA National Council members (25 percent) are affiliated with NYU and vocally campaigned for the resolution. In particular, the ASA President-Elect, Lisa Duggan, is NYU Professor of Social and Cultural Analysis. This means that in the next couple of years, NYU will become the semi-official host to most activities of this organization, and will be perceived as the academic lighthouse from which this group will be broadcasting its irresponsible, anti-coexistence, and anti-academic ideology.

I represent a group of professors who are particularly affected by the ASA boycott resolution. As part of my recent appointment to visiting professor at the Technion – Israel Institute of Technology, I am engaged in joint scientific projects with the Technion and its research staff. I also collaborate with Israeli universities on journalistic projects, named after my late son, Daniel Pearl, which aim at bringing Israeli and Palestinian journalists together.

I think you can appreciate how demoralizing the ASA action has been for me, as well as for other professors in my position. It is not that we view the ASA action as a danger to the continuation of our research projects—scientific collaboration has endured many hecklers in the past, much louder than the ASA drummers, and the latter are clearly more interested in defamation than in an actual boycott. What we do consider dangerous is the very attempt to contaminate our scientific explorations with a charge of criminality, and to bring that "criminality" for a so-called "debate" in the public square, on our own campuses. We view this attempt as a new form of McCarthyism that is aimed at intimidating and silencing opposing voices, and thus threatens academic freedom and the fundamental principles of academic institutions.

When a group of self-appointed vigilantes empowers itself with a moral authority to incriminate the academic activities of their colleagues, we are seeing the end of academia and the end of the sacred academic principles that have been painstakingly developed over centuries.

It is for this reason that I was personally disappointed with your letter which, while expressing opposition to boycotts in general and the ASA resolution in particular, failed to identify the ASA action as an imminent threat to NYU's reputation. Your letter did not state whether the ASA will be able to continue using NYU facilities and services as its de facto national headquarters, and what action you plan to take to restrain its leaders from re-staining the name of NYU with similar actions in the future.

In the name of many NYU alumni who wish to remain proud of their alma mater, I strongly urge you to remove NYU's name from the ASA "institutional member" list (as other universities have done), and to voice a strong and unequivocal condemnation of the pro-boycott activities of the ASA leadership.

Sincerely,

Judea Pearl
UCLA

This letter to President Sexton was intended to close a gap between what university administrators say about the boycott and what they have done about it thus far. If the boycott stands contrary to basic academic principles, then, surely, boycott advocates are undermining those principles and should be exposed.

Of course, no one expects university administrators to discipline professors who violate academic principles. Academic freedom survives by leaving its principles vulnerable to abuse. What one nevertheless expects campus leaders to do is to *define* the norms of a desirable campus environment and to identify activities that do not contribute to such an environment. I hope that activities that undermine academic principles are classified in this category.

I have recently come to understand how campus norms are shaped by willing administrators without infringing on anyone's free speech and without curtailing anyone's academic freedom. It came to my attention in a letter that the chancellor of UC Davis sent to the campus community. The occasion was an event planned for January 13, 2017, featuring Milo Yiannopoulos, an editor at Breitbart News, known for his provocative anti-Leftist commentary. In a masterfully worded letter, Davis's interim chancellor, Ralph J. Hexter, said this: "A university is at its best…when it listens to opposing views, especially ones that many of us find upsetting or even offensive." Thus, Yiannopoulos is a welcome guest. But then came the punchline: "This does not mean, however, that we take an approving or even neutral position with respect to speech intended to express hate or to denigrate or offend others….Such speech we unequivocally condemn." In other words, we are not censoring nor excluding, not even condemning, this ugly speaker, not least because doing so will invite complaints, if not legal action, from organizations such as Council on American-Islamic

Relations (CAIR) and the American Civil Liberties Union (ACLU). No. We are noble, inclusive, and absolutely viewpoint-neutral. What we can do, however, is tell the campus community which speakers we believe are radioactive and which are safe, and we do so only if it is true that their "speech [is] intended to express hate or to denigrate or offend others."

I call this approach selective neutrality. The neutrality is just right, I think, and both wise and effective. But why selective? Because such a message was not sent by Davis's chancellor in the week preceding the anti-Zionist speech of Azka Fayyaz, who spoke at UC Davis in January 2015, at the invitation of SJP. Nor was such a letter sent by the UCLA chancellor in the day preceding the offensive appearance of Roger Waters on November 30, 2016, who spoke at UCLA at the invitation of SJP.

A first step for university administrators who are serious about restoring campus civility, then, must be to internalize the equation: Zionophobia = Islamophobia. The antipathy to Jewish self-determination is no less heinous than the antipathy to Islam and to Muslims. Religion, in other words, has no monopoly on human sensitivity. All identity-defining symbols should be equally respected, and equal protection should be applied against all forms of discrimination, including anti-Zionism, Islamophobia, white supremacy, and more.

Selective neutrality should be the instrument with which the university administration distinguishes those who contribute to a respectful campus climate and productive discourse and debate from those who disrupt such a climate and discriminate against various identities. It must be selective, not in the sense of being inconsistent but in the sense of defining and shaping appropriate campus norms. So understood, it is perhaps the only legitimate means by which academic norms can be reestablished on campus.

Peace and the Future of Israel/Palestine

For those who are curious about my own thoughts on the prospects of peace in the Middle East, they can be summed up in one sentence: "Two states for two peoples, equally legitimate and equally indigenous."

When Palestinian leadership gathers the courage to utter the magical words *equally indigenous*, peace will become unstoppable—not even BDS will be able to stop it.[12]

12 Acknowledgement: This article benefited substantially from discussions with David Brandes.

34. "Israel @ 60 (Yes, 60): Confronting Denial," *Jewish Journal*, April 11, 2018

This article, which was re-published to commemorate Israel's 70th birthday, originally ran in the June 20, 2008, edition of the Jewish Journal. *It deals with a despicable pattern, created and perpetuated by the Western media. In the name of "balance," each year Israel's birthday is bombarded with debates on its right to exist. Do we need to "balance" each celebration of Martin Luther King, Jr. Day with articles by white supremacists?*

Each year, in preparation for Israel's birthday, newspaper editors feel an uncontrolled urge, a divine calling, in fact, to invite Arab writers to tell us why Israel should not exist. This must give them some sort of satisfaction, such as we might have in inviting officials of the Flat Earth Society to tell us why Earth is not, could not, or should not really be round, and to do so precisely on Earth Day, lest the wisdom would escape anyone's attention. Evidently, the banalization of absurdity has its kicks. It is sporty, "out-of-the-box-ish," admirably "Jewish," and, if only we were not dealing with a dangerous experiment involving the lives and dignity of millions of human beings, could easily have earned its authors the National Cuteness Award.

But the issue before us is an adult matter, and the result is a depressing Kafkaesque choreography in which Israel, the heart and soul of Jewish peoplehood, is put on trial for its very existence, while pro-coexistence commentators, if they are invited, deal with the future of Israel and its achievements, but leave the accusations unanswered. There is some wisdom to ignoring insults and unfounded accusations. By answering, one tacitly bestows credence, however minimal, upon the arguments that put you on the accused bench—the last bench that Israel's birthday deserves, even ignoring her accusers' record. So, perhaps it is wise to write chapter and verse about Israel's achievements and let the "colonial" and "apartheid" accusations hang there, unanswered, as living witnesses of the Orwellian mentality of the accusers?

I am not totally convinced.

I am concerned about the possibility that a non-negligible percentage of *Los Angeles Times* readers, especially the novice and the hasty, would interpret the publication of Saree Makdisi's call for dismantling Israel ("Forget the Two-State Solution," *Los Angeles Times*, Opinion, May 12, 2008) as evidence that his arguments and conclusions are deemed worthy of consideration in the eyes of the editors of the *L.A. Times*, whose judgment the public has entrusted to protect us from Flat Earth-type deformities. This concern became especially acute after reporters Richard Boudreaux and Ashraf Khalil ("For Some Palestinians, One State With Israel Is Better Than None," *Los Angeles Times*, World News, May 8, 2008) had already touted the "one-state" slogans in the same newspaper, with unmistaken sympathy, under the cover of "World News."

I am concerned because evil plans begin with evil images. Once the mind is jolted to envision deviant images, it automatically constructs a belief structure that supports their feasibility and desirability. The first phase of Hitler's strategy was to get people to envision, just envision, a world without Jews—the rest is history. Today, we are witnessing a well-coordinated effort by enemies of coexistence to get people to envision, just envision, a world without Israel—the rest, they hope, will become history.

The American press seems to fall for it. In fairness to the editors of the *L.A. Times* (unlike the *Nation* and the *Christian Science Monitor*), articles calling for the elimination of Israel are often balanced by articles calling for peaceful coexistence. But, ironically, this "balance" is precisely where the imbalance occurs, for it gives equal moral weight to an immoral provocation that every Jew in Israel considers a genocidal death threat and most Jews in the world view as an assault on their personal dignity, national identity, and historical destiny. After all, we do not rush to "balance" each celebration of Martin Luther King, Jr. Day with articles by white supremacists, and we do not "balance" a hate speech with a lecture on peaceful breathing technique. A hate speech is balanced with a lecture on the evils of hate.

A true, albeit grotesque, moral balance would be demonstrated only if for every "down with Israel" writer the newspaper were to invite a "down with Palestinian statehood" writer. But editors may have strange takes on morality. For some, questioning the legitimacy of Israel's existence is a mark of neutrality, while questioning the legitimacy of Palestinian aspirations is a social taboo. Decency should somehow inform these editors that both "down with" calls are morally reprehensible and insulting to readers' intelligence, hence, both should be purged from civil discourse and marginalized into the good company of white supremacy and Flat Earth rhetoric. But until decency reigns, we can be sure to see them again at Israel's birthdays, the predators of peace, paraded by the press, demanding their annual prey: Once more to envision, just envision, a world without Israel.

Ironically, in this context, Arab commentaries published around Yom HaAtzmaut can actually be of great service to Israel, for they provide a faithful mirror of the prevailing sentiments in the elite ranks of Palestinian society, and thus gauge precisely how ready it is to accept a peace agreement, whatever its shape, as permanent. This year, the *L.A. Times*, the *Nation*, the *New York Times*, the *Washington Post*, the *Christian Science Monitor*, and others lured an impressive group of Arab intellectuals into unveiling their worldview to American readers. These authors are highly educated, mostly secular champions of modernity and masters of communication—yet keenly attuned to grassroots sentiments. Enticed by the limelight, and seemingly caught off guard, they revealed the naked landscape of the Palestinian mindset.

Sadly, what they revealed in 2008 is not what Mahmoud Abbas would have liked us to think. They revealed what we feared all along but were afraid to admit: The notion of a two-state solution never began to penetrate the surface of Palestinian consciousness. In vain would one search these articles for an idea, or a shred of an idea, that morally justifies a two-state solution, or that acknowledges some historical ties of Jews to the land, or that makes an intellectual investment contrary to the greater Palestine agenda. One by one, the articles depict a culture forged by five generations of rejection and denial, a culture in which compromise means defeat and national identity means denying it to others.

This does not mean that the two-state solution is dead—after all, it is the only proposal worthy of the word "solution"—but it means that the current efforts to reach a peaceful settlement are absolutely futile unless they address the real obstacle: The ideological landscape as revealed to us by our Arab brethren on Yom HaAtzmaut.

35. "Faculty Corner: Zionophobia—Our Only Fighting Word," *Ha'Am*, May 14, 2018

Today, after October 7, when we really want to rebuke an anti-Zionist we call him or her "pro-Hamas" or "antisemitic." Things were less clear before October 7, when anti-Zionists enjoyed an aura of originality. This article explains why the term "Zionophobe" is more effective than the others. It reminds anti-Zionists that their views are racist to the first degree, regardless of whether they are "antisemitic" in the classical sense. It is a word that applies to Hamas, the Palestinian cause, Arab rejectionism, and Western gullibility.

In this inaugural opening of the Student-Faculty Corner of *Ha'Am*, I would like to elaborate on an idea that I advocated in my interview two weeks ago. The idea is simple: From my observations of campus life in the past few years, it seems clear that we are losing the moral fight against BDS and its cronies. It's also clear to me that we will continue to lose unless we assert our moral stature clearly, unabashedly, and effectively by using the magic word "Zionophobia"—the irrational fear of Zionism coupled with an obsessive commitment to undermine the right of Israel to exist.

We do not have another word that describes the moral pathology of those who deny us statehood or even peoplehood. The word "antisemitism," despite the State Department definition, and despite its common usage by Israel's defenders, lost its punch twenty years ago. Every time we label an attack against Israel "antisemitic," I see people yawning: "Here we are, the Jews are using this 'cry-wolf' card again—how boring." Every time we label an attack against Israel "antisemitic," I see hordes of BDS cronies volunteering to fight for the right of Jewish students to have a kosher cafeteria, to pray three times a day, and to wear yarmulke in public. And they truly mean it, as long as the yarmulke is not decorated with blue and white Magen David.

Every time we label an attack against Israel "antisemitic," I hear our enemies cheering: "I am a Semite too!" or "Don't conflate anti-Zionism with antisemitism" or "Some of our board members are Jewish" or "Even a prominent Jewish professor in UCLA's history department wrote that anti-Zionism is normative in Jewish thinking." In short, every time we label an attack against Israel "antisemitic," we lose the high moral ground, and the conversation drifts to where we cannot win.

How about the word "anti-Zionism"? This word, unfortunately, has ceased to be an indictment of bad taste and has become a badge of honor, even in some respectable circles. "Anti-Zionism," or even "anti-Israelism," sounds like a legitimate political position, like anti-tax reform or anti-Republican. Worse yet, our ineffectiveness in winning the BDS debate has turned Zionism into a dirty word, so dirty that even Jews are sometimes hesitant to use it without some qualification. (I personally counted the number of Jewish professors at a reception in the Center for Jewish Studies who uttered the words "I am a Zionist" without fear or apology. The count is frightening).

There remains only one fighting word: Zionophobia.

Zionophobia describes precisely the ideology promoted by BDS activists on campus. More importantly, it rhymes with Islamophobia, the cardinal sin in liberal circles. It has an element of irrationality and an element of bigotry. In short, Zionophobia has all the foul flavors that are normally attributed to Islamophobia and that Israel's enemies are trying to stick to Zionism. My experience in debating hard-core Zionophobes has taught me that the mere mention of the word Zionophobia creates an immediate and drastic change of conversation, from the standard accusations against Israel's policies to the moral core of the dispute: Jews' right to a homeland versus the bigotry of those who deny them that right.

I read what goes on at neighboring campuses, and my heart goes out to the students who need to defend themselves with cotton bullets. For example, at Cal Poly, a registered student group demanded that the university raise all student cultural clubs' budgets "except those aligned with Zionist ideology." I read the reactions of the Jewish and pro-Israel organizations, including Hillel of San Luis Obispo, Chabad of Cal Poly, and others. "We are innocent," they all plead. "Zionism is not guilty," they beg. "We are hurt," they bemoan. "It is antisemitic," some complain. "It is illegal," others note. The one word I am not hearing is "Zionophobia," the word that can turn this whole circus into a match among equals. It is a word that shames the excluder for moral deformity as severely and universally as Islamophobia.

BDS's new tactics of isolating and excluding Jewish students "aligned with Zionist ideology" has also infected NYU's campus, and it is approaching UCLA despite the strength of our community. In February this year, I happened to enter the Green Room in Schoenberg Hall, where BFI (Bruins for Israel) leaders met with invited speaker CNN journalist Fareed Zakaria and described to him some of their difficulties as Jews on campus. The student I heard speak described the social isolation that Hillel students face when they try to collaborate with other campus groups. To paraphrase: "The rejection persists," the student said, "even when you have nothing to do with Israel, even when you criticize Israel, or disavow any connection to Israel." I do not know the name of that student, and I did not hear Zakaria's response, but one thing I do know: People will start respecting you when you are assertive about your rights, and a litmus test of your assertiveness is your readiness to challenge the moral standing of your abusers.

Zionist students will be respected when they stop accusing their abusers of bigotry they conveniently deny—antisemitism—and start indicting them for a bigotry they cannot deny: Zionophobia.

You have your fighting word. Use it.

36. "Inspiration and a Rallying Cry for Graduates," *Jewish Journal*, June 26, 2019

This is the text of my speech at the fourth annual UCLA Jewish Graduation, held June 16, 2019. It covers both the nature of Jewish identity and the central role of Zionism in it. I still use this text in every meeting with students on campus, including Jews and non-Jews.

I am deeply honored by the opportunity to address this graduating class and to speak to you on topics that are so very dear to my heart. I know that I am speaking today to a unique group of graduates. Unique, because all of you felt the need to add a distinctly Jewish color to one of the most memorable days of your life.

And the question you are probably asking is: What is the nature of this extra color we call Jewish? Is being Jewish some sort of a birthmark with which one is burdened or blessed for life? A genetic incident? How can one be proud of a genetic incident? Is it a religious belief? An ethnic loyalty? A commitment to a certain mode of behavior or perspective? An attitude? Is it just a collection of sweet childhood memories, decorated with mother's cooking? Or a language to communicate with our ancestors and decode their wisdom and experience? Most importantly, could a coherent, meaningful answer ever emerge from a community whose members view the question through such diverse prisms?

The question is not trivial, and it shook up the core of my soul seventeen years ago, when our son Daniel was murdered in Karachi, Pakistan, and his last words, facing his abductors' camera, were: "My father is Jewish, my mother is Jewish—I am Jewish. Back in the town of Bnei Brak, there is a street named after my great-grandfather, Chaim Pearl, who was one of the founders of the town." These words have since become an identity banner to every Jewish soul, to every lover of Israel, and to every scholar of peoplehood. But at the time, they raised more questions than answers. What did he mean? What do any of us mean when we say, "I am Jewish"?

So, we asked three hundred people from all walks of life—journalists, comedians, rabbis, musicians, even kids in summer camp—what it means to them to be Jewish, and one hundred fifty of them responded and gave honest answers, compiled in the book, *I Am Jewish: Personal Reflections Inspired by the Last Words of Daniel Pearl.* The answers were as diverse as Jews love to be—two Jews, three opinions—but they have a common denominator, which can be read clearly in the essays of Shimon Peres, Amos Oz, and A.B. Yehoshua, and which happen to coincide with my own answer.

To me, being Jewish means to identify with the past, present, and future of a collective of individuals who happen to call themselves "Jews." This might sound a bit circular, but it is not. Many definitions in logic sound circular and still convey profound meanings. As an act of choice, I select a certain thread of history and label it "mine," that is, relevant to me. Similarly, I imagine the destiny of other members of the collective and label it "ours," that is, relevant to our children. This is indeed what "peoplehood" means: A collective bonded by common history and common destiny.

But who are we? And how did this historical bondage shape us?

I look down the history of ideas, and I find our little subculture scoring an impressive list of accomplishments. I see Jews as the scouts of civilization, the ones who question conventional wisdom and constantly seek the exploration of new pathways. Abraham questioned the wisdom of idolatry; Moses questioned the wisdom of servitude and lawlessness; the prophets questioned institutional injustice; and so the chain goes on from the Maccabees, Jesus, and Spinoza to Marx, Herzl, and Freud down to Einstein, Gershwin, the Zionist Chalutzim, who created the miracle of Israel, and down to the civil rights activists of the 1960s.

As individuals, we do not consciously choose this lonely role of scouts, border-challengers, or idol-smashers. It has penetrated our veins, partly from the Bible and the Talmud through their persistent encouragement of curiosity, learning, and debate, and partly from our free-spirited parents, uncles, and historical role models. But mostly, this role has been imposed on us by the travesties of history. Conventional wisdoms were mighty unkind to us, so our sanity demanded that we challenge those conventions and, in due course, we have learned to challenge all conventions.

Thus, is my Jewishness a blessing or a burden? Do I prefer the trails of the scouts to the safety of the bandwagon? You bet I do. It is only from those trails that I can see where the voyage is heading, and it is only from there that I can discover greener pastures. I am Jewish, and I doubt I would be in my element elsewhere.

This combination of loneliness and creativity brings me to discuss the painful situation in which we, Zionist Jews, find ourselves on this campus vilified and demonized by BDS cronies, betrayed by our longtime progressive allies, and abandoned to exclusion and namelessness by those who should promote equity, diversity, and inclusion on our campus. As many of you know, you and I were recently labeled "white supremacists" by a top BDS ideologist who was a guest lecturer at the Department of Anthropology. I repeat: UCLA Department of Anthropology. Let shame rest with those who earn it. As of today, that lecturer has not yet been asked to apologize to the literally thousands of students and faculty at UCLA who are devout Zionists, champions of human rights and social justice, whom she labeled "white supremacists."

I feel obliged to share with you my rather optimistic assessment of this situation, since many of you will be facing a similar climate in graduate schools or in industry or the business environment. I am optimistic because we have learned to pinpoint precisely what strategy will snap us out of this predicament and, fortunately, the strategy is not unrealizable. It involves two elements. First, recognition of identity. Second, word power.

Let me elaborate. First, we should stop using the term antisemitism in our arguments and complaints, because it makes us easily dismissible by anyone who wishes to take cover under the slogan "anti-Zionism is not antisemitism." Why make it easy for them? Instead, we should demand explicit recognition as "Identity Zionists." Since Jews are a history-bonded collective, and Israel is the culmination of Jewish history, elementary high school algebra dictates that Zionism is an essential component of Jewish identity. Zionist students and faculty should, therefore, be recognized as legitimate participants in UCLA's tapestry of inclusion and diversity.

I said "Zionist," not "Jewish," which is easy to pay lip service to. This means that in all matters concerning code of conduct, Zionism should attain the same protection status as any religion or nationality or identity-distinct collective, and anti-Zionism should turn as despicable and condemnable as Islamophobia, women inferiority, or white supremacy.

This idea is not mine. Such recognition was accepted by California State University in a recent legal settlement of a lawsuit filed by students at San Francisco State. It is now binding, and we should insist that an identical wording be accepted by the UCLA administration. "For many Jews, Zionism is an important part of their identity." We should insist on it in every meeting with UCLA officials, relentlessly, incessantly, before we even make an appointment. It is a prerequisite for any discussion of our posture on campus, and it is the litmus test for our inclusion or exclusion in or out of the Bruins family. I should add that the administration's failure to grant us this recognition is not entirely their fault. No one has asked them to do it. We naively assumed that it is self-evident so, as time passed, they forgot how to spell "Zionism." No more! Zionism has a spelling.

Our second weapon is word power. We should not beg for safe space but create one, through assertiveness and self-awareness of our just cause. He who does not defend his identity from slander cannot expect to be respected. Remember that to an outside observer silence is interpreted as an admission of guilt. The term "antisemitism" connotes submissive begging for protection and should be replaced by a fighting word "Zionophobia"—the irrational fear of a homeland for the Jewish people. It rhymes with Islamophobia on purpose, of course. When you call someone a "Zionophobe," it means: "If you deny my people's right to a homeland, something is wrong with *you*, not me." Jewish students will regain respect only when "Zionophobia" becomes the ugliest word on campus. It depends on us. If we use it often enough, it *will* become the ugliest.

In summary, I believe that once we insist on recognition of our identity and once we arm ourselves with a powerful fighting word, "Zionophobia," campus climate will change dramatically, and the words "I am Jewish" will ring again as a mark of pride, creativity, and accomplishment. I wish you much success in your future careers as you continue the long and heroic journey of our people, a journey of dignity, creativity, and excellence.

37. "Chanukah—Our Trust Deed to History," *Jewish Journal*, December 22, 2019

The story of Chanukah, on which all Jewish children are raised, reinforces the definition of indigenousness as presented in "The Balfour Declaration at 100 and How It Redefined Indigenous People" (see p. 100), according to which holidays provide an unassailable litmus test of historical connection to a land. This piece on Chanukah may be regarded as a companion to the Balfour Declaration piece.

My grandson asked why we make such a big fuss about Chanukah. By the tone of his voice, I could tell that a juicy recipe of latkes and donuts will not work this year, nor will another story of the miracle of the lonely oil vessel, nor even the victory of the Maccabees over the Syrian army in 161 BC. After all, the Bible is full of miracles, miracle makers, wars and battles, winners and losers.

Why Chanukah? I told him honestly what Chanukah means to me: "Chanukah is our *trust deed* to the birthplace of our history, more solid even than the ancient synagogues they are excavating in Israel or the Arch of Titus in Rome, with the Temple ornaments carved in marble."

"Stones can be faked," I told him, "not so a continuous collective memory, passed on from father and mother to son and daughter, over one hundred ten generations. An unassailable proof that no one can fake."

Recollecting back, this was also the answer my mother gave me when I asked what Chanukah meant to her. "I came to Israel on the eve of Chanukah, 1935," she said. "The first day after my arrival, I met a neighbor, a teacher who invited me to visit her kindergarten. There I experienced one of the happiest days of my life. Scores of children were standing there, loudly singing Chanukah songs, in Hebrew, as if this was the most natural thing to do, as if they were singing those songs for hundreds of years."

"Why the wonder?" I asked. "Didn't your family celebrate Chanukah in Poland?"

"Not exactly," she said. "Yes, we lit the candles, but it was in a dark corner, with my father whispering the blessings and mumbling Ma Oz Tzur quietly. You see, the neighbors were Gentile, and he did not feel comfortable advertising that we celebrated a Jewish holiday. And here I come, and suddenly find these toddlers singing 'Maccabee Gibbor!' ['Maccabee, My Hero'] at full volume and in the open courtyard."

Only those who have gone through the exhilarating experience of a people returning to its homeland could truly appreciate the gift that history has bestowed upon the Jews: singing "Maccabee Gibbor" in the language in which it was sung in Jerusalem two thousand two hundred years ago. And only those whose homecoming saga has been undermined and distorted can understand the power of this historical connection.

Israel's neighbors, lacking such biblical connection, have understood the power of trust deeds. This was apparent at the 2000 Camp David Summit, when Palestinian leader Yasser Arafat could not contain himself and whispered in President Clinton's ear: "Everyone knows that Jews did not have a Temple in Jerusalem." At some point, Dr. Saeb Erekat, the chief Palestinian negotiator, decided that the Palestinians are descendants of the Canaanite tribes conquered by Joshua. This, he said later, prevents him and any Palestinian from ever accepting Israel as a Jewish state.

When I first heard about the Palestinian-Canaanite connection, I could not help but imagine how lonely it must be for a Palestinian boy not to be able to sing "Canaanite Gibbor!" in the language of his ancestors, not to have Canaanite role models after which to name songs, towns, and holidays, and, lonelier yet, to be taught by teachers who had never heard of his Canaanite ancestors when they went to kindergarten.

Just four days ago, December 18, 2019, the same Dr. Erekat tweeted a video titled "Merry Palestinian Christmas," saying: "Jesus was one of us. He didn't have blonde hair and blue eyes, he wasn't from Kentucky, he looked like DJ Khaled, minus two hundred pounds. Mary, too, was a Palestinian, Mary's grandmother—a Palestinian. John the Baptist, St. George, the apostles—all Palestinians. Palestine has so much history...." and on and on.

This is not a joke. It is, in fact, the cause, the root, and the essence of the Palestinian tragedy. The feeling of unworthy claimants has haunted their leadership since my grandfather arrived in 1924 to rebuild the biblical town of Bnei Brak and the Grand Mufti of Jerusalem understood that these Jewish emigrants are no crusaders, nor Mongolian invaders, but the original owners of the place, with biblical names to name towns and with kindergarten toddlers singing "Maccabee Gibbor."

The tragedy is that rather than accepting Ben-Gurion's plea, "You don't need to build Temples to be equally indigenous; centuries of physical presence is your trust deed," they chose to reject mutual recognition and go for exclusive endogeneity status. Unable to celebrate any holiday connected to the land to which they claim sole ownership, unable to chant a single hymn authored in the days of Jesus or Judah Maccabee, lacking, in fact, any cultural connection to those days, Palestinian leadership has been laboring relentlessly to fabricate such connection and to seize, misappropriate, and distort the heritage of their neighbors.

The tragedy is that they are still hoping to be taken seriously and as well-intentioned if and when they return to the negotiating table. If only Dr. Erekat understood what his circus is doing to Palestinian credibility. Standing tall above this circus, Chanukah remains the one unchallenged trust deed to the birthplace of our history. Let's think about it this week when we sing the song "Maccabee Gibbor!" that my mother so loved.

38. "Two New Weapons for Reclaiming Israel's Posture on Your Campus," *Jewish Journal*, February 10, 2020

This op-ed is based on a speech I gave at the Alums for Campus Fairness (ACF) conference in Los Angeles. The "two new weapons" the title refers to are: 1) the emancipation of our identity as Zionists from the debate about antisemitism and 2) the moralization of our cause by moving our fight from the legal to the moral arena. I've cut the first part of the op-ed, because it repeats the points I made in "Inspiration and a Rallying Cry for Graduates" (see p. 122). I feel that the final part, which is new, is important to include because it serves as a concrete example of the action we should ask campus administrators to take in helping us to moralize our cause.

How can campus administration help in the process of moralizing our cause?

Let me assure you, every university administrator hates what the Boycott, Divestment, and Sanctions (BDS) circus is doing to campus life. Administrators care about two things only: funding and ranking, neither of which is helped by BDS hostilities. What they don't understand is that they can stop the BDS circus overnight by making it very, very costly to them.

How?

Let me ask around: What is the thing BDS fears the most? Does anyone care to guess?

Of course, it is the truth about Israel. Imagine how they would react if after every one of their Purim shpiels the university issues a public statement of how inspiring Israel is to every decent person on this planet.

Blue sky? Far-fetched? Not really. Selective affirmation of norms and values is an instrument that has been used effectively by campus administrators, even at UCLA. When Milo Yiannopoulos came to speak on campus in 2018, his views were denounced explicitly on moral grounds, and the cultural contributions of Latinos to our city and our country were highlighted proudly by UCLA Chancellor Gene D. Block and communicated to the entire campus community through all the horns and media outlets that chancellors can orchestrate. Block could have used the same instrument to denounce the National Students for Justice in Palestine (SJP) conference and tell the campus community how central Zionism is to the collective identity of students and faculty on campus, and how inspirational Israel is to him, personally, as an American who cares for democracy and human rights.

Block did not do this, but Martha Pollack, the president of Cornell, did. After SJP made its perennial demand to divest from Israel, she issued a public statement from which SJP has not recovered yet. In addition to the standard arguments of BDS being "non-academic" and "divisive," as if anyone cares for those, she added that BDS "often conflates the policies of the Israeli government with the very right of Israel to exist as a nation, which I find particularly troublesome."

This simple sentence, written in the first person, was sufficient for Cornell students to understand that Israel's existence is a moral imperative and opposition to it is morally reprehensible. If there is anything that may stop the BDS crusade of intimidation and criminalization it is precisely the fear that each time they launch one of those funny "resolutions" or "petitions," a university leader will remind the campus who they are, who you are, what they stand for, what you stand for, and why demonizing Israel is a moral deformity. Cornell is your second weapon—use it!

39. "The Year Everything Changed" and "The Year Everything Changed—Continued," *Moment Magazine*, June 2020

I was one of thirty "thinkers" invited by the editors of Moment Magazine *to reflect on which years changed the course of Jewish history. I wish the directors of our Holocaust museums would read the last sentence of my response, where they will discover how they could empower young Jews with a sense of pride and rightness by celebrating the revival of the Jewish people in the State of Israel. As I have repeatedly argued, if the narrative of the Gospel had ended with the Crucifixion, not the Resurrection, Christianity would have never become a world religion.*

1948

I can't think of another moment in time when Jewish history held its breath with greater anxiety and expectation than on Friday, May 14, 1948, at 4 p.m., when David Ben-Gurion pronounced: "We hereby proclaim the establishment of a Jewish state in Eretz Israel, to be known as the State of Israel."

We eleven-year-olds knew that something was brewing, but not what or when. Our parents told us only to play close to home because "times are not the same." We were old enough to listen to the radio and read newspapers, but still unable to grasp the seriousness of the messages that came from Beirut and Cairo of "rivers of blood" and "monumental massacre." Even the fall of the four Etzion Block kibbutzim (in the Judean hills between Jerusalem and Hebron) the day earlier and the execution of its one hundred twenty seven defenders by the Arab Legion did not shock our naive minds to the reality of the time.

Yes, we had heard what happened in Europe. Each of us had family members who had perished (my maternal grandparents included), but our parents kept us shielded from the horrific face of reality. They vowed to bring us up as "normal Jews," unscarred by faraway European antisemitism. We sang and screamed as loudly as we could: "Free Aliyah!! Free Aliyah!!" But when survivors started arriving from inferno Europe, we did not understand why their skin was so white, why they walked so meekly, and why they could not talk like us.

My mother was right, I should have played closer to home. The next day, May 15, my playmates and I found ourselves hugging each other in a staircase while Egyptian warplanes bombarded our town. A neighbor opened the door and said: "Children, it's going to get much worse, but we will prevail." We could not possibly imagine how anything could get worse, but it did. Our neighbor's nineteen-year-old son came back in a coffin two weeks later, and his mother stood glued to her window for the next five years, awaiting her son's return.

Some six thousand dead, one percent of the population, was the price of independence, mostly young men, kids from around the block who smiled at us warmly, waved goodbye, and went to fight five armies. It is only now, as a grandfather, that I begin to understand the magnitude of that historical event on May 14, 1948, and how it empowered a scattered tribe of beggars and peddlers to lift itself from the margin of history and create a world center of art, science, and entrepreneurship. It is only now that I understand what the miracle of Israel did to the posture of every Jew worldwide and how it currently sustains the collective identity of American Jewry.

***

Writing these recollections makes me realize that I, and my 1948 generation, are becoming an endangered species. Like Holocaust survivors, our number declines by the day, and there will soon be very few of us left to tell our stories. Whereas the Holocaust story resonates in hundreds of museums and memorials across the U.S., none is dedicated to the story of Jewish revival—Israel—and how it came into being in the years 1917 to 1948. For some Jewish youngsters, and to most non-Jewish youngsters, a visit to a Holocaust museum is their only exposure to Jewish history, and that exposure skips over the story of Jewish redemption. We must therefore insist on having each and every Holocaust museum expanded with a "From the Ashes" exhibit to empower us and our grandchildren with the most life-sustaining chapter in our collective psyche.

40. "My Rabbi Hat," *Jewish Journal*, February 12, 2021

This meditation is my rabbi-esque interpretation of one of the most profound sentences in the Torah: "And thou shall not oppress the stranger, and you know how it feels to be a stranger, because you were a stranger in the land of Egypt." This sentence captures how universal morality is embedded within Jewish particularity. It offers a scientific basis for grounding universal humanistic values in ethnic identity.

This week, Parashat Mishpatim, I can't resist putting on my rabbi hat and sharing my commentary, because this Parasha contains the core of Jewish ethics and the secret of Jewish survival. The verse I am targeting is: "Ve Ger Lo Tilchats, VeAtem Yedaatem Et Nefesh Hager, Ki Ger Hayita Beerets Mitrayim" ("And thou shall not oppress the stranger, and you know how it feels to be a stranger, because you were a stranger in the land of Egypt.") The message is clear: universal morality emanates from personal empathy, "you know how it feels to be a stranger."

And where does personal empathy emanate from? Here comes the second part to answer those who argue, "I am an American and have never been a stranger anywhere," and reminds them: "personal empathy emanates not from personal experience but from our collective, peoplehood memory." Individual experience is not rich enough to cope with the complexity of human life and the ups and downs of human history. Collective memory is what is needed. "You were once a stranger in the land of Egypt; we all were there, remember?"

Our record, performance, survival, and resilience attest to the power and wisdom of this symbiosis of universal values and people-based memories.

41. "My Purim Rabbi's Hat," *Jewish Journal*, February 25, 2021

"And, who knows, perhaps you have attained to royal position for just such a crisis." Who knows, perhaps the talents and prominence given to Jews in

Hollywood, the media, business, politics, academia, and other spheres of influence were destined for this very moment of world madness, moral confusion, and all-out assault on Jews and Israel.

Throughout my upbringing—and I am sure it has been the same for you—Purim meant fun, parties, clowns, masks, and noise makers (groggers), a sort of Jewish Halloween, save for the costumes being less scary and a bit more civilized. In the past few years, however, I have come to see a profoundly personal meaning in the story of Purim, especially in this powerful message that Mordecai sends to Queen Esther: "Do not imagine that you, of all the Jews, will escape with your life by being in the king's palace," says Mordecai. "For, if you keep silent in this crisis, relief and deliverance will come to the Jews from another quarter, while you and your father's house will perish. And, who knows, perhaps you have attained to royal position for just such a crisis."

It has been several years now that this breathtaking message of Mordecai, not the Purim parties, has come to my mind whenever the story of Purim is narrated. So much so, that I began chanting it to myself whenever I had to utter words or take action that involved risking career opportunities or social acceptance. Personally, I have drawn tremendous courage from the fantasy that some two thousand six hundred years ago, a wise Jew experienced a similar predicament and concluded that the decision was not entirely theirs: "Who knows, perhaps you were destined for this very moment."

More recently, since the rise of academic McCarthyism, I have started using Mordecai's words on friends and colleagues who remain silent upon seeing their students intimidated by BDS cronies or their junior colleagues "cancelled" or interrogated by various vice squads. Mordecai's words resonate in my ears when I explain to colleagues: "We owe our academic stature to many who spoke out in such crises before. It's now time for us to pay back our debt to the community by making our voices heard, despite the risks involved, or we'll all perish." I remind my academic friends that only sixty years ago, Ivy League universities had quotas on Jewish enrollment, and that these quotas were lifted by hardworking members of the Jewish community, many of them volunteers, who wrote letters, petitioned lawmakers, and pressured university administrators to make admission equitable to all. Those volunteers expected our voices to be heard in the protection of their great-grandchildren on college campuses, currently facing the worst crisis since the days of quotas.

And it goes way beyond academia. Be it business, the arts, writing, or law, we owe part of our professional success to community support, and such support comes with expectation and responsibilities. We are expected to make our voices heard in support of those who are more vulnerable to the storm. And when we hesitate, let us remember Mordecai's words: "And, who knows, perhaps you have attained to royal position for just such a crisis."

42. "How Did Hamas Become the Darling of the West?" *Jewish Journal*, June 2, 2021

We in academia are partly responsible for allowing Hamas to dig miles and miles of propaganda tunnels under our campuses. Few of us understood before October 7 the explosive potential of Hamas culture and the power of the "rhinoceros" way of thinking to overtake even the finest of our institutions. "Honk, Honk!"

In February 2009, I wrote an essay about a symposium at UCLA that marked the beginning of Hamas's penetration into academic circles. I also described the culture of fear that had overtaken many of my colleagues who felt it was unsafe to admit to supporting Israel. Twelve years later, in the wake of the most recent conflict between Israel and Gaza and the ensuing antisemitism carried out on our campuses and in our streets, I have revised and updated my original essay, which is just as relevant today as it was when it was first written.

Remember Eugène Ionesco's *Rhinoceros*? Written in the late 1950s, the play describes the transformation of a quiet, peaceful town into anarchy when one after another of its residents is transformed into a lumbering, thick-skinned brute. Only Bérenger, a stand-in for the playwright, tries to hold out against the collective rush into rhinocerism.

First, the townspeople notice a stray rhinoceros rumbling down the street. No one takes a great deal of notice other than to say that it "made a lot of dust." It's a "stupid quadruped not worth talking about," although it does trample one woman's cat. Before long, an ethical debate develops over the rhino way of life versus the human way of life. "Why not just leave them alone," a friend advises Bérenger. "You get used to it." The debate is quickly muted into blind acceptance of the rhino ethic, and the entire town joins the marching herd. Bérenger finds himself alone, partly resisting, partly enjoying the uncontrolled sounds coming out his own throat: "Honk, Honk, Honk."

These sounds from Ionesco's play have echoed in my ears twice. First in 2009, when Hamas gave its premiere performance at UCLA and, second, this past week, when rhinos roamed the streets of Los Angeles shouting: "Honk, Honk, Honk."

Let's start in January 2009, when an email from a colleague at Indiana University queried: "Being at UCLA, you must know about this symposium…pretty bad." Attached was Roberta Seid's report on the now infamous "Human Rights and Gaza" symposium held a day earlier at UCLA. To refresh readers' memory, this symposium, organized by UCLA's Center for Near Eastern Studies (CNES), was billed as a discussion of human rights in Gaza. Instead, the director of the center, Susan Slyomovics, invited four speakers with long histories of demonizing Israel for a panel that Seid describes as a reenactment of a "1920 Munich beer hall." Not only did the panelists portray Hamas as a guiltless, peace-seeking, unjustly provoked organization, but they also bashed Israel, her motives, her character, her birth and conception, and led the excited audience into chanting, "Zionism is Nazism," "Fuck, fuck Israel," in the best tradition of rhino liturgy.

But the primary impact of the event became evident the morning after, when unsuspecting, partially informed students woke up to read an article in the campus newspaper titled, "Scholars Say Attack on Gaza an Abuse of Human Rights," to which the good name of the University of California was attached, and from which the word "terror" and the genocidal agenda of Hamas were conspicuously absent. This mock verdict, presented as an outcome of supposedly dispassionate scholarship, is where Hamas culture scored its first triumph—the first inch of academic respectability, the first inroad into Western minds.

Naturally, when students complained to me about how abused and frightened they felt during the symposium, and how concerned they were about the direction taken by the Center for Near Eastern Studies, I felt terribly guilty. "We should have anticipated such travesties," I told myself. "We, the Jewish faculty at UCLA, should have preempted it with a true symposium on human rights, one that honestly tackles the tough moral and legal dilemmas that the Gaza situation presents to civilized society: How does society protect the human rights of a civilian population in which rocket-launching terrorists are hiding? How does one reconcile the right of a country to defend itself with the wrong of killing women and children when the former entails the latter? What is a legitimate military target?"

In 2009, these were new dilemmas that had not surfaced prior to the days of rockets and missiles, and we, the Jewish faculty, ought to have pioneered their study. Instead, we allowed Hamas's sympathizers to frame the academic agenda. How can we face our students from the safety of our offices, I thought, when they deal with anti-Israel abuse on a daily basis—in the cafeteria, the library, and the classroom—and as alarming reports of mob violence are arriving from other campuses? Burdened with guilt, I called some colleagues, but quickly realized that a few had already made the shift to a strange-sounding language, not unlike "Honk, Honk." Some had entered the debate phase, arguing over the rhino way of life versus the human way of life, and the majority, while still speaking in a familiar English vocabulary, were frightened beyond anything I had seen at UCLA in the forty years that I had served on its faculty.

Colleagues told me about lecturers whose appointments were terminated, professors whose promotion committees received "incriminating" letters, and about the impossibility of revealing one's pro-Israel convictions without losing grants, editorial board memberships, or invitations to panels and conferences. And all, literally all, swore me to strict secrecy. Together, we entered the era of "the new Marranos."

Exaggeration? Jewish paranoia? Hardly. I invite skeptics to repeat the private experiment that I conducted among Jewish faculty in a reception hosted in 2008, by the Center for Jewish Studies at UCLA. I asked each of them privately: "Tell me, aren't you a Zionist?" I then counted the number of times my conversant would look to the right, then to the left, before whispering: "Yes, but..." I am sure that anyone who repeats this experiment will be as alarmed as I was about the level of academic terror that has descended on U.S. campuses, especially in the humanities and political and social sciences. Our generation of Jewish students is paying dearly for the failure of our academic leadership to acknowledge, assess, and form a unified front to combat this academic terror.

And this brings me to 2021, and to the latest war in Gaza. To the *New York Times* front page depicting the victims of Israel's defense operation, as if they had never heard the word "Hamas" or read Hamas's charter. To CNN anchor Fareed Zakaria asserting that Israel is a military superpower, hence Hamas does not pose an existential threat to it. To *New York Times* analyst Nicholas Kristof asserting in an interview with Bill Maher that Israel, too, positions its military headquarters among civilians. To UCLA's Department of Asian American Studies stating on its official university website its "Solidarity with Palestine" and its authoritative understanding that such "violence and intimidation are but the latest manifestation of seventy-three years of settler colonialism, racial apartheid, and occupation." To the statement of scholars of Jewish Studies and Israel Studies from various universities who, in the *Forward*, condemned "the state violence that the Israeli government and its security forces have been carrying out in Gaza." To members of IfNotNow, saying Kaddish for fallen Hamas fighters (among other victims). And, finally, to the mob roaming the streets of Los Angeles and shouting, "Honk, Honk, From the River to the Sea."

Looking back on the past twelve years, there is no question that Hamas has gained a major uplift in status and respectability. It has become, in fact, the darling of the West. True, seasoned commentators remember to add the obligatory, "We are not condoning Hamas, of course, but..."

"But what?" I ask.

Doesn't Zakaria imply that it is not the end of the world if three hundred thousand Israeli children continue to bleed sleeplessly for another twenty years under Hamas rockets? Didn't Nicholas Kristof imply that if those children suffer post-traumatic scars for the rest of their lives that it is Israel's problem, because Israel, too, positions its headquarters in civilian areas? Western analysts will go to any absurd lengths to fabricate symmetry between Israel and Hamas, because symmetry is our new goddess of right and wrong.

But let's not forget that it all started in academia, with a herd of passionate intellectuals who managed to hijack the name of their academic institution, which hardly cared. Do not blame them. After all, intellectuals are trained to cheer their peers when the marching band starts playing, and academic institutions are too slow to understand what is being done in their names. Sadly, as Ionesco understood so well, we are all herd-honking organisms. Please take another look at the rhinos roaming the streets of Los Angeles and see for yourself how hard it is to hold back and not join them with: "Honk, Honk!"

43. "What Should the Role of American Jews Be with Respect to Israel Today?" *Moment Magazine*, November 2021

The question of whether anti-Israel Jews should be officially excommunicated by the rest of the Jewish community has been raised by many in the wake of October 7. This piece addressed this issue relative to supporters of BDS. The schism between the March for Israel rally in Washington, D.C., on November 14, 2023, and the "Jews for intifada" demonstrations warns us of the "two-fate solution" prophesied in this article.

The future of American Jewry rests critically on its connection to Israel and its embrace of Israel as the spiritual compass of Jewish identity. Religion used to be the cement that glued us together, but we have given up that cement. Most Jews today are secular, living in different countries and speaking different languages. The one glue that binds us together is our collective memory of our common history. Israel is both the culmination of that history and its custodian, holding and nurturing our precious trust deeds: holidays, language, sites, landscapes, lore, heroes, and miraculous revival. Sadly, half of American Jewry seems to have given up on this last remaining glue and is starting to see Israel as a liability as opposed to an inspiration.

I predict American Jewry will soon undergo a profound, painful, and irreparable split. I cannot think of another period in Jewish history where the schism was so deep, and growing deeper so rapidly. I see the split in every aspect of life and on many levels. Zionist families who have lost a member to Jewish Voice for Peace cease to function as a family. The split is even deeper in academia. The animosity between Jewish professors who support BDS and those who fight for the good name of Israel has reached frightful intensity. On the surface, most of our faculty and students are still sitting on the fence, true, but the polarization is growing. The Zionist group is becoming more assertive and is closing ranks rapidly, while the Zionophobic group is becoming louder, more organized, and more aggressive.

Today's attitude toward Israel is really the most critical personal decision for every Jew concerned with the future of our people: Do I want to be part of the Jewish people in the next generation or not? While surveys indicate that most American Jews do not consider Israel their first priority, deep in their heart they know that the time for the inevitable decision is rapidly approaching. This is why the conversation is so intense, so fierce, and so loud, ready for its final eruption. The eruption may actually be healthy, resulting in two barely communicating communities: Israel-inspired forward-looking Jews on the one hand and Israel-bashing yesterday-Jews on the other. A "two-fate solution" for what once was one people.

44. "The State of the Jewish State," *Moment Magazine*, Spring 2023

Some people ask: "What's the big deal about statehood?" For the Zionist pioneers, the big deal was the right to bear arms (self-defense) and the right to control immigration (the return of Jews to their homeland) and trade. Here I introduce a third element: the right to normalcy.

Seventy-five years ago, I was a schoolboy living in Bnei Brak when independence was declared. "Be careful," my mother told me the next day. "Do not play too far from home because there are things in the air which are uncertain." I remember huddling with my friends in a staircase when Egyptian warplanes attacked our town. One of the neighbors said, "Kids, it's going to get much worse, but we will prevail." Warplanes bombarded us, shrapnel flew all around, and the house was vibrating and shaking. Things did get much worse. And we prevailed.

It's a miracle that Israel has lasted for seventy-five years. Every historian will tell you that we never had this luck before. We have to preserve it, realizing that it's given to us as a gift, perhaps even as a trial.

Getting sovereignty is really returning to ourselves, because we are a special kind of tribe. Unlike other ancient civilizations, we were always a collective that was bound by common memories and by land. There is no individual redemption, there is no afterlife. Listen carefully to what God tells Abraham, the first Jew: "Follow Me to the land where I'm going to show you how I'm going to make you into a great nation."

I think that Jews everywhere appreciated this return to ourselves and the transformation from being a scattered tribe without identity into something that is very important and not usually mentioned—normalcy. What is a normal form of identity? Sovereignty. The striving for sovereignty is a yearning for normalcy, proof that we carry with us seeds of resilience and rebirth that other tribes do not. That was the idea of Zionism and the idea of establishing a State of Israel.

Before the Holocaust, in the 1930s, Israel already had a healthcare system, education, transportation, electrical supplies. Everything was built by people who were not exactly experts in those fields, but, for all intents and purposes, it was a state, there to receive the survivors. It's a mistake to present ourselves as victims of a tragedy rather than a tribe capable of rebirth and hope and resilience. It's a miracle that the State of Israel has enabled a scattered tribe of middlemen and peddlers to become a world center of art, entrepreneurship, and science. It's how we express ourselves that combines our roots in history and our legends with modernity. This is the key element to every aspect of Israeli lives—the combination of our past with the future.

45. "Oslo Failed Because It Never Started," *Jewish Journal*, September 20, 2023

The Western mind cannot grasp the essential, deeply ingrained Arab rejection of Jewish sovereignty in any part of Eretz Israel. This is one of a number of pieces I've written in which I bemoan Arab rejectionism, as well as its invisibility to most people. I call it "the first elephant in the room." The Oslo Agreement is an example of how this first elephant led to painful disappointment.

September 2023 marks thirty years since the signing of the Oslo Peace Agreement between Israel and the PLO. Dozens of pundits are authoring scholarly articles on "why the Oslo Peace Process failed to bring peace." To these I would like to add my own opinion: It failed because it never started.

The Palestinians never intended to follow the agreement and certainly not to pursue a process toward peace. Evidence for "intention" is hard to come by, but a 2001 interview with a top Palestinian negotiator made it quite clear. Faisal Husseini, the Palestinian Authority minister for Jerusalem affairs, explicitly stated in an interview with *Al-Arabi* (2001) that "the Oslo Accords were a Trojan Horse. The strategic goal is the liberation of Palestine from the river to the sea." Arafat's famous Johannesburg speech conveyed the same intention.

However, on this anniversary of the Oslo Agreement, I would like to draw attention to another, almost forgotten, but perhaps more significant, interview which describes the actual steps Palestinians took to sabotage the idea of peace. I am referring to an interview with Haim Shur (*Maariv*, June 6, 2001), a prominent leader of Israel's peace camp, excerpts of which are given below:

> **Shur:** The Palestinians deceived me, personally, and the entire Israeli Left as well. They lied to us, they scammed us, maneuvered and manipulated us. Personally, I will never forgive them for this. A genuine man of the Left is a man who should accept the reality for what it is, and not see it the way he wishes to. They are not yet ripe for peace, and my duty as a man of the Left is to realize this truth. The Left is not a synonym for deceit.
>
> **Interviewer:** In what way did the Palestinians deceive you, personally?
>
> **Shur:** I had countless meetings with Palestinians. If someone conducted a study on the top ten Israelis who visited Palestinians most frequently, I am sure I would be among them. [I met with Palestinians] more frequently than Shimon Peres, chief Oslo negotiator Yossi Beilin, and Oslo Agreement architect Ron Pundak did. During all of my meetings with them, the Palestinians said that we will find a mutually accepted formula regarding the right of return, but the truth is that this never happened.
>
> **Interviewer:** What do you mean by that?

Shur: They never tried to reach a mutually accepted formula. Everything they said was just a part of the phased plan. I was one of those who opened the American doors for the PLO. When we organized an Israeli-Palestinian conference in Washington, in 1987, the State Department refused to give them entry visas. We took it upon ourselves [to take care of all the necessary details] so that they could get the visas. And then they entered the U.S. and took it by storm with our assistance. This is what they wanted, that was the target, to capture the goodwill of the American Jewish Left. I, personally, invited them to social gatherings at the homes of Jewish Americans. Their success was owed to our help. Without our assistance they would never succeed.

Interviewer: Was that a mistake?

Shur: Not only that this was a mistake, but merely two or three years following [our meetings with the Palestinians in the U.S.] Nabil Sha'ath appeared in front of an audience in Gaza and told them that [their meetings with us] were just a tactical move. [Sha'ath explained to his audience in Gaza that] the Palestinian plan is to make piecemeal gains for the ultimate goal of conquering the entire State of Israel. It became clear to me that the speeches made by Nabil Sha'ath—the same person who was my best friend in America, and who came to hug me and kiss me following my pro-peace speeches—were worthless. He did not mean anything he said.

Interviewer: Does this lack of trust represent a shift for a man of the Left such as yourself?

Shur: There is one thing that no one will ever be able to take away from me, and that is my [commitment to the] truth.

Interviewer: When you said, "they deceived me," were you referring to all of them?

Shur: I referred to an entire group of people, who do not care about anyone or anything, who deceived me. The fact that Nabil Sha'ath is an opportunist is clear to me. The fact that Ziad Abu Zayyad is an opportunist is also clear to me. [The answer to the question of] whether Hanna Seniora is also one? It is not clear to me. [The answer to the question of] whether these professors I met in the U.S. are the same? That I don't know. I don't know if they disagree with Yasser Arafat. I do know I have never heard them [say it].

Interviewer: The Israeli Right is blaming the Left for misleading the nation, for orchestrating some kind of a messianic peace movement. Do you accept the charges?

Shur: To a certain degree, yes. We wished for peace so much that we ended up turning our wishes into factual reality.

Shur's interview was quite traumatic to us Israelis in 2001, a year after the outbreak of the Second Intifada. But it has since disappeared from public conversation. On this thirtieth anniversary of the Oslo Agreement, I feel compelled to bring it back into the limelight. Shur's confession gave Israelis a rare glimpse of the core issue fueling the conflict with their neighbors—a profound and inherent Palestinian rejection of the very idea of Jewish sovereignty in any part of Palestine.

It was a very short glimpse, because it immediately got overshadowed by debates over pressing, albeit peripheral, matters. The Israeli Right blamed the Left for ignoring Palestinian terrorism, internal corruption, and overt antisemitism, while the Left blamed the Right for Rabin's assassination, settlement expansion, and harsh conditions under occupation. Westerners, with hardly any exception, have taken Palestinian rejectionism to be a negotiation tactic, a form of rhetoric, perhaps a rallying point, but not a foundational principle. Shur's haunting words, "They never tried to reach a mutually accepted formula," remind us today of the depth of Palestinian rejectionism and why Oslo never had a chance.

Epilogue: The Crater of October 7

Science tells us that the extinction of dinosaurs occurred approximately sixty-six million years ago when an asteroid struck the Earth, forming a huge crater in the Yucatán Peninsula. An enormous dust cloud blocked the sun, cooled the planet, and disrupted food chains, ultimately leading to the extinction of about 75 percent of all plant and animal species, including the dinosaurs.

Science tells us much about disasters that occurred millions of years ago, but, sadly, it tells us almost nothing about how our lives will be shaped by the giant crater created by the blow of October 7. Looking into its depths, we find ourselves clueless and bewildered about what future might emerge from the dust cloud that still obscures our sun—and what species, movements, or ideas will perish or evolve from the darkness, winter, and confusion it has left behind.

Some say they were surprised by the brutality and hatred of October 7. Others were shocked by the scale of the operation and how close it came to its goal. As a native Israeli, raised on the stories of the Hebron Massacre (1929) and haunted by the horrific images of the Ramallah lynching (2000), I was not surprised by the brutality and savagery of Israel's enemies. Nor was I surprised by the depth of their hatred and inhumanity—a reality I painfully experienced in the murder of my son, Danny. Likewise, I already saw the early and deep infiltration of Hamas's ideology into Western thought. Indeed, this book documents my premonitions about this process and the extent to which Hamas's ideology mirrors the essential Palestinian mindset: "From the river to the sea."

What, then, shocked me about the crater of October 7?

I was shocked by how swiftly Zionophobia—the absolute denial of Israel's right to exist—became normalized, mainstream, and even respectable in Western discourse, precisely at Israel's moment of greatest vulnerability. I've witnessed many attacks on Israel before, but they always followed her victories and achievements. Those attacks I could understand; people instinctively side with the underdog. But the post-October 7 attacks were different. This time, they were driven by a wholehearted desire for Israel's demise—with all its genocidal implications. The scent of blood, it seems, triggered a hunger for more. Hordes of predators emerged from their ideological tunnels, rushing to indict, sentence, and lynch Israel in the finest tradition of herd madness.

Can the Jewish people survive this madness? Can Western civilization endure the dangers rising from these tunnels?

Ideologies, once metastasized, are deadlier than the sword. We have heard Western intellectuals brand the Bibas family as "settlers," thus, legitimate targets. Others went even further, labeling them "Nazi guards of a concentration camp." A civilization capable of generating such images has lost all moral bearings and may not endure for long.

Yet I refuse to say that we are doomed.

Not because the threats aren't real, but because alongside the spreading moral decay I have also found islands of moral clarity, primarily among my fellow Jews, my students, and my academic colleagues. The crater of October 7 has created a deeper appreciation of Israel's centrality in Jewish life, along with a sharper understanding of the outbreak of Zionophobia in its aftermath. This renewed awareness encompasses not only Israel's historical, cultural, and spiritual significance to Jewish identity but also its role as the embodiment of Jewish "normalcy." In these islands of moral clarity, the existence of Israel is now understood to be essential to ensuring that Jews everywhere are treated as equals, not as a unique, tolerated, respected, or admired minority, but as equals. In short, no Jew can be truly equal in the family of man before Israel stands equal in the family of nations.

I cannot end without evoking the victims. I see them, the children of Western civilization, sons and daughters of Isaac and Prometheus: my son, Danny, Ilan Halimi, the Bibas family, the one thousand two hundred murdered on October 7. I imagine them standing up, waiting for me, for us, to say something meaningful. All I can say is *Yitgadal Ve'Yitkadash Shmai Rabah*—the Jewish prayer of mourning recited in memory of the dead. A prayer that does not mention death or mourning, but glorifies God and expresses hope for a good life and universal peace. It is a humble confession of our inability to comprehend God's cruel ways of playing with human lives and world order.

I sang this prayer at Danny's funeral. I said to Danny: "I'll sing it to you in the special melody that your great-grandfather chanted on Yom Kippur." It's a melody that rattles the gates of Heaven and pleads for mending our broken world order.

Yitgadal Ve'Yitkadash Shmai Rabah

Timeline of Key Moments in the History of the Jewish People

Jewish history is a thread that runs through many of the writings in this book. I regard Jewish history as the face of the Jewish people—here we provide a glimpse as a condensed timeline. It describes the chain of events that left an impression on me and my generation and, more broadly, on the Jewish world. These events made us who we are.

We begin the timeline with biblical stories and move into historical events. The biblical stories constitute the fabric into which much of Jewish wisdom, teachings, and philosophy has been woven. Naturally, these dates—from Abraham up to King David, or about 1000 BCE—are approximate. Further, the role of God in these stories should be understood as a metaphor through which the author(s) expressed the pressing philosophical and social questions of their time.

1800–1700 BCE | Abraham

The Book of Genesis relates how God spoke to Abraham, bidding him to leave his home (in what is now Iraq): "Go for yourself from your land, from your birthplace and the house of your father, to the land that I will show you."[1] This land was Canaan, a region including modern-day Israel. Abraham moves to Canaan, establishes neighborly relations with the locals, and purchases and develops a parcel of land. He devotes himself to God and His guidance. God rewards him by designating him to be the builder of a new nation: "I will make you there into a great nation, and all the peoples on Earth will be blessed through you."[2]

For most Jews, this journey signifies the beginning of monotheism, Jewish nationhood, and collective responsibility—the revolutionary Jewish idea that adherence to moral behavior leads to collective rather than personal reward.

1600–1500 BCE | Jacob and His Sons in Egypt

Genesis continues with the story of Jacob, grandson of Abraham, who left famine in Canaan and, following his favorite son Joseph, traveled

1 Genesis 12:1.

2 Genesis 12:2.

with the rest of his family to Egypt, where there were food reserves. God promises Jacob that he will return to Canaan one day.

While in Egypt, Jacob and his twelve sons—who become the twelve Tribes of Israel—live as subjects of a benign Pharaoh. The Israelites grow and prosper.

1400–1300 BCE | Exodus from Egypt and Mount Sinai

The Book of Exodus relates that after more than two hundred ten years of hard labor and oppression under hostile Pharaohs, God commands an initially reluctant Moses to demand his people's freedom. The Pharaoh refuses to release the Israelites until God brings down ten plagues on him and his people.

Led by Moses, the Israelites flee Egypt and journey through the Sinai Desert on their way back to Canaan. At Mount Sinai, Moses receives the Ten Commandments, a concise encoding of basic Jewish laws, beliefs, and moral principles. The reception of the Ten Commandments is considered a key event in the formation of the Jewish people.

God commands the Israelites that in addition to worshipping Him, they must never forget their enslavement and liberation, essentially arguing that if they forget their history, they abandon their religion. At this point the Jews become storytellers, recounting their liberation every year during the holiday of Passover. Bonded by their history, the Jews further solidify into a people with mutual responsibility and a common destiny.

1300–1200 BCE | Arrival in The Promised Land

The Israelites reach the Jordan River along the eastern border of Canaan, where Moses dies and Joshua takes over. According to the Book of Joshua, God facilitated their successful entry into Canaan by drying the river's waters to allow them to cross. After crossing, the Israelites begin the conquest of Canaan, starting with the town of Jericho. They divide the land into areas governed by the twelve Israelite tribes and begin to coalesce into one nation.

> "I vividly remember crossing the Jordan River with Joshua. I wish [the Palestinians] had similar memories, as vivid as mine, so they wouldn't think I'm faking it."[3]
>
> —JP

3 Judea Pearl, Post on X, March 5, 2024, https://twitter.com/yudapearl/status/1765006280442479026.

1200–1000 BCE | Tribes, Judges, and Consolidation into a Monarchy

The twelve tribes, previously ruled by independent judges, consolidate into a sovereign kingdom when the prophet and judge Samuel anoints their first king, Saul, from the tribe of Benjamin.

1000–970 BCE | Jerusalem Becomes the Capital City

David, the second king of Israel, establishes his kingdom in Hebron. Seven or eight years later, he conquers the city of Jebus from the Canaanite tribe of the Jebusites, makes it his capital city, and expands his rule over the entire land of Israel. David renames Jebus Jerusalem, meaning "They will see peace."

970–930 BCE | Solomon's Reign and the Building of the First Temple

King Solomon, son of David, builds the First Temple in Jerusalem. It becomes the focal point of the Israelite state, religion, and culture.

Solomon further expands the kingdom's territory and develops trade relations with its neighbors, including the Phoenicians and the Ethiopians.

930 BCE | Israelite Monarchy Splits

The Israelite Monarchy splits into two separate kingdoms: Israel and Judea.

Israel, a kingdom composed of ten of the twelve tribes, establishes itself in the northern part of the land, with its capital in Samaria (about fifty miles north of Jerusalem). Judea, a kingdom composed of the two tribes of Benjamin and Judah, establishes itself in the southern part of the land, with its capital in Jerusalem.

734–720 BCE | The Assyrians Conquer Israel

The Assyrians undertake a series of assaults on both Israel and Judea, ultimately conquering the kingdom of Israel. They exile its people, forcibly scattering them throughout the Assyrian Empire, ranging from modern-day Syria to Iraq.

597–586 BCE | Babylonian Diaspora

Babylonian King Nebuchadnezzer conquers the kingdom of Judea, destroys the First Temple, and sends its people into exile and servitude in Babylonia. Some people flee to Egypt, while a small number remain in their conquered Judean kingdom.

This was the start of the first Jewish diaspora and the concomitant yearning to return to their homeland as expressed in the Book of Lamentations, as well as in other books of the period, e.g., "If I forget thee, O Jerusalem, let my right hand forget its skill!"[4]

539–516 BCE | Second Temple

Judea becomes a province of the Persian Empire, ruled by Cyrus the Great, which superseded the Babylonian Empire. Cyrus decrees that all exiled nations may return to their homelands. Taking advantage of this decree, Ezra, a scribe and priest, leads his fellow Jews back to Judea. Many Jews choose to stay where they have settled instead of returning with Ezra. Those that do return rebuild the Temple in Jerusalem, ushering in the period of the Second Temple.

336–323 BCE | Reign of Alexander the Great

Alexander the Great, king of Macedon, overthrows the Persian Empire. Judea becomes part of his vast Macedonian Empire, which extends from Sicily in the west to India in the east. He allows the Jews to manage their internal affairs and practice Judaism, while also introducing and encouraging them to adopt Hellenistic culture.

Upon Alexander's death in 323 BCE, his generals go to war to supersede him. Three main victors emerge: Ptolemy establishes the Ptolemaic Empire, based in Egypt; Seleucus establishes the Seleucid Empire, based in Syria; and Antigonus establishes the Antigonid Empire, based in Greece. Eretz Israel falls under control of Ptolemy.

198 BCE | The Seleucids Conquer Judea

Antiochus III, king of the Seleucid Empire, captures Judea from the Ptolemaic Empire.

175–164 BCE | Reign of Antiochus IV Epiphanes

Antiochus IV Epiphanes, nicknamed the "Mad One" for his eccentricities, assumes the kingship of the Seleucid Empire and expresses hostility toward the Jews in Eretz Israel.

---

4 Psalm 137.

167 BCE | Judah the Maccabee

Antiochus IV defiles the Jewish Temple by erecting an altar to Zeus inside and forcing the Jews to worship this ancient Greek god.

A small part of the Jewish population refuses to succumb to Antiochus's religious edicts. They coalesce behind a warrior called Judah the Maccabee, who leads them in a successful rebellion against the overwhelming force of Antiochus's Syrian army.

161 BCE | Chanukah

Judah and his small army, the Maccabees, retake the Second Temple and restore its Jewish character. To this day, Jews commemorate this successful rebellion during the holiday of Chanukah.

> "Chanukah is our *trust deed* to the birthplace of our history, more solid even than the ancient synagogues they are excavating in Israel or the Arch of Titus in Rome,[5] with the Temple ornaments carved in marble. Stones can be faked…not so a continuous collective memory, passed on from father and mother to son and daughter, over one hundred ten generations. An unassailable proof that no one can fake."[6] —JP

142 BCE | Judea's Sovereignty Reestablished

The Maccabees reestablish Judea as a sovereign Jewish kingdom, with its territory extending up to southern Syria. The kingdom is ruled by the Hasmonean Dynasty, composed of descendants of Matityahu, father of Judah the Maccabee. They maintain independence for roughly eighty years fraught with internal feuding and intrigue, which often results in foreign intervention from their neighbors, including the Egyptians, the Syrians, and the Edomites.

63 BCE | Roman Domination

Led by Roman general Pompey the Great, the Romans enter Jerusalem and turn Judea into a much-diminished province of the Roman Empire.

---

5 A triumphal arch built in c. 82 CE commemorating Roman Emperor Titus's victory over the Jews. One of the arch's carved marble panels shows Titus's soldiers processing through Rome holding the sacred objects of the Second Temple, including its menorah, high above their heads.

6 Judea Pearl, "Chanukah—Our Trust Deed to History," *Jewish Journal*, December 22, 2019, see p. 126.

40 BCE | Herod the Great Appointed King of Judea

The Romans appoint Herod the Great as king of Judea (client king of Rome). Herod, of Edomite descent, renovates and expands the Second Temple built by Ezra in an attempt to restore it to the grandeur associated with the First Temple and solidify his own standing among his subjects. The renovated Temple becomes the monumental center of Jewish life.

29–33 | Christianity, a New Jewish Sect

Jesus (born Jehoshua), a Jewish carpenter from the town of Nazareth in the Galilee, becomes an itinerant preacher, folk healer, and leader of a new Jewish sect eventually called the Christians. Considering him a threat to their power, the Romans crucify him on charges of treason. After his death, Jesus's disciples deem him a messiah, testify to his resurrection, and propagate his teachings throughout the Roman Empire.

The Christians ultimately diverge from their Judaic roots. They deemphasize their attachment to Eretz Israel and the Temple services, elevate belief in the divinity of Jesus and original sin over the Mosaic code of conduct, and emphasize universal principles of compassion and forgiveness over peoplehood. Further, they make proselytizing an important part of their religious practice. These revisions help Christianity grow into a major world religion.

66 | Jewish Rebellion Against the Romans

Tired of harsh treatment by Gessius Florus, the Roman governor of Judea, a significant part of the Jewish population launches an ambitious but ultimately unsuccessful rebellion against the Romans.

67–70 | Second Diaspora

Determined to crush the rebellion, Roman Emperor Nero dispatches Vespasian to lay siege to Jerusalem. Vespasian succeeds Nero as emperor and deputizes his son, Titus, to defeat the Jews once and for all. Titus razes Jerusalem and the Second Temple and kills or exiles nearly every Jew living in and around the city. As with the Babylonian exile, a mostly agricultural community of Jews remains in their vanquished homeland. This is the start of the second Jewish diaspora.

Forced from their homeland by the Romans, the Jews become a dispersed nation without a territory. Bereft of their Temple, they make their religion transportable, transmitted through prayers, Torah study, holidays, and the synagogue, which become a kind of stand-in Temple and center of Jewish life.

132 | Bar Kochva Revolt

Led by Shimon Bar Kochva, the Jews who remained in Judea launch another ambitious but ultimately ill-fated rebellion against the Romans. They are endorsed by Rabbi Akiva, the spiritual leader at the time.

Bar Kochva and his army achieved an early but short-lived independence from the Romans, which he marked by minting coins. This success is commemorated in the Jewish psyche through the holiday of Lag B'Omer, a twenty-four-hour period of joyful celebration featuring bonfires, play with bows and arrows, dancing, and weddings.

135 | Roman Victory and Revenge

Under Emperor Hadrian, the Romans crush the Bar Kochva Revolt, which devastates the countryside and leads to the massive expulsion of the Jews. Hadrian changes the region's name from Judea to Palestina (later called Palestine by the Ottomans) in reference to the Philistines, longtime enemies of the Jews—e.g., the biblical giant Goliath was a Philistine—who had disappeared centuries ago. The Jews, however, continue to call their land Eretz Israel (The Land of Israel) or Eretz HaKodesh (The Holy Land). The Romans build a new city on the ruins of Jerusalem and call it Aelia Capitolina.

With these name changes, the Romans intended to erase the connection of the Jewish people to the land. Ironically, the arch that Titus built to signify this erasure ended up becoming one of the most vivid historical proofs of that connection.

200–220 | The Mishnah

Jewish life continues, principally in the Galilee, under relatively benign Roman rule. Taking advantage of the favorable political climate, Rabbi Judah HaNasi ("The Elevated") compiles Jewish oral law and commentary on the biblical scripture into a text known as the Mishnah.

325 | Council of Nicaea

Roman Emperor Constantine the Great convenes the first council of the Christian church in the ancient city of Nicaea, during which he declares Christianity the official religion of the Roman Empire and designates Alexandria and Jerusalem as seats of Christian authority. He establishes a significant Christian presence in Jerusalem in part by building basilicas and churches, including the Church of the Holy Sepulchre (still active today).

Constantine regards the Jews as false descendants of the ancient Israelites for their refusal to accept Jesus as the Messiah. He issues laws that make it punishable by death for the Jews to prevent their own from converting to Christianity or for any citizen of the Roman Empire to convert to Judaism.

410 | Sack of Rome

The Visigoths (a Germanic people) sack Rome, and the empire splits into western and eastern parts. Byzantium, the eastern part of the empire, with its capital in Constantinople, retains control of Palestina.

Several richly decorated synagogues from this period have been excavated by Israeli archeologists, indicating a thriving Jewish community under Byzantine rule.

613–622 | Advent of Islam

Mohammed starts a new religion on the Arabian Peninsula that becomes known as Islam, based partly on the Hebrew Bible. Mohammed declares Islam to be a supersession of Judaism and Christianity, a purer replacement for both religions, and begins the Muslim conquest of the Middle East and North Africa. Under Islam, Jews are deemed *dhimmi*, a protected minority of lower status.

638–1291 | The Muslims, Crusaders, and Mamluks Rule The Holy Land

638 | Byzantium loses Palestina to the Muslims. Much of the Jewish population is coerced into converting to Islam in order to retain their land.

1099 | The Muslims lose Jerusalem to the Crusaders, a Christian movement that started in Europe with the aim of reclaiming The Holy Land for Christendom.

1187 | Under the powerful Egyptian sultan Saladin, the Muslims retake Jerusalem from the Crusaders, reestablishing control over Palestina.

1193 | The Crusaders regain a foothold in Jerusalem, at Christian holy sites, and in a network of fortified castles.

1291 | The Crusaders are finally pushed out of Palestina by the Mamluks, a military caste descended from Turkish slaves that ruled Egypt and Syria for around two hundred sixty years.

Whether they reside in or outside of Palestina, the Jews are at the mercy of the rulers of the day. Sometimes, as in Moorish Spain, they are granted a degree of autonomy that allows them to thrive: they practice Judaism openly, attain important positions in society, and produce some of the greatest leaders and thinkers in Jewish history, including Moses Maimonides (the Rambam). At other times the Jews endure forced conversions to Christianity, second-class citizenship under Muslim rule, and eruptions of persecution, expulsion, and massacre across the Diaspora. All throughout this period, they never stop yearning for Eretz Israel. For example, the Rambam insisted that he be buried in Tiberia, and the Spanish rabbi and poet Yehuda HaLevi wrote in a famous twelfth-century poem: "My heart is in the East, and I in the uttermost West."[7]

1492 | Spanish Expulsion and Inquisition

The new rulers of Spain, King Ferdinand and Queen Isabella, issue an edict to their Jewish subjects: accept conversion into Catholicism or leave. As a result, more than one hundred sixty thousand Jews are expelled from the country. The Jews who convert ("Conversos") are brutally harassed and interrogated under suspicion of practicing Judaism in secret, which is why this period became known as the "Inquisition." (In 1536, Portugal follows Spain in launching its own Inquisition).

The exiled Spanish and Portuguese Jews resettle principally in the Netherlands, Italy, the Balkans, and North Africa, becoming known as Sephardic Jews for their Spanish and Portuguese roots.

---

7 Yehuda HaLevi, "My Heart Is in the East," Jewish Virtual Library, https://www.jewishvirtuallibrary.org/quot-my-heart-is-in-the-east-quot-yehuda-halevi.

1500–1600 | Tzfat Revived

Some of the most distinguished rabbis in Jewish history resettle the northern town of Tzfat, turning it into a center of Jewish mysticism (Kabbalah) and culture. The first moveable-type printing press in Asia is established in Tzfat and allows for the dissemination of key texts throughout the Jewish world. These include Rabbi Joseph Caro's *Shulchan Aruch* (*The Table Prepared for a Meal*), a book codifying Jewish customs and practices, and liturgical songs like "L'Cha Dodi" ("Come, My Beloved") by Rabbi Shlomo Alkabetz, with which Jews welcome Shabbat to this day. Such texts further unify the Jews as a people.

1517 | The Ottoman Conquest

The Ottomans (modern-day Turks) conquer The Holy Land, call it Palestine, and absorb it into their empire, which includes the Balkans and the entire Middle East. Sultan Bayezid II welcomes exiled Sephardic Jews to resettle in the Ottoman Empire.

1648–1649 | The Chmielnicki Pogroms in Ukraine

Led by Bogdan Chmielnicki, nicknamed "Chmiel the Wicked" by the Jews, masses of Cossacks and Ukrainian peasants rise up against the repressive rule of the Polish nobility in Ukraine. Fired by antisemitism and resentment toward the Jews for providing services to the Polish nobility, Chmielnicki and his followers wipe out hundreds of Jewish communities as they wage their rebellion against the Poles. These pogroms have come to be known as "the decrees of 1648–1649."

1665–1676 | The Messianic Cult of Shabbetai Zvi

Reeling from the Chmielnicki pogroms, the Jewish community latches onto Shabbetai Zvi, who declares himself the Messiah in 1665. He gains a significant following throughout the Jewish world. In 1666, he is brought before the Ottoman Sultan Mehmed IV and threatened with death or conversion to Islam. He chooses conversion and slanders the Jewish community, for which he is excommunicated by the rabbinical authorities. A small percentage of his followers continue Zvi's messianic cult for at least a century after his death. His messianic stint makes the Jewish community more sensitive to deviation from rabbinical orthodoxy than it had ever been before.

1789–1791 | Emancipation in France

The French Revolution explodes in full force with the storming of the Bastille in Paris in 1789. Two years later, on September 27, 1791, the Jews are granted emancipation. They become equal citizens of the French Republic, though they are not recognized as a nation. As Comte de Clermont-Tonnerre argued during the National Assembly debate about Jewish emancipation: "The Jews should be denied everything as a nation, but granted everything as individuals....The existence of a nation within a nation is unacceptable to our country."[8]

1853 | Publication of *Ahavat Tzion* (*The Love of Zion*)

Considered to be the first modern Hebrew novel, Abraham Mapu's *Ahavat Tzion* imagines life in Jerusalem during the time of Judean king Chizqiyyahu. The book becomes a surprise hit throughout the Jewish world, because it describes Jewish life as that of any normal nation, with people from all walks of life, among them army officers, thieves, noblemen, beggars, and prostitutes. The novel inspires yearning for the life of a normal people in its own land. Many early Zionists credit *Ahavat Tzion* with awakening their zeal for normalcy.

1879 | Publication of "She'ela Nichbada" ("A Serious Question")

Writer, lexicographer, and Zionist leader Eliezer ben Yehuda publishes the essay "She'ela Nichbada" ("A Serious Question"), in which he argues that Diaspora Jews should emulate the oppressed European populations fighting for political freedom and national revival by reestablishing themselves in Eretz Israel and regenerating their culture and language.

1881 | Hebrew Revived

Eliezer ben Yehuda moves to Jerusalem, where he launches a one-man effort to restore Hebrew as a spoken language.

1881–1882 | Czar Alexander II Assassinated and the "May Laws" Enacted

On March 13, 1881, Czar Alexander II of Russia is killed in St. Petersburg when his carriage hits a bomb planted by a group of

8 Comte de Clermont-Tonnerre, in Jewish Virtual Library, "Emancipation: France," https://www.jewishvirtuallibrary.org/emancipation#France.

radicals. His assassination, falsely blamed on the Jews, ignites mass pogroms throughout the Russian Empire, some carried out spontaneously by the public and others organized with the help of the new czarist government of Alexander III (son of Alexander II).

On May 15, 1882, Czar Alexander III enacts the "May Laws," which codify professional and educational restrictions against the Jews. He also forces them out of the cities and back into the Pale of Settlement, a rural region in the western part of his empire.

Spurred by these events, some two million Jews flee the Russian Empire in one of the largest migrations in history. Most find refuge in America, with a much smaller number moving to Eretz Israel. In America, their great numbers overwhelm the existing Jewish population of two hundred fifty thousand, transforming the face of American Jewry.

1882 | First Aliyah

Organized by Hovevei Zion (Lovers of Zion), an Odessa-based movement established in 1881, thirty five thousand Jewish immigrants relocate to Eretz Israel. Most come from Russia, which they leave to escape crushing poverty, antisemitism, persecution, and pogroms. Among the leaders of Hovevei Zion is Leon Pinsker, who advocates in his 1882 pamphlet, "Auto-Emancipation," that Jews should not wait for the Messiah to free them but, rather, should take emancipation into their own hands.

From this point forward, significant waves of Jewish immigration from Europe and Russia, as well as a trickle from Arab and Muslim countries in the Middle East and North Africa, feed a developing Jewish presence in Palestine.

> "We must humbly admit that homecoming after two thousand years is rather unprecedented in the history of nations. We must strongly insist, though, that yearning for two thousand years is equally unprecedented, and perhaps doubly relevant to what counts as 'indigenous.'"[9] —JP

1897 | Zionism Catalyzed

Zionism is catalyzed when Austro-Hungarian lawyer, journalist, and author Theodor Herzl convenes the First International Zionist

9 Judea Pearl, Post on X, May 2, 2023, https://twitter.com/yudapearl/status/1653457589429211136?cxt=HHwWgMDQodm6ofltAAAA.

Congress in Basel, Switzerland on August 29. At the congress, the delegates define its aim: "Zionism seeks to establish for the Jewish people a publicly recognized, legally secured homeland in Palestine."[10] This sets in motion a political process that will ultimately give rise to the modern State of Israel.

Herzl was motivated by the danger of rising antisemitism in Europe and Russia, particularly after covering the Dreyfus Affair for the *Neue Freie Presse*, in which Alfred Dreyfus, an assimilated Jewish captain in the French army, was falsely convicted of espionage and humiliated in front of a crowd shouting, "Death to Judas, death to the Jews!" A year after this event, in February 1896, Herzl published *Der Judenstaat (The State of the Jews)*, in which he argued that the only way to guarantee a future for the Jewish people is for them to reestablish sovereignty. As he wrote: "The whole plan is in its essence perfectly simple....Let the sovereignty be granted us over a portion of the globe large enough to satisfy the reasonable requirements of a nation; the rest we shall manage for ourselves."[11] In the first edition of *Der Judenstaat*, Herzl debated between Argentina and Palestine as the location for the Jewish nation. In the Hebrew translation, published in August 1896, he insisted that the state must be in Palestine, after listening to the sentiments of Eastern European Jews.

> "If I had to choose the single most significant impact that the Basel Congress has had on our lives...I would name one forgotten statement that Herzl made in his first speech....On the morning of Aug. 29, 1897, after fifteen minutes of wild cheering, Herzl took the stage and said, 'Zionism is a homecoming to the Jewish fold even before it becomes a homecoming to the Jewish land....'It was the future of the Jewish people, not just of Israel, that was forged there in Basel...."[12] —JP

1903 | Kishinev Pogrom

Incited by a blood libel, and tacitly encouraged by the central government, a mob rampages through the town of Kishinev, Russia

---

10 Judea Pearl, "The Basel Congress's Unexpected Result, 120 Years Later," *Jewish Journal*, August 30, 2017, see p. 97.

11 Theodor Herzl, *The Jewish State*, trans. Sylvie D'Avigdor (New York: Skyhorse Publishing, 2019), 8.

12 Pearl, "Basel Congress's Unexpected Result," see p. 99.

(modern-day Moldova) for nearly three days, murdering forty-nine Jews and injuring hundreds, raping at least six hundred Jewish women, and destroying and looting Jewish property. Hayim Nahman Bialik (who would later become Israel's national poet) travels to Kishinev from his home in Odessa to document the atrocities. The experience leads him to write one of his most famous poems, "In the City of Slaughter," in which he condemns the Jews as cowards for not defending themselves.

News of the pogrom makes a notably strong impact around the world, including in America, strengthening recognition that Zionism may be the only solution to Jewish persecution. In Ottoman Palestine, the Yishuv forms a self-defense group called Bar-Giora, forerunner of the Israel Defense Forces (IDF).

In the months following the pogrom, one of its chief instigators, the publisher Pavel Krushevan, publishes the notorious antisemitic forgery, "The Protocols of the Elders of Zion," which portrays Jews as a cabal aiming to control the world. This forgery and its lies have been adopted by many antisemitic leaders and movements ever since, from Henry Ford to the Nazis to Islamic governments to Hamas.

1909 | Tel Aviv Founded

Sixty-six families from Jaffa found Tel Aviv—the first modern Jewish city—on sand dunes north of the city. Tel Aviv will blossom into a major urban center of entrepreneurship, culture, and modernity.

The city's name comes from writer and Zionist leader Nahum Sokolow's Hebrew translation of a novel by Theodor Herzl titled *Altneuland* (1902), in which Herzl depicts his vision of the future Jewish state. Sokolow translated the novel's title as "Tel Aviv," meaning "Spring Hill," in reference to a verse in the book of Ezekiel.

1917 | Balfour Declaration

In anticipation of the British capturing Palestine from the Ottomans, and due mainly to the efforts of Chaim Weizmann, the British government publicly endorses Zionism. In a short letter to Lord Walter Rothschild, a scion of one of the world's most prominent banking families and an active Zionist, British Foreign Secretary Lord Arthur James Balfour writes,

> Foreign Office
> November 2nd, 1917
>
> Dear Lord Rothschild,
>
> I have much pleasure in conveying to you, on behalf of His Majesty's Government, the following declaration of sympathy with Jewish Zionist aspirations which has been submitted to, and approved by, the Cabinet.
>
> His Majesty's Government view with favour the establishment in Palestine of a national home for the Jewish people, and will use their best endeavors to facilitate the achievement of this object, it being clearly understood that nothing shall be done which may prejudice the civil and religious rights of existing non-Jewish communities in Palestine or the rights and political status enjoyed by Jews in any other country.
>
> I should be grateful if you would bring this declaration to the knowledge of the Zionist Federation.
>
> Yours,
> Arthur James Balfour[13]

This letter becomes known as the Balfour Declaration. It encourages the third aliyah, when Diaspora Jews take its declaration seriously as a license to move to Eretz Israel.

> "By focusing on the Jewish narrative, the [Balfour Declaration] broadened the concept of indigeneity to include peoples who have maintained vivid collective memories of past civilizations and who shaped their identity through dreams of returning to the cradles of those civilizations.... Balfour understood that Eretz Israel is an inextricable part of Jewish identity. Accordingly, he also understood that indigeneity is based on intellectual attachment and historical continuity no less than on physical presence or genetic lineage."[14] —JP

---

13 Letter from Lord Arthur James Balfour to Lord Walter Rothschild, November 2, 1917, in Jewish Virtual Library, "Balfour Declaration: Text of the Declaration (November 2, 1917)," https://www.jewishvirtuallibrary.org/text-of-the-balfour-declaration.

14 Judea Pearl, "The Balfour Declaration at 100 and How It Redefined Indigenous People," *Jewish Journal*, November 3, 2017, see p. 101–102.

1920–1921 | Arab Riots

Led by Haj Amin al-Husseini (later appointed Mufti, the top religious leader, of Jerusalem) and fearing Jewish return to Palestine, the Arabs launch a series of violent attacks against the Jews in Jaffa and Jerusalem. This begins a relentless, obsessive rejection of Jewish sovereignty that continues to this day. As a result of the riots, the idea of Jewish self-defense gains new urgency, and the Jews form a paramilitary organization called the Haganah (Defense).

Under the pretense that the Jews planned to destroy the Al Aqsa Mosque (Dome of the Rock), the Mufti exploited his connections with the Muslim communities of India, Egypt, and Iraq to enlist their support in his rejection of Zionism, thereby turning this rejection into a religious conflict.

1922 | British Mandate of Palestine

The League of Nations (predecessor to the United Nations) meets in London and votes to grant Great Britain an official mandate to administer Palestine. The land becomes known as the British Mandate of Palestine or the British Mandate of Palestina EY, with "EY" standing for Eretz Yisrael.

Article 2 of The League of Nations mandate reads: "The Mandatory shall be responsible for…secur[ing] the establishment of the Jewish national home…and the development of self-governing institutions, and also for safeguarding the civil and religious rights of all the inhabitants of Palestine, irrespective of race and religion."[15]

To pacify the Arabs, the British give them Transjordan (modern-day Jordan), which the British carve out of what was originally supposed to be part of the Jewish national home in Palestine. They grant the kingship of Transjordan to the Hussein family of Saudi Arabia, from which the current royal family is descended.

15 Text of the Mandate, Article 2, in Jewish Virtual Library, "British Palestine Mandate: Text of the Mandate (July 24, 1922)," https://www.jewishvirtuallibrary.org/text-of-the-british-mandate-for-palestine.

1929 | Hebron Massacre

Incited by the Mufti, an Arab mob massacres eighty-one Jews in Hebron and riots in Jerusalem near the Wailing Wall.

David Ben-Gurion and the Zionist leadership remain hopeful for reconciliation after the massacre, but for a portion of the Yishuv, it dispels the dream that peaceful coexistence could be achieved with the local population.

1933 | Assassination of Chayim Arlosoroff

Chayim Arlosoroff is assassinated on the beach in Tel Aviv. The identity of the assassin(s) remains a mystery. Accusations about who did it polarize the Yishuv. One theory connects his assassination to his controversial negotiations with Germany.

As head of the Political Department of the Jewish Agency for Palestine, Arlosoroff had entered into negotiations with Hitler deputy Hermann Goering shortly before his assassination in order to secure a deal for Jewish immigration from Germany. Called the Ha'Avara (Transfer) Agreement, it permitted approximately sixty thousand German Jews to immigrate to Mandate Palestine with their capital between 1933 and 1939. Their capital and intellectual and industrial expertise led to the development of commerce and industry, creating many jobs, which allowed some two hundred thousand impoverished Jews from Eastern Europe to immigrate. Further, the German-Jewish immigrants developed the civil service and infrastructure for the nascent Jewish state, without which the size and status of the Jewish community in Palestine would not have justified a claim for a state, and the Jewish community would not have been able to repel the 1948 Arab assault.

1936–1939 | Arab Riots and the Peel Commission

The Jewish population in the British Mandate of Palestine reaches four hundred fifty thousand. In response, the Arabs launch large-scale riots against the Jews and the British Mandate authorities, which they continue for three years. The British army eventually quashes the riots, severely weakening Arab fighting capabilities.

The British dispatch Lord William Peel to lead a commission to discover the cause of the violence and propose solutions to stop it. In

1937, after completing interviews with dozens of prominent Arab and Jewish leaders, Peel and his commissioners recommend that the land be partitioned into two separate territories, one for the Jews, one for the Arabs. The portion allotted to the Jews is about 30 percent of present-day Israel.

This is the first time the idea of partition is proposed. Jewish leadership reluctantly agrees to the plan, while the Arabs reject it out-of-hand.

1939–1945 | The White Paper, World War II, and the Holocaust

With Hitler's rise to power in 1933, increasing numbers of Jews seek safe haven. On May 23, 1939, the British government, anxious not to provoke the Muslim populations of Egypt, Iraq, and India, capitulates to Arab pressure and issues a White Paper. Among other things, the White Paper rejects Lord Peel's partition plan and severely curbs Jewish immigration to Mandate Palestine. European Jews are forced into a bind: they cannot remain where they are but they are barred from entering almost every country or territory that could offer them refuge, especially Mandate Palestine. There the Yishuv is prepared to receive them, but a British naval blockade prevents their entry. As a result, one-third of world Jewry is stranded in Europe, most of whom (six million) are murdered in extermination camps.

> "Tomorrow [January 27, 2023]…is International Holocaust Remembrance Day, marking the seventy-eighth anniversary of the liberation of Auschwitz-Birkenau. I'll share two personal notes. 1. I find solace thinking that my grandparents weren't entirely hopeless when they were pushed into their death train, in Kielce, [Poland], August 1942. I know that they were thinking about me, six years old, growing up free in Israel, singing Hebrew songs at school, in contrast to the humiliating experience they had had at their school. I cherish the thought that I was there for them, to comfort their last hours. 2. I find the words 'never again' somewhat hollow when spoken at Holocaust museums and education centers that memorialize the destruction of European Jewry, yet fail to document its resurrection—Israel."[16] —JP

16 Judea Pearl, Post on X, January 26, 2023, https://twitter.com/yudapearl/status/1618759846849032192.

1945 | World War II Ends

On May 8, 1945, Germany surrenders to the Allies (France, Great Britain, America, and the Soviet Union), ending World War II in Europe and leaving the surviving Jews homeless, scattered throughout Europe, or stranded in Displaced Persons (DP) camps.

1946 | Kielce Pogrom

On July 4, incited by a blood libel against the remnants of the Jewish community in Kielce, Poland, a mob of soldiers, police officers, and civilians murder at least forty-two Jews and injure more than forty. It is the worst outburst of antisemitic violence in postwar Poland and is intended to discourage Jewish Holocaust survivors from returning to their homes. It convinces many Polish Jews that they have no future in Poland and sparks the mass migration of hundreds of thousands of Jews from Eastern to Western Europe.

The pogrom also convinces U.S. President Harry Truman that Jews have no future in Europe. Truman instructs his generals to allow the Jews free passage across American zones from Eastern Europe to the ports of France and Italy. From there, many Jews manage to board one of the one hundred twenty illegal ships that sailed to Palestine to try to break the British naval blockade. About one hundred thousand Jews enter Palestine by this and other routes. The Yishuv welcomes them. Their harsh experience makes international news and is instrumental in the U.N. sending special commissions to the area and eventually proposing a Jewish state.

1947 | U.N. Partition Plan

On November 29, the General Assembly of the United Nations votes to adopt U.N. Resolution 181, also known as the Partition Plan, calling for the end of British rule in Palestine and the creation of two states in the land, one for the Jews, one for the Arabs.

The vote takes place after a major diplomatic effort by the Zionist movement, which welcomes the plan wholeheartedly. The Arabs apply their own pressure to oppose the plan. A month before the vote, Azzam Pasha, the secretary general of the Arab League, vowed in an interview with an Egyptian newspaper that the Arabs would undertake "a war of extermination and momentous massacre which will be spoken of like the Mongolian massacre and the Crusades."[17]

On the announcement of the vote, the Jews react with jubilation, while the Arabs resort to hostilities against the Yishuv in line with Azzam Pasha's threat, leading to heavy casualties on both sides. Alarmed by these hostilities, and fearful of an all-out Arab invasion, the U.S. State Department advises the Zionist leadership to postpone declaring a state until things quiet down. After a fierce debate, the Zionist leadership rejects the advice by one vote.

> "[O]ne of the most significant events in Jewish history, perhaps the most significant since the Exodus from Egypt—Nov. 29, 1947—the day the U.N. General Assembly voted thirty-three to thirteen to partition Palestine into a Jewish state and an Arab state."[18] —JP

1948 | Declaration of Independence and War of Independence

Upon the ending of the British Mandate, Israel is officially reconstituted into today's modern state. On Friday, May 14, in the events hall of the Tel Aviv Museum, David Ben-Gurion (soon to be elected Israel's first prime minister) reads aloud The Declaration of the Establishment of the State of Israel, opening with: "The Land of Israel was the birthplace of the Jewish people. Here their spiritual, religious, and political identity was shaped. Here they first attained to statehood, created cultural values of national and universal significance, and gave to the world the eternal Book of Books."[19]

On Saturday, May 15, the last British soldiers leave the country and the Israeli War of Independence begins when five Arab armies—from Egypt, Syria, Jordan, Lebanon, and Iraq—plus a small contingent from Saudi Arabia launch an attack on Israel with the proclaimed aim to annihilate the State. As a result of this war, approximately seven hundred thousand Arabs are displaced. The majority either leave Israel to wait out the war in safer areas or are encouraged to leave by the Arab

---

17 Abdul Rahman Azzam, in David Barnett and Efraim Karsh, "Azzam's Genocidal Threat," *Middle East Quarterly* 18, no. 4 (Fall 2011): 85.

18 Judea Pearl, "The Forgotten Miracle: Nov. 29, 1947," *Jewish Journal*, December 18, 2008, see p. 59–60.

19 The Declaration of the Establishment of the State of Israel, May 14, 1948, in *The Times of Israel*, "Israel's Declaration of Independence—May 14, 1948," https://www.timesofisrael.com/israels-declaration-of-independence-may-14-1948/.

forces to clear the path for the invasion. Some are expelled from strategic locations by local Israeli troops. This displacement, and the failure of the Arab attacks, has become known as the Nakba (Disaster) in the minds of the Palestinians, whose "right of return" remains a contested issue to this day.

1949 | War of Independence Ends

Israel prevails, albeit at a steep loss of six thousand young lives. Israel, Jordan, Egypt, and Syria establish a ceasefire line, which becomes known as the "Green Line" reportedly because the negotiators of the armistice agreement used a green pen to mark it out. The Arab refugee issue is left unresolved, in part because of the refusal of the Arab League to negotiate directly with Israel, which would be tantamount to recognition.[20]

The ceasefire agreement leaves the West Bank under Jordanian control and the Gaza Strip under Egyptian control. Supported by these governments and the Syrian army in the Golan Heights, the Arabs continue attacking Israeli communities inside the Green Line.

> "Had the partition plan been accepted, the humiliating defeat of the five Arab armies that attacked Israel in May 1948 would have been avoided, fears of Arabs' genocidal designs would not have settled into the Israeli mindset, the Palestinian refugee problem would not have emerged, and efforts toward reconciliation and collaboration would have moved the region to a new era of dignity and prosperity."[21] —JP

1949–1952 | Flight of the Mizrahi Jews

With the establishment of the State of Israel, Mizrahi Jews—those from Arab and Muslim countries—become targets of increased Arab and Muslim hostility. Expelled outright or compelled to leave by increasing violence and intimidation, more than eight hundred thousand Mizrahi Jews pour into the fledgling Jewish state from countries across North Africa and the Middle East, e.g., Morocco, Egypt, Iraq, and Yemen. Most of them are forced to leave all of their possessions and capital behind.

---

20 See Adi Schwartz and Einat Wilf, *The War of Return: How Western Indulgence of the Palestinian Dream Has Obstructed the Path to Peace*, trans. Eylon Levi (New York: All Points Books, 2020).

21 Judea Pearl, "Israel, Starting from Scratch," *Los Angeles Times*, May 12, 2008, see p. 44.

1964 | PLO Established

Aided by the Russian KGB, and modeled on the Algerian National Liberation Front, the Palestine Liberation Organization (PLO) is established in Cairo on May 28. Its aim is to continue the war to annihilate Israel. The KGB had previously singled out Zionism for defamation as a cover for its antisemitism. They helped the PLO formulate its charter and forge a Palestinian national identity based in antisemitism and Zionophobia.

In its charter, the "Palestinian National Covenant," the PLO's first chairman, Ahmed Shukeiry, defines its goals to be the eradication of Israel and, thereby, the "liberation" of Palestine.

> "Palestinian national identity, because it is only [one hundred three] years old [1920], has shallow historical roots. It's sad, because roots make nations secure and pragmatic. Instead, it revolves around negating their neighbor—a futile battle, given the neighbor's stubborn insistence on life."[22] —JP

1967 | Six-Day War and "The Three Nos" of Khartoum

In response to Egyptian President Gamal Abdel Nasser closing the Strait of Tiran to Israeli shipping, vowing to annihilate Israel, expelling U.N. peacekeeping forces from the Sinai, and massing his army along Israel's border, the Israeli Air Force preemptively attacks the Egyptian airfields, wiping out much of its air power. As Syria and Jordan join the fight, six days of fighting ensue (June 5 to 10) during which Israel defeats the Egyptian, Jordanian, and Syrian armies and captures the Golan Heights (from Syria), the West Bank and East Jerusalem (from Jordan), and the Gaza Strip and Sinai Peninsula (from Egypt). With the reunification of Jerusalem, Jews are once again able to access their holiest site, the Wailing Wall (the remnant of the mount of the Second Temple).

This decisive victory also results in Israel's military control over a large Arab population. Israel makes overtures to return the captured territory in exchange for a formal peace under a rubric that becomes known as "land-for-peace." From August 29 to September 1, the Arab League convenes for a summit in Khartoum, Sudan, to coordinate a response. They rebuff Israel's land-for-peace overtures with a resolution known

---

22 Judea Pearl, Post on X, March 21, 2023, https://twitter.com/yudapearl/status/1638115256475209728?cxt=HHwWgMDStbHJ4LstAAAA.

as "The Three Nos:" No peace with Israel. No recognition of Israel. No negotiations with Israel. This rejection is traumatic for Israelis and gives rise to the settlement movement, whose rationale is: If we are destined to live by the sword until the end of time, we had better do it from a position of strength.

1968 | PLO Campaign of Terrorism

The PLO commits itself to terrorism against Israelis at home and abroad. It revises its charter accordingly, declaring in Article 9 that "armed struggle is the only way to liberate Palestine. This is the overall strategy, not merely a tactical phase."[23]

1972 | The Munich Olympics Massacre

On September 5, during the Summer Olympic Games in Munich, Germany, a PLO faction calling itself Black September infiltrates the Olympic Village, kills two members of the Israeli team, and takes nine members hostage. The Palestinians later murder all nine Israeli hostages during a botched German rescue operation.

The Mossad eventually catches or kills most of the perpetrators.

1973 | Yom Kippur War

On Yom Kippur, the holiest day of the Jewish year, Egypt and Syria launch coordinated surprise attacks on Israel, which retained control of the Sinai Peninsula and the Golan Heights. They are backed by the Soviet Union, which provides them with advanced weaponry. The Syrian army advances through the Golan Heights, while the Egyptian army crosses the Suez Canal into the Sinai Peninsula.

After three weeks of fierce fighting, Israeli forces gain the upper hand: they cross the Suez Canal, advancing to within sixty-two miles of Cairo, and they enter Syria, advancing to within twenty-five miles of Damascus. U.S. Secretary of State Henry Kissinger pressures Israel to halt further advances and begin ceasefire negotiations.

The Israeli victory comes with heavy casualties, with about two thousand seven hundred dead and about eight thousand wounded. After

---

23 The Palestine National Charter, in Jewish Virtual Library, "Palestine Liberation Organization: The Palestine National Charter (July 17, 1968)," https://www.jewishvirtuallibrary.org/the-palestine-national-charter-july-1968.

the war, criticism of the government leads to the resignation of Prime Minister Golda Meir and the convening of a public inquiry to determine how Israel could have been caught so unprepared.

1976 | Entebbe Rescue Operation

Together with members of the far-Left German terror group, the Baader-Meinhof Gang, Palestinian terrorists hijack Air France flight 139 en route from Tel Aviv to Paris and divert it to Entebbe, Uganda. The terrorists separate the Jews and Israelis from the rest of the two hundred forty eight passengers, allowing the latter to go free. They demand a ransom of $5 million for the release of the plane, while for the release of the hostages they demand that Israel free forty convicted Palestinian terrorists held in its prisons and an additional thirteen terrorists held in various other countries. After a risky, nearly eight-hour flight at altitudes below one hundred feet to evade radar detection and crossing over Kenya, a country not entirely friendly to Israel, Israeli commandos execute a successful rescue operation. All but four of the hostages survive and are returned to Israel.

1977 | Menachem Begin Elected Prime Minister

Menachem Begin, leader of the right-of-center Likud Party, is elected prime minister. His win becomes known as "The Upheaval," since it breaks the rule of the left-of-center Labor Party, which had run Israel since its independence. Begin's win also reflects a major societal shift, since it is the first time that the Mizrahi sector takes political power from the elite Ashkenazi sector, primarily associated with the Labor Party.

1979 | Peace with Egypt

Egyptian President Anwar Sadat lands in Israel and addresses the Israeli Knesset (Parliament) as Egypt becomes the first Arab state to make peace with Israel. As part of the treaty, Israel agrees to withdraw from all of Sinai, returning it to Egypt. Sadat paid for peace with his life, as a group of Islamic extremists, led by Egyptian army lieutenant Khaled el Islambouli, assassinates him two years later.

Though the peace agreement holds, it remains a cold peace, e.g., few Egyptian tourists visit Israel, Egyptian journalists are discouraged from traveling to Israel, and the Egyptian people are exposed to pervasive antisemitic and Zionophobic propaganda incorporated into school curricula and popular culture.

1982 | First Lebanon War

In an attempt to halt hostile operations from southern Lebanon, Israel launches Operation Peace for the Galilee, also known as the First Lebanon War. Israel's goal is to clear the PLO and other Palestinian and Lebanese terrorist organizations and Syrian army forces out of southern Lebanon, which had been their base since the late 1960s for ongoing terror attacks on northern Israel and worldwide.

Israel conquers southern Lebanon, enters Beirut, and encircles the PLO. Under internal and international pressure, Israel allows Yasser Arafat and other PLO leaders to relocate to Tunis, where they reestablish their headquarters. Israel maintains a military presence in southern Lebanon until 2000, when Prime Minister Ehud Barak unilaterally withdraws IDF forces.

1987–1993 | First Intifada

Mass rioting breaks out in a Palestinian refugee camp in Gaza, sparking wider unrest and violence against Israelis in Gaza, the West Bank, and Jerusalem in what the Palestinians call an intifada ("uprising"). It results in thousands of Israeli casualties (mainly injuries) and crushes hopes that cohabitation would eventually lead to coexistence. The intifada also affects Palestinian society, as the PLO kills its own people for suspected collaboration with Israel or mere contact with Jews and Israel. Under the policies of Defense Ministers Yitzhak Rabin (elected prime minister in 1992) and Moshe Arens, Israel puts down the intifada with heavy force. Ultimately, the violence and chaos within Palestinian society becomes so serious that the PLO itself attempts to end the intifada.

1991 | Madrid Peace Conference

U.S. President George H.W. Bush, with Soviet President Mikhail Gorbachev as co-chair, convenes a conference in Madrid aimed at ending the Arab-Israeli conflict. It is attended by Israeli, Egyptian, Syrian, Lebanese, and joint Jordanian-Palestinian delegations and marks the first time that all of the parties to the Arab-Israeli conflict gather for direct negotiations. While no agreements are reached, the conference leads to the outlining of steps to peace and helps pave the way for the Oslo Accords and the Israeli-Jordanian peace agreement.

1993 | The Oslo Accords

On September 13, Israeli Prime Minister Yitzhak Rabin and PLO Chairman Yasser Arafat sign the Declaration of Principles on Interim Self-Government Arrangements at the White House. Popularly known as the Oslo Accords, because negotiations had begun in Oslo, Norway, the arrangements aim to resolve the Israeli-Palestinian conflict by initiating direct talks between Israel and the PLO and outlining steps to peace, including the PLO formally recognizing Israel and renouncing terror and Israel withdrawing its military from some parts of the West Bank. Within two years, Israel and the PLO agree to divide the West Bank into three areas: A, B, and C. Area A, encompassing the major Palestinian cities and towns (e.g., Ramallah, Jenin, Bethlehem), is controlled exclusively by the Palestinian Authority (PA). In Area B, covering around four hundred fifty Palestinian towns, villages, and refugee camps, the PA controls all public order and civil affairs, while Israel controls security in coordination with the PA. Area C includes all of the Jewish settlements and military installations, with Israel controlling all aspects of governance except for the civil affairs of the Palestinian residents. The three core issues—the future of Jerusalem, the status of Palestinian refugees, and formal acceptance of Jewish right to sovereignty—are left to be resolved at a later date.

Contrary to the goal of the agreement, the Palestinian public is made to believe that the Oslo Accords are merely the first step toward the eventual dismantling of Israel. As Faisal Husseini, one of the leading Palestinian negotiators, stated in a 2001 interview with *Al-Arabi* reporter Shafiq Ahmad Ali, they regarded the Oslo Accords as a Trojan Horse concealing their unwavering goal of "the liberation of all historical Palestine from the [Jordan] River to the [Mediterranean] Sea, even if this means that the conflict will last for another thousand years or for many generations."[24]

---

24 Faisal Husseini, in The Middle East Media Research Institute (MEMRI), "Faysal al-Husseini in His Last Interview: The Oslo Accords Were a Trojan

"The Palestinians' greatest mistake, which has caused them tragedy after tragedy, was and is to conceptualize Israel as a colonizer, rather than a home-comer. This conception dictates that if you make its life miserable enough, the colonizer will quit, like [the French in] Algiers. Palestinians (and their supporters) fail to grasp that Israelis do not have a France to go back to. They are determined to stay or die trying to stay. Therefore, all talks about 'decolonizing' Palestine boil down to talks about a genocide of eight million human beings."[25]

"We can say it even more concisely: 'We don't have a France to go back to; Israel for us means survival. Another assault on us means another tragedy for you.'"[26]

—JP

1994 | Arafat Returns from Exile and Peace with Jordan

In compliance with the Oslo Accords, Israel allows Yasser Arafat to return to the Palestinian Territories from his Tunisian exile. He eventually establishes his headquarters in Ramallah, where he remains until his death in 2004.

On October 26, Jordan becomes the second Arab state to make peace with Israel. As with Egypt, it is a cold peace.

1995 | Rabin Assassinated

On November 4, Yigal Amir, an Israeli extremist who is against the Oslo Accords, assassinates Prime Minister Yitzhak Rabin as he is leaving a peace rally in Tel Aviv. The assassination culminates a period of incitement against Rabin, in which the political Right accused him of betraying Israeli interests and marked him as a traitor.

2000 | Camp David Negotiations and the Second Intifada

U.S. President Bill Clinton, Israeli Prime Minister Ehud Barak, and Palestinian Authority (formerly PLO) Chairman Yasser Arafat gather for a summit at the Camp David presidential retreat in the summer,

---

Horse; the Strategic Goal Is the Liberation of Palestine from the [Jordan] River to the [Mediterranean] Sea," https://www.memri.org/reports/faysal-al-husseini-his-last-interview-oslo-accords-were-trojan-horse-strategic-goal#_edn1.

25 Judea Pearl, Post on X, March 4, 2024, https://twitter.com/yudapearl/status/1764560153863725548.

26 Judea Pearl, Post on X, March 4, 2024, https://twitter.com/yudapearl/status/1764637755739668898.

and again in the winter, to negotiate a final settlement of the Israeli-Palestinian conflict in accordance with the Oslo Accords. Both rounds of talks fail, with Arafat rejecting Barak's offer without making counteroffers. Arafat then launches the Second Intifada, unleashing terror attacks on Israelis that persist for the next five years and result in thousands of casualties.

> "The Palestinian national movement is the only national movement in human history whose ultimate goal is not to win independence but to dismantle another people's independence."[27] —JP

2002 | Operation Defensive Shield

Precipitated by the relentless terror attacks of the Second Intifada, and in direct response to a suicide bombing that killed thirty and wounded one hundred fifty people attending a Passover Seder at the Park Hotel in Netanya, Israel launches Operation Defensive Shield, a large-scale military operation in the West Bank aimed at preventing further Palestinian terror. The IDF establishes presence and intelligence operations in Palestinian cities and towns throughout the West Bank, thereby foiling plans for terrorist operations before they are executed. Though it did not stop all West Bank terror attacks, it was the first time in Israel's history that terrorist activities were brought largely under control. Operation Defensive Shield stands as a role model for counter-terrorism to this day.

However, terrorists continued attacking Israeli forces stationed in Gaza, which led Israelis to question the rationale of maintaining a presence there.

2005 | Withdrawal from Gaza

Under Prime Minister Ariel Sharon, Israel unilaterally withdraws from Gaza, leaving it under Palestinian sovereignty with the exception of the movement of goods and people across its borders. As part of the withdrawal, Israel removes about nine thousand Jewish settlers residing in twenty-one settlements inside Gaza. While the majority of these settlers follow instructions and leave on their own, one-third must

---

27 Judea Pearl, Post on X, October 17, 2023, https://twitter.com/yudapearl/status/1714208850759561309.

be forcibly removed by the IDF. Though Sharon's removal policy is controversial and could not guarantee peace, it is backed by a majority of the Israeli public.

Israel and Egypt maintain control over ground, sea, and air traffic into Gaza to prevent arms smuggling.

2006 | Second Lebanon War

Israel and Hezbollah—a paramilitary force supported by Iran and Syria entrenched in southern Lebanon—engage in a thirty-four-day war in Lebanon. The war is instigated when Hezbollah operatives cross into Israel under cover of a barrage of rocket attacks from inside Lebanon, kill eight IDF soldiers, and abduct two others.

The war ends inconclusively, with a ceasefire arrangement from the U.N. Security Council (Security Council resolution 1701), according to which the United National Interim Force in Lebanon (UNIFIL) and Lebanese forces would control the region, and Hezbollah would not be allowed south of the Litani River. Hezbollah totally ignores the resolution while the U.N. stands by, allowing them to rearm with weapons from Iran, funneled through Syria.

2007 | The Annapolis Conference and Hamas Takes Power in Gaza

U.S. President George W. Bush convenes an international conference in Annapolis, MD, to officially revive the moribund Israeli-Palestinian peace process. By the end of the conference, Israeli Prime Minister Ehud Olmert and Palestinian Authority President Mahmoud Abbas agree to continue negotiations with an aim to conclude a peace treaty by the end of the following year. Once again, these negotiations fail. According to Olmert, three issues remained unresolved: 1) Palestinian refusal to recognize Israel as a Jewish state, 2) Palestinian insistence on full right of return to Israel proper, 3) Palestinian refusal to regard a peace agreement as a formal "end of all claims."

Hamas, a military branch of the religiously fanatic Muslim Brotherhood movement, violently overthrows Fatah leadership and takes power in Gaza. It institutes an ongoing campaign of rocket attacks aimed at civilian targets throughout southern and central Israel. The Hamas charter calls for armed struggle toward the destruction of Israel, the expulsion of most Jews from Israel, and the institution of Islamic law across the land. Israel launches multiple operations to stop the rockets, none of which achieve lasting results.

2020 | Abraham Accords

Led by the administration of U.S. President Donald Trump, Israel normalizes relations with the United Arab Emirates, Bahrain, Morocco, and, later, Sudan. Unlike the cold peace agreements with Egypt and Jordan, the Abraham Accords result in warm peace, including tourism, journalism, cultural exchange, and long-term business contracts. Unlike the Oslo Accords, which pushed the thorniest disagreements to future negotiations, the Abraham Accords began by addressing the core of the dispute: Israel's indigenous place in the Middle East, as symbolized by the evocation of the name Abraham.

2023 | Hamas Invasion and Massacre

On October 7, under cover of a barrage of rocket attacks from inside Gaza, thousands of Hamas terrorists breach Israel's southern border and execute the worst massacre perpetrated against the Jewish people since the Holocaust. They rampage through Israeli cities and towns, raping girls, women, and some men and brutalizing and murdering everyone they encounter (mostly civilians ranging from months-old babies to the elderly), torching everything they can, and kidnapping more than two hundred Israelis and foreign nationals. In response, Israel declares war on Hamas, with the aim of ridding Gaza of Hamas control, thus preventing future attacks.

Surprising to some, this massacre evokes sympathetic support for Hamas among many Westerners, especially in higher education and on the political Left, revealing a latent unacceptance of Israel's existence, a willful dismissal of Israel's struggle for survival, and, more broadly, deep anti-Western sentiments.

> "Historically speaking, the Palestinian national ethos is consistently genocidal in intent and aims, from birth (1920) to puberty (1947) to maturity (2023). In 1947, Azzam Pasha promised 'a monumental massacre and rivers of blood,' explaining: 'it's not a shame to try and fail, it's a shame not to try.' Today, pro-Hamas activists want them finally to succeed."[28]
>
> —JP

28 Judea Pearl, Post on X, January 13, 2024, https://twitter.com/yudapearl/status/1746189123910525301.

Glossary of Key Terms

Antisemitism: Upholding a belief in the inferiority or evil nature of the Jewish people, or advocating acts that harm the Jewish people as a collective. This includes stripping Jews of their homeland, i.e., Zionophobia.

Apartheid: A policy of separating communities based on qualities such as race or ethnic identity, for example, the policy formerly practiced in South Africa against non-whites.

Arab Rejectionism: The deeply entrenched ideology dominating Palestinian society, according to which a Jewish homeland in any border must be rejected and fought against as the highest priority.

Colonialism: A policy or practice by which a foreign power exerts its control over another territory to which it has no indigenous connection. The central characteristic of colonialism is allegiance to a motherland, the place of origin from which the colonizers come.

Colony: A newly established settlement, typically agricultural, on previously uncultivated land. During the period of the New Yishuv, it was the term for a newly established agricultural community.

Diaspora: The Jewish community living outside of Israel. A state of dispersion considered temporary and abnormal throughout Jewish history.

Eretz Israel: Also Eretz Yisrael. Hebrew for The Land of Israel, the historic homeland of the Jewish people. See Zion.

Indigenous: Living or occurring naturally in an area or environment. Intrinsic; innate. When applied to land ownership claims, indigenousness is based on three factors: geographical residence, genetic lineage, and intellectual or historical attachment. Jewish indigenousness is based on vivid collective memories of a past civilization and continuous expectation of returning to the cradle of that civilization.

Jew: A member of the widely dispersed people sharing collective memories centered around Eretz Israel, a sense of mutual responsibility, and a commitment to a common destiny. Throughout their dispersion, religion was the carrier of those memories and commitments. For some Jews, religion still plays an essential role in their Jewish identity, however, the majority of contemporary Jews are secular.

Judaism: The religious aspect of Jewishness. Judaism traces its origins to the monotheism embraced by Abraham and has its spiritual and ethical principles articulated chiefly in the Torah and the Talmud. In the Diaspora period, the practices and beliefs of Judaism were the main carriers of Jewishness.

Moral Relativism: The view that moral judgments are true or false only relative to some particular standpoint (for instance, that of a culture or a historical period) and that no standpoint is uniquely privileged over others. It has been associated with the denial of universal moral imperatives to be upheld by every human society and the insistence that we should refrain from passing moral judgments on beliefs and practices characteristic of cultures other than our own. Taken to the extreme, moral relativism would tolerate such practices as female circumcision, honor killing, and slavery.

Nakba: Arabic term for "disaster." Originally coined in 1956 by the Syrian intellectual and Arab nationalist Constantine Zurayk to describe the humiliating failure of the Arab states' attack on Israel in 1948. Later adopted, and continually evoked, to describe the displacement and human suffering that resulted from this attack.

Palestine: A name given by the Ottomans to a region in the Middle East formerly coined Palestina by the Romans and formerly named Eretz Yisrael by the Hebrews.

Palestinian: Literally, a person who comes from Palestine, including members of the Yishuv during the British Mandate period. Collectively, a term characterizing the national movement of the Arab residents of Palestine that emerged in the 1920s, led by the Mufti of Jerusalem Haj Amin al-Husseini, with two goals: 1) to establish an Arab state in all of Palestine and 2) to prevent the Jews from establishing their own state in any part of the land.

Racism: The belief that race (e.g., skin color or genetic lineage) accounts for differences in human character or ability and that a particular race is superior to others. More broadly, discrimination or prejudice based on other immutable characteristics, such as sexual orientation, ethnic heritage, or deeply entrenched cultural traits and mores.

Sovereignty: The right and power of a governing body to handle the needs of a given society without outside interference. The two essential features of a sovereign government are self-defense and control of immigration.

Terrorism: The ideological license to elevate one's grievances above the norms of civilized society through the use or threatened use of force. Typically, terrorism refers to extra-governmental organizations seeking to intimidate or coerce societies or governments to accede to their demands. Often takes the form of violence against civilian populations to advance some ideological or political cause.

Yishuv: The Jewish community in Palestine before the establishment of the State of Israel. Two distinct periods define the Yishuv. The period of the Old Yishuv refers to the community residing in Palestine before the First Aliyah (1882), largely composed of observant Sephardic and Ashkenazic Jews who focused on Torah study and lived on charity from the Diaspora. The period of the New Yishuv refers to the community composed of the waves of Zionist pioneers who founded self-supporting agricultural communities and new towns and cities (e.g., Tel Aviv) with the ultimate aim of reestablishing Jewish sovereignty in Eretz Israel. While it lacked control over its own defense and immigration, the New Yishuv otherwise featured all the attributes of a modern democratic state, including elected leadership, town councils, and a Rabbinical Council; educational and healthcare systems; a robust independent press; arts and cultural centers; and considerable economic activity. The strong institutional structure established by the New Yishuv enabled the smooth transition from British Mandate rule to independence in 1948.

Zion: Biblical name for both Jerusalem and Eretz Israel, also used as a symbol for the Jewish people itself.

Zionism: The continuous yearning of the Jewish people for self-determination and normalcy in their historic homeland. The political manifestation of Zionism was catalyzed in 1897 by Austro-Hungarian lawyer, journalist, and author Theodor Herzl (1860–1904) and realized with the establishment of the modern State of Israel in 1948.

Motivated by the danger of rising antisemitism in Europe and Russia, Herzl argued a two-part purpose for Zionism: 1) to establish for the Jewish people a publicly recognized, legally secured homeland in Palestine and 2) to rekindle Jews' connection to the fold of their peoplehood.

Zionophobia: A form of racism denying the Jewish people a home in Eretz Israel.

Related to but distinct from antisemitism, Zionophobia earns its discriminatory character by denying the Jewish people what it grants to other historically bonded collectives: the right to nationhood, self-determination, and legitimate coexistence with their neighbors. The "phobic" component in the word Zionophobia highlights the irrational obsession with which most Zionophobes pursue their genocidal goal of stripping Israeli Jews of their sovereignty.

Index

Bibliography and Recommended Reading

Bibliography

Barnett, David, and Efraim Karsh. "Azzam's Genocidal Threat." *Middle East Quarterly* 18, no. 4 (Fall 2011): 85–88.

Ben-Gurion, David. *Anachnu U'Shcheneinu.* Tel Aviv: Davar, 1931.

——. "Leberur Motsa Ha'Falahim." *Der Yidisher Kemfer* (January 22, 1918). Reprinted in David Ben-Gurion, *Anachnu U'Shcheneinu.* Tel Aviv: Davar, 1931.

——. "Zechuyot Ha'Yehudim Ve'Zulatam B'Eretz Yisrael." *Der Yidisher Kemfer* (January 23, 1918). Reprinted in David Ben-Gurion, *Anachnu U'Shcheneinu.* Tel Aviv: Davar, 1931.

Doherty, Benjamin. "Watch: Omar Barghouti on 'Ethical Decolonization' and Moving Beyond Zionist Racism." *The Electronic Intifada* (September 29, 2013). https://electronicintifada.net/blogs/benjamin-doherty/watch-omar-barghouti-ethical-decolonization-and-moving-beyond-zionist-racism.

Dysch, Marcus. "Finkelstein Disowns 'Silly' Israel Boycott." *The Jewish Chronicle* (February 16, 2012). https://www.thejc.com/news/uk-news/finkelstein -disowns-silly-israel -boycott-1.31716.

HaLevi, Yehuda. "My Heart Is in the East." Jewish Virtual Library. https://www.jewishvirtuallibrary.org/quot-my-heart-is-in-the-east-quot-yehuda-halevi.

Herzl, Theodor. *The Jewish State.* Translated by Sylvie D'Avigdor. New York: Skyhorse Publishing, 2019.

Jabotinsky, Ze'ev. *Medinah Ivrit.* Tel Aviv: T. Kopp, 1937.

Jewish Virtual Library. "Balfour Declaration: Text of the Declaration (November 2, 1917)." Jewish Virtual Library. https://www.jewishvirtuallibrary.org/text-of-the-balfour-declaration.

Jewish Virtual Library. "British Palestine Mandate: Text of the Mandate (July 24, 1922)." Jewish Virtual Library. https://www.jewishvirtuallibrary.org/text-of-the-british-mandate-for-palestine.

Jewish Virtual Library. "Emancipation: France." Jewish Virtual Library. https://www.jewishvirtuallibrary.org/emancipation#France.

Jewish Virtual Library. "Palestine Liberation Organization: The Palestine National Charter (July 17, 1968)." Jewish Virtual Library. https://www.jewishvirtuallibrary.org/the-palestine-national-charter-july-1968.

Markland, Dave. "Chomsky on BDS: A Transcript." *Z Blogs* (July 4, 2017). https://zcomm.org/zblogs/chomsky-on-bds-a-transcript/.

Muir, Diana. "A Land without a People for a People without a Land." *Middle East Quarterly* 15, no. 2 (Spring 2008): 55-62.

Myers, David N. "U.S. Academics Should Not Boycott Israeli Universities." *Jewish Journal* (December 18, 2013). http://jewishjournal.com/opinion/I25482/.

Seid, Roberta. "Omar Barghouti at UCLA: A Speaker Who Brings Hate." *Jewish Journal* (January 16, 2014). http://jewishjournal.com/opinion/126186/.

Shlaim, Avi. *The Iron Wall: Israel and the Arab World*. New York: W.W. Norton and Company, Inc., 2001.

The Middle East Media Research Institute (MEMRI). "Faysal al-Husseini in His Last Interview: The Oslo Accords Were a Trojan Horse; the Strategic Goal Is the Liberation of Palestine from the [Jordan] River to the [Mediterranean] Sea." MEMRI. https://www.memri.org/reports/faysal-al-husseini-his-last-interview-oslo-accords-were-trojan-horse-strategic-goal#_edn1.

The Times of Israel. "Israel's Declaration of Independence—May 14, 1948." *The Times of Israel* (August 4, 2018). https://www.timesofisrael.com/israels-declaration-of-independence-may-14-1948/.

Torok, Ryan. "Eritrean Solidarity Rally Underscores Community Divisiveness Over Israel." *Jewish Journal* (January 22, 2014). http://jewishjournal.com/news/los_angeles/126278/.

USC Shoah Foundation. "Intl Day to End Crimes Against Journalists | Iraqi Jewish Survivor Ruth Pearl | USC Shoah Foundation." USC Shoah Foundation. https://www.youtube.com/watch?v=NvXlhf01jE4.

Weizmann, Chaim. *Devarim*. Vol. 1. Tel Aviv: Mizpah Publishers, 1936.

Recommended Reading

Ha'am, Ahad. *Selected Essays*. Jerusalem: Sefer ve Sefel Publishing, 2003.

Halevi, Yossi Klein. *Letters to My Palestinian Neighbor*. New York: Harper, 2018.

Herf, Jeffrey. *Israel's Moment: International Support and Opposition for Establishing the Jewish State, 1945-1949*. Cambridge: Cambridge University Press, 2022.

Landes, Richard. *Can "The Whole World" Be Wrong?: Lethal Journalism, Antisemitism, and Global Jihad*. Boston: Academic Studies Press, 2022.

Lévy, Bernard-Henri. *Israel Alone*. New York: Wicked Son, 2024.

——. *Who Killed Daniel Pearl?*. Translated by James X. Mitchell. New Jersey: Melville House Publishing, 2003.

Lewis, Bernard. *What Went Wrong? Western Impact and Middle Eastern Response*. Oxford: Oxford University Press, 2002.

Morris, Benny. *1948: The First Arab-Israeli War*. New Haven: Yale University Press, 2008.

Pearl, Daniel. *At Home in the World: Collected Writings from The Wall Street Journal.* Edited by Helene Cooper. New York: Simon & Schuster, Inc., 2002.

Pearl, Judea, and Ruth Pearl, eds. *I Am Jewish: Personal Reflections Inspired by the Last Words of Daniel Pearl.* Woodstock: Jewish Lights Publishing, 2004.

Pearl, Mariane. *A Mighty Heart: The Inside Story of the Al-Qaeda Kidnapping of Danny Pearl.* New York: Scribner, 2003.

Pessin, Andrew, and Doron S. Ben-Atar, eds. *Anti-Zionism on Campus: The University, Free Speech, and BDS*. Bloomington: Indiana University Press, 2018.

Schwartz, Adi, and Einat Wilf. *The War of Return: How Western Indulgence of the Palestinian Dream Has Obstructed the Path to Peace*. Translated by Eylon Levi. New York: All Points Books, 2020.

Senor, Dan, and Saul Singer. *Start-Up Nation: The Story of Israel's Economic Miracle*. New York: Twelve, 2009.

Sokolow, Nachum. *History of Zionism, 1600-1919*. London: Longmens, Green and Company, 1919.

Troy, Gil. *The Zionist Ideas: Visions for the Jewish Homeland—Then, Now, Tomorrow*. Lincoln: University of Nebraska Press, 2018.

Weiss, Bari. *How To Fight Anti-Semitism*. New York: Crown, 2019.

About the Author

Judea Pearl is Chancellor's Professor of Computer Science and Statistics at the University of California, Los Angeles (UCLA) and Director of the UCLA Cognitive Systems Laboratory. He is known internationally for his contributions to artificial intelligence (AI), human reasoning, and philosophy of science and has received numerous scientific awards, including the 2011 ACM A.M. Turing Award, equivalent of the Nobel Prize in computing, "for fundamental contributions to artificial intelligence through the development of a calculus for probabilistic and causal reasoning." In 2012, his alma mater, the Technion-Israel Institute of Technology, awarded him its Harvey Prize, and in 2021, he won the BBVA Frontiers of Knowledge Award for "laying the foundations of modern artificial intelligence so computer systems can process uncertainty and relate causes to effects." He holds honorary doctorates from seven universities, among them Yale, Carnegie Mellon, and the University of Toronto. He is a member of the National Academy of Sciences and the National Academy of Engineering, and a fellow of the Royal Society, the Royal Statistical Society, the Cognitive Science Society, and the Association for the Advancement of Artificial Intelligence.

Dr. Pearl was born in 1936, in the town of Bnei Brak, Israel, which his grandfather, Chaim Pearl, founded in 1924, alongside twenty-five other Hasidic-Polish families. Inspired by the legacy of the ancient biblical town of Bnei Brak, the seat of rabbinical scholarship and learning in the second century CE, they bought the land where the town used to sit and created a community combining modern life, agricultural work, and religious devotion. Most of his mother's side of the family perished in the Holocaust. Dr. Pearl was eleven years old when the United Nations General Assembly voted to adopt the Partition Plan, ending British rule in Mandate Palestine and formalizing the creation of modern-day Israel. This remains a foundational event in his life.

From 1953 to 1957, Dr. Pearl served in the Nachal Division of the Israel Defense Forces (IDF), combining military service and agricultural work. Upon completion, he enrolled in the Technion, where he earned a Bachelor's degree in Electrical Engineering (1960) and met his wife, Ruth

Rejwan, whose family had fled antisemitic hostility in Iraq and come to Israel in 1951. After marrying and completing their degrees, they moved to America for their graduate studies.

Dr. Pearl was hired by RCA Research Laboratories in 1961, where he worked on superconductive storage and logic devices for computers. He earned a Master's in Electrical Engineering from Newark College of Engineering (1961), a Master's in Physics from Rutgers University (1965), and a Doctorate in Electrical Engineering from the Polytechnic Institute of Brooklyn (1965). In his doctoral dissertation, he developed a "vortex theory of superconductive memories." This research led to his discovery of a new phenomenon in superconductivity, later called the "Pearl Vortex." From 1966 to 1969, Dr. Pearl served as the director of advanced memories at Electronic Memories, Inc., in Hawthorne, California. He was hired by UCLA in 1969, where he began teaching and research in pattern recognition, image coding, decision theory, and AI.

Dr. Pearl has written three fundamental books in AI, *Heuristics: Intelligent Search Strategies for Computer Problem Solving* (1984), *Probabilistic Reasoning in Intelligent Systems: Networks of Plausible Inference* (1988), and *Causality: Models, Reasoning, and Inference* (2000, 2009), winner of the London School of Economics Lakatos Award in 2001, for its "outstanding contribution to the philosophy of science." More recently, he co-authored *Causal Inference in Statistics: A Primer* (2016, with Madelyn Glymour and Nicholas Jewell) and *The Book of Why: The New Science of Cause and Effect* (2018, with Dana Mackenzie), which brings causal analysis to a general audience. *The Book of Why* has been translated into fifteen languages, including Hebrew, Turkish, and Chinese.

Dr. Pearl is the father of slain *Wall Street Journal* reporter Daniel Pearl and president of the Daniel Pearl Foundation, which he co-founded in April 2002 with Ruth and their daughters, Tamara and Michelle, "to continue Daniel's life work of dialogue and understanding and to address the root causes of his tragedy." The Daniel Pearl Foundation sponsors journalism fellowships, organizes worldwide concerts, and promotes a hate-free world through lectures and public dialogues. In 2006, Dr. Pearl was a co-recipient of the Purpose Prize for forming the Daniel Pearl Dialogue for Muslim-Jewish Understanding with Pakistani diplomat and scholar Akbar Ahmed, with whom he traveled through the U.S., Canada, and the U.K., aiming to forge bridges between Jews and Muslims based on their common heritage.

Together with Ruth, Dr. Pearl co-edited *I Am Jewish: Personal Reflections Inspired by the Last Words of Daniel Pearl* (2004), winner of the 2004 National Jewish Book Award. The book comprises a collection of essays from a cross-section of the Jewish people reflecting on Daniel's last words: "My father is Jewish, my mother is Jewish, I am Jewish." Dr. Pearl lectures and writes frequently on Jewish identity, the Arab-Israeli conflict, the history of Zionism, and Israel on campus.

Acknowledgements

Thank you to the editors of the newspapers, magazines, journals, and books who made room for me in their pages—especially Nadine Epstein of *Moment Magazine* and Rob Eshman and David Suissa of the *Jewish Journal of Los Angeles*—giving voice to many of my articles, even the heretical ones that other publications would not touch.

Thank you to David Kedmey for making the connection to his sister, Karen Kedmey, my editor, without whom the ideas in this book would be scattered across the internet, homeless and hard to find. Einat Wilf, Yossi Klein Halevi, Gil Troy, and Bernard-Henri Lévy helped shape my understanding of many aspects of the topics covered in this book, and I am fortunate to call these enlightened thinkers my friends and mentors.

While this might come as a surprise, I'm truly grateful for the readers of my "educational channel" on X, whose challenges and feedback sharpened my arguments and kept me honest.

No acknowledgement would be complete without paying my debt to my high school and college teachers in Israel, who exposed me to the marvels of scientific thinking. I am a fortunate product of the greatest educational experiment in history. My high school teachers, in particular, were displaced academics from Germany, who had been at the top of their fields before the Nazis came to power. They knew the joy of scientific discovery, and they understood that this joy would no longer be part of their professional life. They viewed us, their pupils, as substitutes for their lost dreams and instilled in me and my classmates the idea that each of us could change the world.

My son, Danny, and my wife, Ruth, have been my guiding lights for my writing and curiosity. And my daughters and grandchildren never fail to remind me why all of this matters—I hope they're proud of their *Sabbah*.